THE GREAT POWER (MIS)MANAGEMENT

The Great Power (mis)Management

The Russian–Georgian War and its Implications for Global Political Order

Edited by
ALEXANDER ASTROV
Central European University, Hungary

Routledge
Taylor & Francis Group
LONDON AND NEW YORK

First published 2011 by Ashgate Publishing

2 Park Square, Milton Park, Abingdon, Oxon OX14 4RN
711 Third Avenue, New York, NY 10017, USA

Routledge is an imprint of the Taylor & Francis Group, an informa business

First issued in paperback 2016

British Library Cataloguing in Publication Data
The great power (mis)management : the Russian–Georgian war
and its implications for global political order.
1. South Ossetia War, 2008--Congresses. 2. World
politics--2005-2015--Congresses. 3. Great powers--
Congresses.
I. Astrov, Alexander, 1960-
327.1'09051-dc22

Library of Congress Cataloging-in-Publication Data
Astrov, Alexander, 1960-
The great power (mis)management : the Russian–Georgian war and its implications for global political order / by Alexander Astrov.
p. cm.
Includes bibliographical references and index.
ISBN 978-1-4094-2467-3 (hardback)
1. South Ossetia War, 2008--Diplomatic history. 2. Georgia (Republic)--Strategic aspects. I. Title.
DK679.S68A88 2011
947.5808'63--dc22

2011003496

ISBN 978-1-4094-2467-3 (hbk)
ISBN 978-1-138-26129-7 (pbk)

Contents

List of Figures and Tables

Figures

Tables

List of Contributors

Pami Aalto is Jean Monnet Professor (International Relations) and Director of the Jean Monnet European Centre of Excellence at the University of Tampere, Finland. His main publications include *The EU-Russia Energy Dialogue: Europe's Future Energy Security* (ed., Ashgate 2007), *The European Union and the Making of a Wider Northern Europe* (Routledge 2006), and *Constructing Post-Soviet Geopolitics in Estonia* (Frank Cass 2003).

Alexander Astrov is Associate Professor at the Department of International Relations and European Studies at Central European University, Hungary, working in the field of international relations and political theory. His publications include *On World Politics: R.G. Collingwood, Michael Oakeshott and Neotraditionalism in International Relations* (Palgrave, 2005) and *Self-Founded Community: Minority Politics vs. Minor Politics* (Tallinn University Press, 2007).

Alan Chong is Associate Professor at the S. Rajaratnam School of International Studies in Singapore. He has published widely on the notion of soft power and the role of ideas in constructing the international relations of Singapore and Asia. His most recent book was *Foreign Policy in Global Information Space: Actualizing Soft Power* (Palgrave, 2007). He is currently working on several projects exploring the notion of 'Asian international theory'. His interest in soft power has also led to inquiry into the sociological and philosophical foundations of international communication.

Pertti Joenniemi, is Senior Research Fellow at the Danish Institute for International Studies. His research interests include transatlantic relations, European neighbourhood, and Denmark's foreign policy identity. Recent publications appeared in *European Journal of International Relations*, *Journal of International Relations and Development*, *Cooperation and Conflict*, and *The Journal of Borderland Studies*.

Jana Kobzova is coordinator of the Wider Europe Programme at the European Council on Foreign Relations. Before joining ECFR, she headed the Belarus Democratization Programme at the Bratislava-based Pontis Foundation. She co-authored a book on a Slovak foreign policy (2010) and has written articles and book chapters on Eastern Europe and EU Eastern policy. She is a co-author of ECFR's latest policy report *The Specter of Multipolar Europe* (2010).

Andrey Makarychev is Professor of International Relations and Research Fellow at the Institute for Eastern European Studies, Free University of Berlin, Germany. He teaches courses in Theories of International Relations and Russian Foreign Policy in Nizhny Novgorod Linguistic University, Syktyvkar University (Russia), Odessa National University (Ukraine) and Azerbaijan Diplomatic Academy. His previous employers were the Centre for Conflict Studies (ETH, Zurich) and the Danish Institute for International Studies.

Irina Papkova is currently an Assistant Professor at the Department of International Relations and European Studies at Central European University. Her research and teaching interests include religion and politics (particularly the intersection of international relations and religion); nationalism and empires; Russian politics; humanitarian intervention; and the political implications of historical memory. She is the author of *The Orthodox Church and Russian Politics* (Oxford University Press, 2010).

Nicu Popescu is Senior Policy Fellow at ECFR, specializing in European Neighbourhood Policy, secessionist conflicts in the post-Soviet space, EU–Russia relations, Moldova and the South Caucasus. He is the author of *EU Foreign Policy and Post-Soviet Conflicts: Stealth Intervention* (Routledge, 2010).

Sergei Prozorov is Academy of Finland Research Fellow at the Department of Political and Economic Studies at the University of Helsinki, Finland. He is the author of four monographs, the most recent being *The Ethics of Postcommunism* (Palgrave, 2009). He has also published articles on Political Philosophy and International Relations in *Philosophy and Social Criticism*, *Continental Philosophy Review*, *Political Geography*, *Review of International Studies*, *Millennium*, *International Theory* and other journals.

Andrew Wilson is Senior Policy Fellow at ECFR working in the field of comparative politics of democratization in the post-Soviet states. His publications include *Virtual Politics: Faking Democracy in the Post-Soviet World* (Yale University Press, 2005), *Ukraine's Orange Revolution* (Yale University Press, 2005) and *The Ukrainians: Unexpected Nation* (Yale University Press, 2009).

Preface

This volume originated from a series of discussions in the Department of International Relations and European Studies (IRES) at Central European University. The initial objective of these discussions was rather modest: to take stock of the various reactions to the Russian–Georgian war of 2008 and to assess them against the background of various theoretical approaches available within contemporary International Relations. Gradually, the emphasis shifted towards the theory part of the equation. Whereas various practitioners reacting to the crisis invariably invoked the idea of 'great power politics', theory, it seemed, had rather little to say about greatpowerhood. Or, at least, whatever it had to say on the subject was scattered across various approaches and lacked the kind of precision which would allow one to say why the Russian–Georgian conflict, rather than, say, the less dramatic but surely more lasting self-assertion of China, should be marking the 'return of great power politics', if indeed a return it was.

Is it indeed the case that the very idea of great power is so inseparable from that of war that the practices of greatpowerhood become recognizable only against the background of military action? Is this the meaning of Prince Gorchakov's aphorism, that great powers are not recognized but rather reveal themselves as such? Or was the aphorism itself, as well as various wars waged by Russia throughout history, a reaction to the lack of recognition by other great powers? And, then, how does the idea of greatpowerhood as a revelation sit together with what Hedley Bull defined as 'great power *management*', a practice whose main objective is to keep wars, at least major wars, at bay? Or, to put it differently, in terms suggested by the title of the volume: Do wars result from some mismanagement of power or are they, as a legitimate instrument of global political ordering, a principled rejection of the managerial approach to power?

These and similar questions were discussed at the Convention of the Central East European International Studies Association (CEEISA) in St. Petersburg, where the volume began to take its current shape. Apart from the authors, many individuals and organizations contributed to this shaping. In fact, the book would not have been possible without the generous support of IRES and CEEISA and the comments and suggestions of Chris Brown, Viktor Friedmann, Matteo Fumagalli, Stefano Guzzini, Maria Mälksoo, Michael Merlingen, Viatcheslav Morozov, Daniele Monticelli, Iver B. Neumann, David Ridout, Paul Roe, Anna Selmeczi, Flemming Splidsboel and Jodok Troy.

Alexander Astrov

Chapter 1

Great Power Management Without Great Powers? The Russian–Georgian War of 2008 and Global Police/Political Order

Alexander Astrov

Right after the outbreak of the Russian–Georgian war of 2008, there was a lot of talk about a paradigm-shift in international relations. The *Financial Times* quoted Estonian president, Toomas Ilves, as saying: 'What we have seen is a complete paradigm shift in the security architecture of Europe. Everything we have done has been based on the assumption that Russia won't engage in aggression ... That premise is no longer operable ... The threat is not military but Russia's jingoistic rhetoric is unsettling. We live in post-modernist 21st-century Europe but we have a Russia which acts in a 19th-century pre-modern way' (Wagstyl et al. 2008). The sentiment clearly echoed an argument advanced already prior to the war and reiterated immediately after it: 'History's back' (Kagan 2008a, 2008b): The final triumph of democracy announced after the end of the Cold War as 'the end of history' was but a brief aberration from the ongoing (hi)story of great-power confrontation in which geoeconomics will never overcome geopolitics, since the enemies of democracy – Putin's Russia among them – have learned the trick of not only achieving economic growth without democratization but also turning their thus enhanced power against democracy, both at home and abroad.

How much credence should we give to such statements though? After all, less than half a year after the war, the new American administration initiated a pragmatic 'reset' of US–Russian relations. In addition, the foreign minister of Poland, a state whose president stood shoulder to shoulder with his Baltic colleagues in Tbilisi, was now boasting of rapprochement with Russia, and was quizzed by his hosts at the influential US Council on Foreign Relations on the possible lessons in pragmatism American foreign-policy makers could take from this (CFR 2009). In light of this, on a more theoretical note, how can we ascertain a paradigm-shift in world politics, generally, and decide whether it was caused by one conflict in particular?

Contemporary International Relations (IR) theory offers more than one analytical tool for answering such questions. The one employed in this volume comes from the English School and there are two interrelated reasons for that. First, the English School presents itself as a broad theoretical church capable of accommodating a variety of approaches without *a priori* committing its members to any of the more restrictive positions (Little 2000). However, for this very reason, many of its tools lack in precision. Yet, why not take this as an invitation for meaningful theoretical work? Especially so, given that the English School, in its 'classical' formulation, does have something to offer which seems to be immediately relevant for the case at hand; namely, the idea of 'great power management'.

Great power management, according to Hedley Bull, is an institution of international society and like other such institutions – war, diplomacy, international law and the balance of power – it is what gives international society its 'visible expression' (Bull 1977: 37). Bull's discussions of the individual institutions invariably culminate in the argument that each represents international society as such. Thus, diplomats, 'even in the pristine form of messengers, are visible expressions of the existence of rules to which states and other entities in the international system pay some allegiance' (172). None of the institutions are immune to change, but when change happens, it signifies a shift in the very structure of the society of states. So, if there is a paradigm-shift in world politics, it should find its expression in the operation of the institutions of international society.

For sure, the Russian–Georgian war can be meaningfully analysed by focussing on any of the five institutions. Still, great power management stands out in this respect, and not only because Russia's blunt assertion of its spheres of influence has stirred most of the paradigm-shift talk. To begin with, from the point of view of successful great power management, as it is presented by Bull, this war should not have happened in the first place. This seems to present an analyst with two choices: either great power management, as a clearly defined set of practices, was mishandled by some of the actors, or, again, as such clearly defined practice, it is no longer working in a changing international society. Therefore, all that is left, is to pick the right methodological tools for an investigation of both options.

Unfortunately, there is no such thing as a 'clearly defined' practice of great power management. For reasons to which I shall return shortly, Bull's initial discussion of it is marked with significant theoretical tensions. Furthermore, it would not be an exaggeration to say that, in spite of some important work published later (Cf.: Watson 1992, Hurrell and Ngaire Woods 1999, Buzan and Wæver 2003), theoretical attention given to great power management is minuscule in comparison to that attracted by other institutions. Therefore, this volume aims at providing prior work in clarifying the meaning of the institution itself.

Needless to say, by calling this exercise 'prior work', I do not mean that all analysis of the Russian–Georgian war should be put to one side until the meaning of great power management is elucidated. Rather, it is by examining the various aspects of the war that individual chapters highlight different sides of Bull's initial analysis or bring in new themes not to be found in it. In so doing, they rely on different (meta)theoretical frameworks, so as to explore the range of possibilities rather than to test a single hypothesis. What, hopefully, still endows the volume as a whole with some measure of coherence, is that all of them are addressed to the same question: What does the Russian–Georgian war of 2008 tell us about great power management as an institution of international society?

To avoid the impression that this is a gap-filling exercise, in the remainder of this introduction, I want to build a case for the importance of great power management as such, and to argue that, far from being a relic of the past or a secondary addition to other institutions, great power management is one of the defining practices of international society, which indeed deserves more theoretical attention. I argue that what makes it significant in a practical sense and theoretically intriguing, is the peculiar dualistic structure of not only the anarchical society of states but the Western mode of ordering generally. The dualism in question may be described as that of anarchical sovereignty and, to allude to Michel Foucault's famous concept, anarchical governmentality. The idea of great power management implies this dualism but does not make it explicit enough. Once explicated, it allows one to see how greatness, power and management, rather than being arbitrarily thrown in to constitute a definition, form an *apparatus*, or *dispositif* in Foucault, crucial for any ordering (Agamben 2009).

I begin by taking a closer look at the history-is-back argument mentioned earlier and showing how it can be related to Bull's account of great power management and Foucault's discussion of the two 'technological assemblages' characteristic of the Westphalian system: politics and 'police'. (Throughout, the latter term is used in inverted commas to distinguish the specific mode of governance denoted by it in Foucault from the more familiar practices of law-enforcement). I then identify tensions in Bull's analysis and address them by drawing on Foucault's one. Throughout, I set Foucault's governmentalist and the English School's broadly juridical approaches to ordering alongside, and sometimes against, each other, so as to show how the idea and practices of greatpowerhood, once taken to stand for more than mere preponderance in force, draw on the resources of both approaches and therefore can only be grasped by reference to both.

Politics and 'Police'

Although the claim that the Russian–Georgian war signifies a return to great power confrontation was advanced from the neoconservative side in the US, it is safe to say that its acceptance went far beyond this particular intellectual grouping. In itself, this is hardly surprising given that Russia has never really concealed its great-power ambitions, or in fact, can hardly imagine itself in any other role (Hopf 2002). On closer reading, however, the argument is marked with important tensions not only in its account of the contemporary situation but also in how it understands that very 'history' which it attempts to bring back. At the very least, its presentation of the nineteenth century significantly differs from almost every major account this period receives in IR. This is not to say that these accounts themselves are unproblematic. In fact, it is two specific tensions in Bull's discussion of great power management that I address in this section by introducing Foucault's analysis of the Westphalian order.

Which history is back?

Returning first to the neoconservative claim of a paradigm-shift, it is based on the premise that 'international order does not rest on ideas and institutions alone' but 'is shaped by configurations of power'. Yet, the specific configuration of power threatened at present by great power autocracies turns out to rest precisely on the balance between ideas and institutions, democracy and autocracy, so that the 'optimists in the early post-Cold War years were not wrong to believe that a liberalizing Russia and China would be better international partners. They were just wrong to believe that this evolution was inevitable' (Kagan 2008a). Put differently, the argument does not question, let alone abandon, the-end-of-history paradigm itself but merely expects its fulfillment in the longer run. In the meantime, since the run might be too long for small states like Georgia to endure, democracies led by the United States should speed up the genuine end of history through decisive political action.

This conclusion might well be welcomed by those who support a certain view of democracy while rejecting the teleology of Hegelian History if it were not for a number of difficulties. First, it does not take a 'great power autocracy' to accept that difference of opinion is in the very nature of democracy (Mouffe 2009), as well as the analytical tools with which we evaluate its quality (Kratochwil 2006). Why, then, present as a threat the fact that 'when Russians speak of a multipolar world, they are not only talking about the redistribution of power. It is also the competition of value systems and ideas that will provide "the foundation for a multipolar world order"' (Kagan 2008a). This is especially so, given that, in the case of the Georgian war, at least some representatives of Russian foreign-policy elites went out of the way to indicate their willingness to forego differences in value systems for the sake of great power cooperation in the field of global security (Lavrov 2008).

Related to this is the second difficulty, best seen once the argument is compared to both realist and liberal positions, which take the interplay of international order and democracy seriously. Thus, for Henry Kissinger, as a representative of realism, the neoconservative contention that 'history is back' in the form of great power competition between democracy and autocracy also characteristic of the nineteenth century, does not make any sense at all. In his theoretical framework, there was no single, homogeneous 'nineteenth century' but three distinct, incompatible configurations of international order: the Concert of Europe, Bismarckian *Realpolitik* and the uncontrolled arms race that followed. Each of these orders not merely had its own technique of power-handling but rested on a distinctive worldview. The 'rationalist' world of Metternich, in which the statesman had to understand the underlying 'order of things' and to bring political organization in accordance with it, was succeeded by the 'empiricist' order of Bismarck, in which no underlying principle of legitimacy was needed since power was believed to be able to legitimize itself. Long before the 'great power autocracies' of today learned how to achieve economic growth without democratization, Bismarck decoupled the binary orthodoxy of his age: liberalism and nationalism. The nationalistic aspirations of Prussia were achievable without liberalization and could, if needed, supply power required for balancing liberalism at home and abroad (Kissinger 1968). So, liberalism, as well as Metternich's rationalism, serves here as an ideational framework for the interpretation of power; that is, as the means for the attainment of an end, which itself remained the same since the Peace of Westphalia order.

In what may well be the strongest liberal affirmation of the role of democracy in the construction of international order, John Ikenberry (2000) retains this ends-means relationship. To be sure, the order he has in mind is radically different from Kissinger's, based not on realist balancing but cooperative institutions buttressed by a 'constitutional bargain' between a dominant power and lesser states. The ambition to achieve such a bargain is present in international relations, again, since the defeat of Napoleon; its success depends on the number of democratic states around. Still, here as well, democracy is neither more nor less than a variable in both practical and theoretical equations which, if balanced, point towards order, stability and peace.

In the neoconservative argument, and in the Bush Doctrine, this relationship between democracy and order is reversed. Analysing this reversal, David Chandler (2004, 2005) notices that in cases when democracy is judged to be lacking, order established for the purpose of its promotion invariably brackets that very contestation of ideas and values which should be part and parcel of democracy. In itself, this dynamic may be dismissed as almost trivial. To enjoy stable order, it is sometimes necessary to go through an upheaval, be it a revolution or a dictatorship; 'traditional' societies have to go through an often torturous process of modernization to reap the fruits of modernity. Whatever the analytical and normative value of such dismissals in general, in the specific context of international relations, the demotion of order from its place as the end of all politics has special significance, not least because of the explicit codification of this place of order in the Westphalian arrangements.

It may well be the case that the Westphalian norm of non-intervention has never really amounted to anything more than a form of 'organized hypocrisy' (Krasner 1999); or that hierarchical relations continued to exist well into the post-1648 world (Lake 2009). However, neither the routine intervention into the affairs of other states, nor the acceptance by some of these states of the authority of such interventions (Hobson and Sharman 2005) repudiates what Foucault (2007: 300) presented as the defining characteristic of the Westphalian system, in which 'instead of a sort of absolute eschatology that posits an empire, a universal monarchy as the culminating point of history, we have what could be called a relative eschatology, a precarious and fragile eschatology, but towards which it really is necessary to strive, and this relative eschatology is, in short, peace. ... Peace will no longer come from unity, but from non-unity, from plurality maintained as plurality'. Whereas contemporary Western diplomats responded to Russia's longstanding ambition to (re)establish its sphere of influence with a stringent dichotomy – 'Either the ex-Soviet countries are independent states, or they are not' (Rachman 2008). Foucault (2007: 299) reads both the inequalities in state-power and the existence of spheres of influence as being not merely compatible with but also necessary for the operation of the Westphalian system.

This is also true with Bull's take on great power management. From the outset, however, this initial take is marked with two tensions. To begin with, while the whole of Bull's discussion of great powers and international order is premised on the explicitly stated idea that great powers are such not merely by fact but also by right, he nevertheless holds to the idea of the sovereign equality of states: 'If states were equal in power as they are in law, ... then it is difficult to see how ... international conflicts could ever be settled and laid to rest, or the claims of any one state definitely granted or denied' (Bull 1977: 205–6). So, while inequalities in power are obvious, it is not clear whether great powers are indeed equal with the rest in law. He then defines great power management as consisting of two distinct practices: 'great powers manage their relations with one another in the interest of international order', and not least by preserving the general balance of power; they 'exploit their preponderance in relation to the rest of the international society', by acting either in concert or unilaterally (206). However, the first of these two practices clearly overlaps with what Bull otherwise defines as a separate institution of international society, balance of power.

Both tensions may result from a certain blind spot in the English School's approach generally. Bull intends to avoid 'domestic analogy' as a way of theorizing international order by analogy with the state. Hence his commitment to the principle of the sovereign equality of states which, although producing an international 'state of nature', does not require further transition to a global commonwealth. So, when 'domestic analogy' sneaks back in, this time in the form of the distinction between the rulers and the ruled, he links it conceptually not to any developments in the international law but to the practice of the balance of power, even at the expense of analytical clarity. Ironically, what is blurred through such linking is a deep historical and conceptual continuity between the practices of balancing and ruling; continuity, central for Foucault's analysis of security to which I now turn, so as to prepare some ground for a possible delinking of great power management from the balance of power.

Instruments and technologies of inter-state governance

As has been mentioned already, the defining characteristic of the Westphalian arrangement for Foucault is plurality. Plurality, neither supported by the previous system of right nor ordered towards some future unity, requires its own principle of organization, and this is what the balance of power is (Foucault 2007: 299). It is maintained through three instruments, and Foucault's analysis of the first two of these – war and diplomacy – is roughly analogous to respective discussions by Bull, pointing in each case to the 'idea of veritable society of states' (303). The third instrument, however, what Foucault calls 'a permanent military apparatus' (305) does not have direct analogues in Bull, and this is where a transition to something rather different from the English School's account of the society of states begins.

The logic of the permanent military apparatus links individual states' domestic systems with the principle of the balance of power. In so far as the Westphalian system is an ever changing relation of forces, it is not enough to know this relation at any given moment (through diplomacy) or to adjust it as need be (through war). States have to possess an entirely different grasp on their own force as well. The need to maintain a navy, a costly venture even in time of peace, necessitates and enables sweeping financial reform in England, for example (Brewer 1989). Similarly wide-ranging legal reforms and new agricultural policies are introduced because, having learned how to mobilize increasingly large armies, early-modern states still had to learn how to disband them without turning major war-endings into civil disorders (Innes 1994). The implications for international order run deeper still.

If the first three instruments of the society of states are classed by Foucault as 'political-military', there also emerges a whole new toolbox that states develop to maintain the European balance – 'police': 'From the seventeenth-century "police" begins to refer to the set of means by which the state's forces can be increased while preserving the state in good order'; but, since in the newly-created field of forces 'there will be imbalance if within the European equilibrium there is a state, not my state, with bad police', action must be taken in the name of the balance of power so that 'there is good police, even in other states' (Foucault 2007: 313–15). Obviously, apart from the suggestion that intervention in the name of good governance may have earlier origins than the Bush Doctrine, the fact that domestic politics may have 'international sources' is not lost on IR (Gourevitch 1978). The connection between 'police', Machiavellianism, mercantilism and the state's ambition to manage its human resources is also well studied (Wallerstein 1980, Hont 1990, Pocock 1990). My interest here is in a somewhat different and more general point related to the continuity mentioned earlier or to another 'domestic analogy'.

Underlying Foucault's exploration of the multifaceted connection between the rise of 'police' and the requirements of the European equilibrium is his more general focus on the relation between ethics, economics and politics that had been destabilized long before the Peace of Westphalia. At least since Machiavelli and reactions to his writings, 'the doctrine of the Prince or the juridical theory of the sovereign constantly try to make clear the discontinuity between the Prince's power and any other form of power, which involves explaining, asserting and founding this discontinuity' (Foucault 2007: 94) as, for example, the discontinuity between ethics (self-governance), economics (governance of the household) and politics (governance of the whole; that is, that state). In contemporary IR, such explanations and assertions usually emphasize the primacy of politics (Buzan and Little 2001). Starting with Hans Morgenthau's insistence on the political character of his realism; through Kenneth Waltz's *Theory of International Politics*, 'political' because international structure, as the organizing principle of international system, is understood in terms of the binary opposition of anarchy and hierarchy, rather than, say, economic opposition of wealth and dearth or the ethical one of good and evil; to Alexander Wendt's *Social Theory of International Politics* in which 'politics' no longer has any specific meaning, apart from being an allusion to Waltz.

In the case of the English School, this affirmation of the primacy of politics is marked with significant ambiguities. When Martin Wight (1966) argued for the non-existence of International Theory, he opposed the state, as the subject-matter of Political Theory, to the realm of international relations, marked with the recurrence and repetition of contingency and in that sense similar to the Aristotelian *oikonomia*, of which there could not be any theory in principle on account of the contingent character of this activity of governing the household. When, however, Bull (1966) invoked contingency in his 'case for the classical approach', contingency appears as a characteristic of genuinely political action, because now politics is opposed to the regularities of economistic scientific modelling. Yet, both texts purport to affirm the same case, based on the discontinuity of politics from other human endeavours. And one would be hard pressed to find in either of them any account of the transformation through which politics was displaced by the alliance of science and economics from its 'classical' position as an activity exclusively concerned with the governance of the whole, be it the whole of the state or the whole of the society of states (even though E.H. Carr's (1939) *Twenty Years' Crisis, 1919–1939: An Introduction to the Study of International Relations* does contain something of this kind).

Foucault's point that in the various 'arts of government', such as ethics, economics and politics, 'one must try to identify both an upward and a downward continuity', opens up theoretical space for such an account. The study of 'downward continuity' leads in the direction of 'police' by acknowledging that the good government of the state has its implications for both family- and self-governance. That of 'upward continuity' develops as a lesson in politics for the Machiavellian Prince who, starting with the art of governing himself, gradually acquires the skills needed for governing the state. By around the eighteenth century, however, both lines began to extend significantly: 'government in respect of its pursuits had come to enjoy a lengthened tether and could browse upon pastures hitherto far out of its reach' (Oakeshott 1993: 11). On the descending line, 'police' developed into biopolitics, while the starting point of this descent was pushed further up, as it were, by the ascending line, now culminating not in the affairs of the state but those of the society of states. Put differently, 'police' begins as 'international police', premised on the recognition that the conditions of international order impact the conduct of both individuals and national economies, and begins immediately where politics now peaks, so that the two lines form, as it were, a full circle, within which the meanings of both politics and economics change dramatically. Thus, if in the sixteenth century, the word 'economy' still designated, as in Aristotle, a *form* of government, 'in the eighteenth century, through a series of complex processes ... it will designate a level of reality and a field of intervention for government' (Foucault 2007: 94–5).

Some define this, by now global, field as a single 'business civilization' (Cox 2000), others, equally provocatively, as an Empire (Hardt and Negri 2001). For the US neoconservatives, this is the 'geoeconomics' which, allegedly, failed to bring about the end of history on its own and has to be supported by democratic geopolitics. But where is this geopolitics to begin in the uninterrupted circular movement of politics and 'police'? Back in the interwar period, Morgenthau (1929) argued *contra* Carl Schmitt – perhaps, the most significant twentieth-century thinker of those attempting to explain, affirm or found the distinctiveness of the 'political' – that anything can be made political, but only through some form of nationalism. Or, perhaps, through some other form of exceptionalism that will allow to clarify the meaning of 'great power' in great power management.

The Story of Two Exceptionalisms

For my purposes, a meaningful distinction between 'politics' and 'police' is needed as well, albeit for reasons different from the neoconservative ones. If made, it will allow for the disentanglement of great power management from the balance of power and thus the removal of one of the analytical tensions in Bull's analysis. The balance of power will then be tied conceptually to the instruments of the society of states identified by Foucault as military-political, above all, war and diplomacy, whereas great power management, as an exercise of great powers' preponderance in relation to the rest of the international society, will be related to 'police'. However, it should be clear by now that to draw such a distinction is not easy, if possible at all, given the tight continuity between politics and 'police' affirmed in Foucault's analysis. Moreover, exceptionalism implied in the idea of great power is at loggerheads with the exceptionalism presupposed, both in theory and in practice, by the 'science of police'. In practice, the clash of these two exceptionalisms may be seen as one cause of the Russian–Georgian war. In theory, this clash is, perhaps, best understood through Iver B. Neumann's (2008) recent revision of Russia's claim to greatpowerhood, if one aspect of this revision, directly related to Foucault's analysis of 'police', is clarified and another characteristic of greatpowerhood, not present in either Foucault or Neumann, is added.

City-citizen and shepherd-flock games

Neumann approaches the idea of great power by focussing not on Russia's well-known and long-standing claim to be one but rather on the difficulties Russia has always had in having this claim recognized by others. 'Others' in question do not include all sorts of realists for whom the issue is decided solely by the state's material capabilities while great powers themselves have existed and will exist always (Mearsheimer 2001) not least because the 'inequality of states ... makes stability possible' (Waltz 1967: 224). It is precisely the ambiguity of Russia's claim that suggests the inadequacy of such a 'quantitative' approach. So, in addition to it, Neumann examines another, qualitative, approach to great powers, in which their 'greatness' is evaluated in terms of the quality of governance. It has a venerable historical pedigree and culminates in Foucault's analysis of liberalism, as a tradition of governing less, governing indirectly, placed by Neumann alongside the 'science of police' (a placement I shall revisit later). Russia, ostensibly committed to direct state intervention, appears outside of this tradition and thus outside of the club of great powers if membership in this club is judged not merely by the state's capacity to project its material power but also by the quality of its government. Importantly, this liberal rejection of Russia's claim is presented by Neumann as a continuation of another, 'civilizational' ranking of states, also focussed on the mode of government and restricting membership in the great powers club exclusively to well-governed, that is, civilized societies.

Although such reading of Foucault is quite possible, it does not make explicit enough one significant development associated with the rise of 'police'. Foucault himself outlines it by citing Catherine the Great: 'Police regulations are of a completely different kind than other civil laws. The things of police are things of each moment, whereas the things of the law are definitive and permanent'; and Foucault's editors do not fail to notice that this quote reproduces almost exactly a passage from Montesquieu (Foucault 2007: 340, 360 n. 18). What it also reproduces, of course, is the Aristotelian distinction between the modes of government appropriate for *polis* and *oikos*, politics and economics; only now, aided by the conjoined operation of statistics and 'police', it is *oikonomia* that is about to become the terrain of scientific certainty and administration. In his pursuit of continuity between the various arts of government, Foucault immediately emphasizes the affinity between 'police' regulations and laws proper; but those intent on making the distinction between politics and economics stress another, rather disturbing, continuity: between liberal democracies and autocracies that in their resort to extra-legal modes of governance transform political worlds into 'deserts' (Arendt 2005: 93–200) – a clear allusion to an ancient statement about Roman practices reported by Tacitus: 'to usurp under false titles, they call empire; and where they make a desert, they call it peace' (Cf.: Ranciere 1994: 27–9). Read this way, is not Russia practicing precisely the techniques of 'police' by seeing to it that the state remains in good order while accumulating the much needed force? And why not read the 'autocratic' delinking of economic growth and particular form of democracy as nothing but one of the techniques of government?

This interpretation would still be compatible with Neumann's conclusions: although 'catching up' with the West in terms of reliance on 'police' mode of governance, Russia is excluded from the league of great powers on account of the non-liberal character of its way of 'policing'. The overall conflict, then, of which the Russian–Georgian war may be an instance, is between the two, liberal and non-liberal, modes of 'police' governance and not between 'police' and politics, as this conflict is often presented in the contemporary Russian foreign-policy discourse, where it is possible to detect a somewhat ambiguous theme positing the strong state as a precondition of the individuals' good life and their very survival, while, at the same time, placing the state, in its relations with other states, on the side of the ultimate good (Morozov 2009).

This theme, in turn, can be read against the background of Foucault's outline of the objective of 'police', which, as the neoconservative promotion of democracy, no longer postulates order as its end. Instead, 'the objective of police is everything from being to well-being, everything that may produce this well-being beyond being, and in such way that the well-being of the individuals is the state's strength' (Foucault 2007: 328). At this point, in the manuscript, Foucault notes that well-being or the 'good' implied in this definition completely changes its meaning from that of Saint Thomas where individual conduct is considered good when it is directed towards the supreme good. Whereas, in drawing this contrast, Foucault (2001: 201–22) is primarily interested in distinguishing the 'good' grounded theologically from the one grounded in the 'reason of state', Aquinas' understanding itself marks a radical change from the ancient one, in which the good constitution of the *polis* allowed for, rather than resulted from, the good life of its members. Put differently, the distinction between politics and 'police' may be understood as that between the 'city-citizen' and the 'shepherd-flock' power-games played out throughout history on the 'bodies politic' of modern states turning them into 'demonic projects' marked with 'the confluence of the murderous power of the sovereign's sword and the productive, vitalist power of biopolitics' (Prozorov 2007: 57). This ambiguous, dualistic character of the modern state, significantly complicates the decision to be made within Neumann's qualitative tradition, whether this or that state belongs to the great powers club or not. Membership may be denied because the state in question does not play the 'shepherd-flock' or 'police' game properly or because it plays an altogether different, 'city-citizen' or politics, game.

One way of addressing this ambiguity is to focus on what Neumann's overall framework does not capture at all: the question of how exactly the decision is made. However, before addressing this question, it is necessary to consider one aspect of greatpowerhood missing from the analyses of both Foucault and Neumann. The proposed polarization between quantitative and qualitative approaches, while allowing for the change in the meaning of great power in principle, does not question the omnipresence of great powers throughout history. We may, following realism, understand Athens as a great power merely because it had the material capabilities that allowed Athenians to get whatever they wanted, thus setting them apart from lesser states that could only hope to adapt to the external environment. Alternatively, we can understand Athenian exploits by reference to the quality of their domestic regime, which will give significantly new meaning to the Melian dialogue (Garst 1989). Yet, in itself, such change of perspective alone cannot account for another difference: the difference in great powers' status within the international society as a whole. And this difference, it seems, requires the re-introduction of the juridical perspective.

When Thucydides' contemporaries read the Melian dialogue, they indeed could have understood that Athenian *hegemonia*, indisputable as far as force was concerned, was no longer a matter of *time*, 'bestowed informally by free consent of the Greek community as reward for achievements, and retained by consent, not by force', as seemed to be the case at the outbreak of the Peloponnesian war. Instead, it became a matter of *arkhe*, connoting 'something akin to our notion of political control', initially applicable only 'to authority within a city state and only later to rule or influence over city states' (Lebow and Kelly 2001: 594–5). They also could have attributed this change to the destruction of the Greek *nomos* (concrete conventional order) caused not only by prolonged warfare but also by a then current wave of democratization that eroded the preceding aristocratic order (Lebow 2001). Finally, they could have read Athenian rejection of Melian friendship – 'your hostility cannot so hurt us as your friendship' – as a blatant violation of law, *dike*, but only in the sense that *dike* mostly regulated procedural arrangements for the restoration of friendship rather than arbitration aimed at achieving 'a technically satisfactory settlement' based on a shared understanding of rights and obligations (Wight 1977: 43–73). All this is in stark contrast to the self-understanding of the great powers at the Congress of Vienna, who saw their alliance as standing 'for the law of nations' (Bridge and Bullen 1980: 20) and framed their rhetoric and provisions in expressly juridical terms.

Put differently, preponderance, established at the Congress of Vienna and maintained within international order ever since can be described as *legalized* hegemony, different from both *time* and *arkhe* of the Greeks in its ambition to translate preponderance into the legal norm (Simpson 2004).

Recognition vs. expertise

Foucault's focus on the 'shepherd-flock' game certainly implies a move away from the juridical theory of sovereignty, and Neumann follows this move. But can we really grasp the idea of great power whose heyday is usually associated with the Congress of Vienna without any recourse to this theory? And who would represent this theory better than Schmitt, for whom the presence of great powers in that period endowed even wars with the character of 'completely legal procedures' (Schmitt 2006: 186). This characterization is based on Schmitt's insistence that genuinely legal procedures are possible only when the formal body of law remains grounded in the concrete order, *nomos*. Since 1815, European great powers succeeded in translating their preponderance in strength into a position of the guardians of this grounding, understood here almost literally, since the *nomos* in question was, in turn, grounded in the territorial divisions of Europe and the practice of land-appropriation.

There was, however, another characteristic of great power presence in the post-1815 world that resonates with Schmitt's understanding of legal order generally; namely, great powers' peculiar position vis-à-vis the rest of the international society. On the one hand, they were immersed in the day-to-day activities of the world, following with 'extraordinary interest' even those conflicts in which they themselves remained neutral (192). On the other, these conflicts seemed to acquire their form as 'completely legal procedures' precisely when the great powers remained neutral, not least because wars between the great powers themselves had a tendency of turning total, in the sense of rupturing the spatial order that served as a foundation of legal order (187). As though great powers had to perform a delicate balancing act indeed, what really had to be balanced was their paradoxical position both inside and outside of the society of states. This corresponds to Schmitt's understanding of the sovereign position within legal order established through the decision on exception.

In the case of international order, however, this decision worked, as it were, in two opposing directions. First and foremost, it was the decision on exclusion by which war was bracketed as exception and order/peace installed in its position of the rule, even if it was recognized that through the practices of land-appropriation and territorial adjustments this rule remained grounded in exception. In addition to this, the sovereign decision became a decision on inclusion – inclusion into the club of great powers itself, so that recognition 'as a Great Power became and remained a legal institution of international law, as important as the recognition of a new state or government' (191). In fact, the tone in which Schmitt discusses the mutual recognition of great powers almost suggests that, far from being a form of quasi-sovereignty, the reign of great powers is an example of perfect sovereignty in which sovereign decision gives shape not only to the concrete situation the sovereign is facing, but also to the sovereign itself, and does so, as in the mythologized instance of the founding of the state, without any extrinsic support from either hereditary right or electoral procedures.

If we accept this strong emphasis on recognition as central for the juridical understanding of both great powers themselves and their legalized hegemony within international society, one of the practical implications of this will follow from Barry Buzan and Ole Wæver's (2003) suggestion that today both NATO and the EU may be considered as great powers. Within a Schmittian framework, accession to these collectively constituted great powers should be subject to recognition by other great powers, certainly those who express their concerns on the issue. With the latest rounds of both NATO and EU enlargements, however, the mantra of both aspiring and existing member-states was: Russia has no legitimate say in this process shaped exclusively by a set of criteria established by these organizations themselves. As the NATO Secretary General reiterated after the 2008 war: 'I would expect the NATO summit ... to reaffirm our position ... that Georgia will become a member of NATO once Georgia fulfills the necessary criteria' (Shields 2010).

This emphasis on set criteria, rather than highly indeterminate political decisions, of which the mutual recognition by great powers is the supreme one, is also characteristic of Neumann's analysis. Although most of what we know about Russia, be it its material capabilities or the quality of its government, we learn from the reports of its 'others', these reports operate with a fixed set of criteria readily available in both quantitative and qualitative approaches. It is tempting, at this point, to argue that here, as in the famous account of the meta-theoretical problems that once plagued IR regime-theory (Kratochwil and Ruggie 1986), the intersubjective character of the subject-matter (mutual recognition) is at odds with objectivist knowledge on the basis of which decisions on greatpowerhood are made. In the juridical theory of sovereignty, Schmitt's understanding of recognition removes this incoherence. Here, statements like 'The only state which did not know its place in the hierarchy of power was the Ottoman Empire' (Bridge and Bullen 1980: 3) should be read literally. The Ottoman Empire was not confused or undecided as to whether it was admitted into the club or not and in accordance with what criteria. It quite literally did not know and in fact could not know its position in lieu of recognition by the great powers, since only this recognition, as with Hobbesian Leviathan (Williams 1996) created meaningful knowledge in matters of power and rank.

Still, it may be premature to charge Neumann with incoherence, because central to the rise of 'police' as an 'art of government' different from juridical sovereignty is precisely the kind of knowledge that rejects Schmittian decisionism in favour of statistical certainty. Here, the various Western observers cited by Neumann represent entities whose own power 'is not political power at all, but purely administrative power – power of the experts and interpreters of life' (Ojakangas 2005: 16).

So it is not really surprising that one such expert and interpreter, Edward Lucas, while summing up possible lessons from the Russian–Georgian war, concluded that 'diplomatic recognition is basically a formality, a technicality, and it doesn't really make much difference' (RFE/RL 2009). And although the Estonian president quoted at the beginning will certainly disagree on this point, he, nevertheless, knows only too well that it is the 'police' expertise that makes all the difference between the 'postmodernist 21st century' and the times when 'it dawned on our 19th-century forebears that Estonians are equal to other nations' (Ilves 2010a):

> And here we are. But this is not the end of history as was believed earlier. We struggled for twenty years to secure our liberty. We met criteria and cleared bars, carried out reforms and did our homework. Estonia was like a student who arrived at school – Europe, in this case – decades after class had begun. By then, the curriculum had long been in place. That era is now over. We are no longer the best student in a remedial class. After 1 January 2011, when the euro is adopted, only self-imposed goals will remain. (Ilves 2010b)

Characteristically, in the years leading up to the Russian–Georgian war, Estonia, as well as the other two Baltic states, actively disseminated expertise and interpretations acquired in the 'school, Europe, in this case' in Georgia and Ukraine. Not surprisingly, when during the war Russia dismissed such practices as 'virtual projects' (Lavrov 2009), this rhetoric itself appeared 'unsettling' even without military intervention: it unsettled that very order of ranks through which states like Estonia were struggling to break so as to secure their independence – the order that ranks 'police' expertise higher than the constitution and stability of the whole from which the idea of 'well-being' is derived in the juridical mode of government.

Still, the goal of securing one's independence as a sovereign people seems to have been paradoxically immune from change since the nineteenth century, even within this paradigm of governance. In fact, it can find its footing in Foucault's (2001: 217, n. 10) own suggestion that the arts of government are always 'in some sense immanent to the population' of a given state that effectively limits the universality of the 'inter-state police' by reintroducing not merely specific state-borders but Westphalian order as such. Yet, this is a tenuous limitation challenged by Foucault's understanding of the 'population' as already a product of 'police' which, unlike the 'people' of juridical sovereignty, does not possess any immanent ways of governance. Further, it cannot be limited to a given state's territory. As with 'economy', 'population' becomes a 'level of reality' and a field of governmental intervention which, in turn, can no longer be limited to state-government.

This latter tendency is reinforced once liberalism is placed vis-à-vis 'police' more precisely than in Neumann. Whereas liberalism clearly inherits from 'police' its focus on the individual well-being as well as diffuse, indirect techniques of governing, its significance and distinctiveness rest on the fact that 'for the first time the arts of government were systematically linked to the practice of freedom' (Rose 1999: 68). It is now that governing as the 'conduct of conduct' becomes an activity distinguished by its ambition to conduct the conduct of individuals themselves recognized as capable of freely conducting their own activities. But as an immediate corollary of this, comes the requirement of a prior distinction, made by way of recognition: distinction between those who, being capable of free conduct themselves, can be governed in this manner and those who, because of their ignorance of or aversion to individual freedom, can only be governed in some other way (Hindess 2005).

As such, this distinction is nothing but a decision, a decision on the worth of life both as 'being and well-being'; a decision which, unlike the 'police' activity of 'conducting conduct' itself, is resolutely political in so far as it presupposes the whole and gives it concrete shape by introducing divisions within it; a decision of which the neoconservative opposition between democracies and autocracies is a type; a decision which, as in the case of Schmitt's great powers, takes the form of recognition. Recognition which, as in Neumann, differs from Schmitt's mutual recognition of great powers in that it neither requires nor grants reciprocity.

Another Domestic Analogy

At this point, it is possible to define great power management as a 'police' mode of governing whereby great powers 'conduct the conduct' of the rest of the international society, whose members, sovereign states, are posited by Westphalian arrangements as free individuals capable of conducting their own affairs. Defined this way, great power management is, in principle, distinct from the political organization of the society of states, be it in the form of the 'classical' balance of power or the liberal distinction between individuals capable and incapable of exercising their freedom. Except that in the latter case, states have to reaffirm their credentials as free individuals in accordance with the new rules: their 'freedom' is now measured in terms of their own capacity for administrative management which, in turn, requires their acceptance of the freedom of their citizens. This, needless to say, introduces a whole gamut of issues related to humanitarian intervention, rogue states and such like. Moreover, by demoting states to the position of administrators, the new rules do not merely modify the restriction on the membership in the great powers club, as in Neumann, but, in a manner resembling Trotsky, tend to consign the establishment as such to the 'waste bin of history'. Hence the array of euphemisms, from the 'leader' to 'indispensable nation', recently introduced by the US in its self-acclamations (Lebow and Kelly 2001: 606) or the way in which Condoleezza Rice (2008) countered Russia's claim to greatpowerhood, threatening it not with the opposite of greatness, whatever that may be, but 'irrelevance'.

But can there be great power management without great powers? Counterintuitive as it may sound, 'yes' is a possible answer, provided we now revisit the second contentious issue in Bull's analysis, that of fact and right, by, again, juxtaposing 'police' and juridical approaches to government.

New nomos *of the globe*

Obviously, the concurrent demotion of states to the position of administrators and reintroduction of politics in the form of decision on the 'suitability' for liberal governance begs the question: Who, then, is to make this decision? The answer given from within 'liberal political reason' itself explicitly takes issue not only with Foucault's defence of the 'immanent' ways of governing but also with the English School's account of the evolution of international society, mobilizing them against each other. The English School's story of the successful expansion of the European society of states to the rest of the world challenges Foucault's argument that the means used by government are 'immanent to the population', while Foucault's account of 'population' is extended to challenge the English School's commitment to the original Westphalian system. The net-result is a 'focus on the governmental character of the modern states system and its continuities with the states system of the colonial era' that affirms the continuity of governance throughout both the domestic and the international spheres:

> What unites the many late-twentieth-century projects of neoliberal reform – the corporatization and privatization of state agencies, the promotion of competition, individual choice, and autonomy in health, education, and other areas of what

> Western states once regarded as the proper sphere of social policy, and so on – is the attempt to introduce not only market and quasi-market arrangements but also empowerment, self-government, and responsibility into areas of social life that had hitherto been organized in other ways. (Hindess 2005: 409)

In other words, the state is not the only decision-maker around. Although this is indeed different from the English School's account, the juridical theory of sovereignty generally has its own version of this story to tell. One of its possible beginnings is with the Salamanca school of international law which responded to the ethical and theological problems of the Conquista by attempting to articulate *ius gentium* as a universally valid, even if man-made, arrangement, and, having rediscovered the Roman notion of *dominium*, not only drew a distinction between public and private international law, but resolutely privileged the latter over the former, thus extending the power of *dominium* beyond Princes towards all humans: 'To disrupt commercial relations is a violation of *ius gentium* that is punishable by war' (Koskenniemi 2009: 23; see also Ortega 1996).

The emphasis placed by the English School on the protestant, Grotian beginnings of international law is in large measure due to the latter's rearticulation of *ius gentium* in the direction of the '*public* law of Europe' (Bull 1977: 33–4, emphasis added) even if the expression is used not in strict legal terms. However, in the nineteenth century, the Salamancas made a mighty comeback when international law, by then separated from natural law and thus significantly relativized, had to respond to the practices of imperialism. Unlike the conquistadors, imperialists did not question the humanity of the locals but had serious doubts about their capacity to possess the European idea of sovereignty, which rendered any transfers of sovereignty problematic. Consequently, the 'scramble for Africa' was conducted mostly by way of privatizations, which granted to the locals their 'human rights', but limited these rights to those of property ownership (Koskenniemi 2001: 98–178).

Despite his, sometimes rather annoying, tendency to put most of the blame on the Americans, Schmitt (2003: 210) was clearly aware of the development: 'After 1900, it became customary to distinguish sharply between *internal* and *external*. The result was that its significance for the reality of interstate international law became muddled. In particular, not enough attention was paid to the fact that the classic form of the state in European international law contained a dualism *within itself*, namely, between public and private law. Neither of these dualisms can be isolated'. By focussing exclusively on the inside/outside distinction (the ground for 'domestic analogy'), international lawyers overlooked the rise of private international law, the economic relations it regulated, and tensions that were created between the two kinds of international law. The connection between these tensions and the erosion of the European *nomos* became most visible in the spheres of influence established in Africa.

Although spheres of influence, the most visible attribute of great power management, are often presented as having their origins in times immemorial. Bull (1977: 219–25) replicates Hume's manner of analysing the balance of power, by suggesting that, perhaps, not only the phrase but the practice itself, in its distinct modern form, is modern and originates in the nineteenth century. Like some later, more elaborate, 'linguistic' analyses (Kratochwil 1986), he then attributes their demise to the lack of explicit agreement on their legitimacy between the great powers of the next century.

Schmitt's account is significantly different. At the Congo Conference of 1885, great powers and lesser states discussed their spheres of influence quite explicitly, but their prolonged deliberations led to the dissolution of the European order. The problem was not with the expansion as such, but with the change in the meaning of land-appropriation. Instead of extending the European principle of territorial organization to the new lands, so that the status of Belgian colonies, if Belgium were to have any, would be consistent with the neutrality of Belgium itself guaranteed by the great powers, Europeans introduced a new principle, 'effective occupation', that turned the whole issue from a public concern of all European states into 'an individual question of Belgian foreign rights' which it addressed through private agencies, as 'a completely practical matter' (Schmitt 2003: 223). Accordingly, the recognition of Congo was no longer a political act, but a matter of conditionality and testing, a precedent that was elevated into a general principle at Versailles (Cf.: Rutherford 1926). In the meantime, the actual practices of 'effective occupation', the establishment of 'death camps' and 'cordons sanitaire' as part of health policies (Lyons 1985) revealed yet again the 'demonic' character of 'police' governing as 'a monstrous unison of the executioner and the physician' (Prozorov 2007: 57).

Not surprisingly, then, IR accounts that take seriously both juridical and biopolitical approaches to global governance, often end up with an outline of a new *nomos* of the Earth: non-Westphalian and non-territorial because decisions as interpretations of life are now often taken by diffused non-state actors, and not at the outer borders of states as 'bodies politic' but on the bodies of humans who find themselves in the zones of indistinction between private and public, inside and outside, *oikos* and *polis*, none of which can be taken for granted in their 'classical' meaning (Edkins 2000, Vaughan-Williams 2009).

An 'angelic project'

Shortly before noting that since 1815, European equilibrium 'explicitly and systematically' begins to 'function as a sort of inter-state police or as right', Foucault (2007: 315) mentions a text from 1611, 'with a curious title of *La Monarchie aristodémocratique*' (313). Perhaps, the title did not sound so curious back in the seventeenth century. When, in 1642, Charles I rejected the demands of the Long Parliament, he did so by claiming that the mixed constitution of England, as conjoined rule of the one, the few and the many, represented a perfect combination of the three pure forms of government, monarchy, aristocracy and democracy, derived from antiquity. In arguing so, he had a tradition to draw upon: this line of argument was in circulation in England already by the fifteenth century. But since

Charles' adherence to it resulted in civil war, Hobbes rejected the idea in favour of absolute sovereignty. Yet, by the time Hume was writing his *History of England*, the mixed constitution was again considered to be the closest approximation to an ideal commonwealth (Weston 1955) and also the original, 'domestic' version of the balance of power.

As it turned out, it was easier to replace a literally beheaded king than the pan-European Empire beheaded, metaphorically, at Westphalia. The ideal society of states, *jus publicum Europaeum*, indeed resembled something like an aristodemocracy, where the aristocratic club of great powers reigned over the democratically organized world of sovereign and equal states. In the best of all possible worlds, great powers' intervention with this world was limited to their 'extraordinary interest' in its affairs, as if, like the best of all possible governments, they ruled by doing nothing. A view, strikingly consonant with that of the founder of US neoconservatism, Irving Kristol (1967: 602): 'a great power is "imperial" because what it does *not* do is just as significant, and just as consequential, as what it does'. Except that, referring to the real world, Kristol immediately added: 'a great power does not have the range of freedom of action derived from the freedom of inaction that a small power possesses'.

So, what is it, then, that keeps the real-world great powers busy? For one, Schmitt knew they *were* doing something else, and this proliferation of functions eroded the practice of their mutual recognition. Thus, when the two wars with China and then with Russia, won by Japan in the beginning of the twentieth century 'were seen by the European Great Powers as reception parties for Japan's entrance into the narrow circle of the Great Powers that sustained international law', for the Japanese themselves, 'the pivotal event was their participation in the punitive expedition of the Great Powers against China' (Schmitt 2003: 191). Similar confusion in domestic politics would be described as 'confusion of powers'.

Now, what interests Foucault in the 1611 book is that, instead of the discussion of the pure forms of government that the title seems to invite, it discusses something altogether different: how already existing governmental offices set up for the administration of justice, finances and armies should be complimented with an office responsible for the administration of citizens' well-being; that is, 'police'. Similarly, when Hume was announcing the general acceptance of the mixed constitution, his friend, Adam Smith, was preparing a book known to us as *Lectures on Jurisprudence* but with its subject-matter defined as 'justice, police, revenue and arms'. If published, the book would have completed the triad that started with the discussion of ethics, continued with the analysis of economics and culminated in the treatise on politics; a sequence Foucault (2007: 94) presents as almost canonical in the education of the French dauphine in the seventeenth century. With Smith, as with some other thinkers of the time, however, the question was no longer that of the forms of government, but a more familiar one of the division of powers.

Something similar was happening, it seems, in the self-understanding of the great powers at the Congress of Vienna where they in effect usurped the proceedings:

> The advantage of this mode of proceeding is that you ... keep the power by concert and management in your own hands, but without openly assuming authority to [others'] exclusion. You obtain a sort of sanction from them for what you are determined at all events to do, which they cannot well withhold ... And you entitle yourselves, without disrespect to them, to meet together for dispatch of business for an indefinite time to their exclusion. (Simpson 2004: 99)

Only the authorship of Castlereagh and the context to which this statement referred, betrayed the fact that it was made on behalf of the European great powers and not some European executive of the time.

Put differently, once their hegemony, legalized in 1815, was stated 'explicitly and systematically', great powers seemed to acquire, as Castlereagh clearly saw, not only the sovereign 'power by concert' but also the task of 'management', as a specific 'executive' function of interstate governance. In their own way, the great powers of the post-World War II world, describing themselves as world-policemen, knew that just as well. And so did the Byzantines, who, in their encounters with numerous restless neighbours, generally preferred procrastination to action (Shepard 1985), but when pressed to get their hands dirty with actual government, considered that to be an expression of the divine *oikonomia* (Obolensky 1963).

In his own genealogy of the modern idea of government, meant to compliment that of Foucault, Giorgio Agamben (2007) stresses that the early Christian meaning of divine *oikonomia* had nothing to do with any preordained plan but rather referred to the *ad hoc*, anarchical management of the world and also to the structure of relations within the Trinity polarized into the dualism of reign and governance; a dualism Agamben relates not only to a wide range of theological and philosophical concepts but also to the juridical and biopolitical approaches to governance. Here, the state, or modern order generally, appears as an 'angelic project' in so far as angels in the theological constructions, just like ministers in the governmental ones, make possible a kind of governance in which the world can only be governed in accordance with the nature of the creatures thus governed, 'simply' because these creatures are also this government's creations.

Bequeathed by Christian theology to the worldly governments of the West, the intra-trinitarian structure of governance introduced not only the distinction between a legislator-god who reigns by setting out general laws-principles and his executives whose activities, to recall Catherine the Great, are 'the things of police' which 'are things of each moment', but also the radical split between all worldly action and its foundations in being, thus rendering all action and all politics anarchical, non-foundational, and also estranged from the world in which it necessarily has to unfold. So that while history lasts, until the judgement day, this mode of government, invariably vicarious in its character, although aimed at global well-being beyond mere survival, produces a kind of collateral effect: 'Whether it is a matter of the breaking down of preexisting constitutional forms or the imposition, through military occupation, of constitutional models considered democratic on peoples to whom these models appear to be impracticable, in every case the essential thing is that a region – and, at the limit, the entire globe – is governed while remaining completely foreign' (2007: 158).

The anarchical character of governance is also the reason why governmental technologies not merely identify subjects suited for the application of these technologies, but create them. Replaying the relation posited by theology between the creator capable of ruling over worldly creatures in ways congenial to their own nature only because this very nature is owed by them to his creation, modern governmental technologies 'must always imply a process of subjectification, that is to say, they must produce their own subject' (Agamben 2009: 11). And one of the privileged techniques of subjectification, again, because of its place within the complex of trinitarian relations, is glorification; that is, production of a subject who is not merely capable of freely moving about his or her own business but a subject who is 'great'. From the early Christian liturgy, through Machiavellian *grandezza* and the early-modern search for everything that gives 'splendour' to the state (identified by Foucault (2007: 313) as one of the beginnings of 'police') to the totalitarian salutations and contemporary spectacle of opinion-polls, glorification has gone hand in hand with modern governance. Unlike the ancients, in whose world, glory occupied a central position but was, in principle, inseparable from action the way action itself was, in principle, inseparable from being, the moderns had to devise the various techniques of acclamation and self-acclamation to make their governance, predicated on the separation of powers, possible (Agamben 2007).

Without going any further into this dense text, we may set the duality of reign and government identified in it against another theological analogy, used by Michael Hardt and Antonio Negri (2000: 36) in which various non-governmental agencies, especially those concerned with representing the whole of humanity, are identifying the sins of the world by offering their interpretations of life, and leave 'to the "secular wing" the task of actually addressing the problems'. Within the corners of this analogy, it is not at all impossible to imagine a world in which 'great powers', whose 'greatness' is now indeed reduced to merely 'quantitative' preponderance, perform the executive managerial role only, while reigning is done by someone else; or, more precisely, it is necessary to investigate the exact manner in which reign and governance, politics and 'police', juridical and governmental approaches to global rule are allocated in today's world and what role 'greatness' plays in such allocations.

Anarchical Sovereignty/Anarchical Governance

It would be interesting to attempt such an investigation by revisiting, for example, a moment in history clearly privileged in realist thinking, the Concert of Europe, and to ask whether or not the major powers of the day recognized in Napoleon's undertaking not only a very old ambition to impose upon Europe a single *authority*, but also a genuinely new one: to establish a European *government* (Cf.: Schroeder

1994 for an historical analysis along these lines). And while resolutely rejecting the former, they stealthily embraced the latter. Hence 'power by concert' *and* 'management' in the hands of the great powers now recognized as 'great' in some distinctly new way. Hence, also, Kissinger's dramatization of the story into a fortuitous personal alliance between Metternich and Castlereagh, which now could be analysed not in terms of the combination of legitimacy and force but rather in terms of reign and governance, general principles invariably compromised by their practical application, and contingent 'police' regulations which can only partake of the character of law through resort to emergency or exception. So that Metternich's lamentation on the occasion of Castlereagh's suicide – 'The man is irreplaceable, above all for me' – should be read not as Kissinger's (1957: 312) thinly veiled affirmation of the 'indispensability' for Europe of an overseas 'insular power', but as a testimony to the dualistic character of ruling.

Anarchical society, in other words, can only be sustained through an interplay of anarchical sovereignty and anarchical governance; all of them 'anarchical' not because of a lack in authority but of a lack in foundations. Accordingly, it can be adequately analysed through a combination of two approaches, juridical and governmentalist, represented here by Bull and Foucault respectively. Read this way, 'great power management' is not a fixed practice in need of precise theoretical definition, but a research programme focussed on unpacking the complex relationship between the three terms involved.

The volume begins such unpacking by examining the positions of Russia and the US. At first sight, these cannot be further apart. For one, while Russia, during the 2008 conflict, seemed to be eager to assert its great power status, the US emphatically rejected the legitimacy of the institution as such. However, according to Sergei Prozorov, Russia's actions had little if anything to do with great power management, if the latter is understood as an activity of shaping the international society as a whole, or even the regional society of states that emerged from the ruins of the Soviet Union. Instead, Russia's conduct is best understood as an opportunistic attempt to manage the exception which has become the rule within its own domestic order. Irina Papkova, in turn, traces American rejection of greatpowerhood to another version of exceptionalism: the ongoing entrapment of US foreign-policy makers in the Cold War discourse, even when – or, perhaps, especially when – this discourse is privileged as an experience in need of overcoming. Furthermore, whereas the Cold War is hardly remembered fondly in Russia either, the peculiar neoconservative equation of it with the great power competition of the nineteenth century left hardly any space for agreement between the two states.

Within the theoretical framework adopted by Andrei Makarychev, discursive constructions that create such 'chains of equivalence' (for example, Cold War/spheres of influence/nineteenth century/greatpowerhood) are specific to the practices of depoliticization that, in principle, leave no room for a meaningful, non-quantitative articulation of greatpowerhood. Makarychev traces these constructions in the discourses of both Russia and NATO during the 2008 war. However, alongside the practices of depoliticization, he also detects the opposing attempts to politicize the situation, again, traceable on both sides of the NATO–Russia relationship. Some balance between the two is what is needed for the operation of great power management. A similar conclusion is reached in a more policy-oriented analysis of the EU–Russia relations by Jana Kobzova, Nicu Popescu and Andrew Wilson. Here, the inability of both actors to balance their use of 'military-political' and technocratic arsenals, or their 'soft' and 'hard' power, is seen as the main reason behind their failure to manage the post-Soviet space.

According to Pertti Joenniemi, however, speaking of successes or failures in the context of the Russian–Georgian war may be itself problematic, given that the post-war discourse, both academic and policy-oriented, is hardly marked by any significant agreement on either the outcome or the meaning of the conflict. Joenniemi himself proposes to analyse the various approaches by examining the various modes of 'security-speak' present in all of them. These, in turn, are arranged according to the image of international society presupposed in each of them. This focus on securitization allows for accentuating the differences not only between the positions of Russia, the EU and the US, but also the resulting differences in EU–Russia, US–Russia and, if only implicitly, EU–US relations. Following this view, the pragmatic post-war rapprochement in US–Russian relations may not only signal a stronger preference for great power management and a corresponding view of international society, but also raise questions about the effect such pragmatism may have for small states and non-state actors.

The issues of pragmatism and small states within international society are then examined in more detail by Pami Aalto and Alan Chong. Apart from general, English-School-inspired theoretical considerations, both authors focus on the empirics of specific regional practices, the Northern Dimension and ASEAN, and arrive at yet another possible, albeit paradoxical, understanding of 'great power management': Under certain conditions, it may denote a set of practices through which small and medium powers manage the conduct of their potentially intrusive 'great' neighbours.

In practical terms, this paradoxical inversion should not be over exaggerated. Theoretically, however, its very possibility highlights yet again the dynamic character of the overall relationship between 'greatness', 'power' and 'management' in Bull's initial construction. So, in the volume's conclusion, I will return to this relationship, this time with a focus on 'greatness', so as to see which specific mode of 'greatness' may be at work in the various traditions of international thought identified by the English School.

Chapter 2
From *Katechon* to *Intrigant*: The Breakdown of the Post-Soviet *Nomos*

Sergei Prozorov

This chapter addresses the 2008 Russian–Georgian conflict in the context of the post-Soviet spatial order, which can be conceptualized with the help of Carl Schmitt's concept of *nomos*. While the war has been analysed in its numerous aspects (pertaining, for example, to the dynamics of Russian domestic politics, NATO enlargement, EU–Russian relations) (see Allison 2008, King 2008, Cornell and Starr 2009, Asmus 2010), the key significance of this event has arguably been obscured by its own apparent self-evidence. The conflict was the first instance of the violation by Russia of the integrity of the post-Soviet territorial settlement, the spatial order established in the Belovezha treaties of December 1991. While this violation appears obvious, its significance has not been fully appreciated (cf. Allison 2008: 1160). In this chapter, the implications of this breakdown of the post-Soviet *nomos* in the wider context of the post-communist condition will be elucidated and the transformation of Russia's international standing that resulted from this breakdown will be traced.

The background, causes, motives and dynamics of the Russian–Georgian conflict shall therefore be bracketed off and its key outcome, that is, the systemic transformation of the post-Soviet spatial order, which has radically modified Russia's standing in this region in the wider context of the 'great power management' of international society, shall be focused on specifically (Bull 1977: 200–29). While from the beginning of the post-communist period Russia arguably functioned as the restraining force in the post-Soviet realm, adequately described by the political-theological concept of the *katechon*, the 2008 war has made the recourse to this function impossible, plunging the post-Soviet space into the condition of anomie, or the state of exception. However, this process should not be understood in terms of the simple dichotomy of nomos and anomie, whereby Russia's war in Georgia effects the collapse of order into disorder and the degradation of the *katechon* into a proverbial 'rogue state'. Contrary to widespread fears outside Russia and some hopes inside it (see Allison 2009, Chesnakov 2008), Russia's rupture of the post-Soviet *nomos* is not a relapse into a Soviet or pre-Soviet imperialism, nor is it a revolutionary attempt to establish any new *nomos* in the post-Soviet space. It shall be argued that Russia's orientation towards the destruction of the post-Soviet *nomos* should be viewed as the continuation of the domestic political process of the stabilization of the state of exception and thus the adaptation of the *modus operandi* in foreign policy to the domestic strategy of the management of anomie. What we observe is neither a collapse of the institution of great power management nor its abuse by a rogue power, but rather the manifestation of the anomic foundation of every *nomos* or, in terms used by Alexander Astrov in the introduction to this volume, the anarchical character of governmentality. This strategy of the management of anomie in the context of the understanding of post-communism as a post-historical condition will be analysed and the transformation of the logic of the *katechon*, ensuing from it, in terms of Walter Benjamin's theory of baroque sovereignty will be probed. In the conclusion, the implications of this strategy for Russia's standing in the international society shall be addressed.

The Russian–Georgian War and the Demise of the Post-Soviet *Nomos*

The Russian intervention in Georgia in August 2008, provoked by its military offensive in South Ossetia, and the subsequent recognition by Russia of South Ossetia and Abkhazia as independent states not only marked the lowest point in the history of Russian–European relations in the post-communist period but also destabilized the overall post-Cold War world order. According to Alexander Stubb, Finnish foreign minister and, as chair of the OSCE, an active participant in the resolution of this crisis, we may even speak of a 'post-080808 world' (Stubb 2008). Even if this statement might appear to be an exaggeration, given the relatively low intensity of this war and the ultimately inconsequential character of Russia's unilateral recognition of the Georgian provinces, it is undeniable that the Georgian crisis has serious systemic implications for Russia's relations with the West and Europe in particular. The rhetoric of integration seemed to be abandoned by both parties, particularly Russia, whose leaders' statements during and after the conflict did not exclude suspending relations with EU and NATO and proclaimed, in the widely reported words of President Medvedev, that Russia 'did not fear a New Cold War'.

This crisis of the integrationist paradigm has been the main focus of the discussion of the implications of the war both inside and outside Russia (see Asmus 2010, King 2008, cf. Joenniemi 2008), serving as yet another nail in the coffin of the naïve belief in Russia's 'transition to democracy' and yet another vindication of the advocates of Russia's inherent imperialism (see Lucas 2008). Yet, this emphasis on the global implications of a local low-intensity conflict has obscured the significance of the war for the mid-level of the post-Soviet region, roughly coterminous with the Commonwealth of Independent States. While the claim about Russia's ultimate 'breaking with the West' as a result of the war is at best hypothetical, the war has had immediately observable actual effects on the structure of spatial order of the post-Soviet realm. In this chapter, this spatial order shall be referred to as the post-Soviet *nomos*.

The concept of nomos is central to the later work of Carl Schmitt, commonly known as the 'concrete order thinking' period that followed the renunciation of the more famous decisionist approach of the Weimar era. With the current revival of Schmitt's political thought, the theory of *nomos* has become increasingly influential in International Relations; particularly insofar as its connections to the more established disciplinary traditions, like the English School, become clearer (see Odysseos and Petito 2007: 1–18). Just as the project of the English School sought to go beyond the opposition between the international system, defined in the abstract manner by the logic of anarchy and the equally abstract designs for a legal world order in favour of the concrete analysis of the emergence and transformation of the European society of states, Schmitt's theory of nomos, defined by Alessandro Colombo (2007) as 'realist institutionalism', examines the conditions of emergence and eventual demise of the concrete spatial order of the *Jus Publicum Europaeum*. Thus, the theory of *nomos* resonates with the Bullean approach of other contributions to this volume, insofar as it seeks to reconstitute the informal constitution of the international society and the practices of great power management involved in its reproduction and transformation.

Going beyond the opposition of normativism and decisionism, in which a lifeless, abstract norm faced the momentary eruption of the concrete force of life, in his classic *Nomos of the Earth* (2003) Schmitt presents *nomos* as a foundational concept, denoting the totality of the historically concrete spatial order, the unity of order (*Ordnung*) and its localization (*Ortung*) in the concrete life of a community (Schmitt 2003: 42–9, 78–9). The *nomos* of a community is not externally imposed either by norms or decisions but is rather a product of spontaneous historical developments, an immediate expression of the historical continuity of concrete existence of a political entity. While this description suggests a renunciation of Schmitt's emphasis on the transcendence of order (see Prozorov 2005), manifested in the sovereign decision, in favour of the immanentism he previously criticized, the situation is rather more complicated. As Mika Ojakangas (2004: 117) has demonstrated, Schmitt's orientation towards the extreme, excessive or transcendent element of order that is simultaneously its foundation survives in the 'concrete order' period of his writing. It does so in the form of Schmitt's construction of the origin of *nomos* itself in the fundamental act of land appropriation (*Landnahme*), which conditions the possibility of law, both public and private (Schmitt 2003: 80–5). In the theory of the *nomos*, land appropriation serves as a precise analogue of the sovereign decision on the exception, which opens the concrete order to what is exterior yet essential to it: 'in its original sense, *nomos* is precisely the full immediacy of a legal power not mediated by laws. It is a constitutive historical event – an act of legitimacy, whereby the legality of a mere law first is made meaningful' (Schmitt 2003: 73).

Thus, we are not very far from the decisionist affirmation of the constitutive outside of any normative order. For Schmitt, the *nomos* is the condition of possibility of legal order that is itself not legal and it is the oblivion of this foundation of the law in Western modernity that leads to its degradation into a mere system of rules and the degeneration of the state into a nihilistic apparatus of administration. In the international domain, the retreat of the *nomos* into oblivion and the replacement of the spatial order by positive law have led to 'a fundamental separation of order and orientation that [alone] can be called 'nihilism' in an historically specific sense' (Schmitt 2003: 66). While Schmitt's nostalgia for the European *nomos* and its problematic aspects has been addressed elsewhere (Prozorov 2006), for the purposes of this chapter, the basic logic of this concept as an extra-legal foundation of law, the unity of order and localization that grants the political community a sense of orientation in the world shall be retained. Further, the figure that in Schmitt's theory maintains this unity against the perpetual threat of its dissolution, that is, the *katechon* shall be specifically focused on. Before delving into this discussion, let us begin with a brief characterization of the post-Soviet *nomos*.

In order to identify the structure of the post-Soviet *nomos* we need to recall that the process of the dissolution of the USSR was marked by a radical contingency. Not only was this dissolution not inevitable, as it tends to be portrayed by liberal transitionalist approaches since the early 1990s, but more importantly, the very *form* that this dissolution took, that is, the fragmentation of the Union along the internal administrative borders of the republics of the USSR, was itself utterly contingent. To see this, we need only recall the heated political debates in the final years of Perestroika about potential border revisions in the process of the dissolution of the Soviet Union. In his widely influential article 'Rebuilding Russia' Alexander Solzhenitsyn (1990) famously argued that the survival of the Soviet Union was unfeasible and charted the potential outline of its gradual dissolution along ethnic and religious lines. According to his scenario, the three Baltic republics, the three Republics of the Caucasus, the four Central Asian republics and possibly Moldova would 'certainly and irreversibly' be separated from the Union state. Somewhat more ominously in the contemporary context, Solzhenitsyn argued that Kazakhstan should be split between a smaller independent state, primarily populated by Kazakhs, and the 'originally' Russian territories of South Siberia and South Urals. Regarding Ukraine and Belarus, Solzhenitsyn issued a passionate plea for the maintenance of their union with Russia. In case the separatist tendency in these republics were to prevail, Solzhenitsyn was only prepared to admit the possibility of the separation of individual regions within the republics, for example, Western Ukraine, whose ethnic and religious ties with Russia were weaker.

While today, with the hindsight of the wars in the former Yugoslavia, this scenario cannot but appear to be a recipe for disaster, this was not the case in 1990–1991. Solzhenitsyn's impeccable anti-communist credentials at the time ensured its respectability even among such esteemed 'democrats' as Sergei Stankevich and Oleg Rumyantsev and such key figures in the Yeltsin administration as Vice President Alexander Rutskoi. Indeed, given the fundamental indeterminacy of sociopolitical life after the demise of Soviet socialism, it was only logical that the borders of the new independent states would be negotiable, *like everything else*, from the economic system to public morality. As Richard Sakwa has argued (1996: 341–3), there was no logical reason why the internal administrative borders of the USSR should be considered adequate for the emerging post-communist nation-states. Most of the post-Soviet states never existed in their present borders, which many of them understandably perceived as absurd. And yet, it was precisely these borders that were declared inviolable in the Belovezha Treaties that finalized the process of the dissolution of the USSR. Russia and other post-Soviet states have thus avoided the Yugoslav scenario by opting for the most formal and meaningless principle of using internal Soviet borders as legitimate borders of the new independent states. The Commonwealth of Independent States that succeeded the USSR was founded on the reciprocal affirmation of the territorial integrity of the member states within these utterly contingent borders. As a result, the possibility of the internal fragmentation of Soviet republics along the lines of Solzhenitsyn's proposal was delegitimized, along with separatist projects within the new post-Soviet states. Thus, the condition of the *impossibility* of the repetition of the Yugoslav scenario in the former USSR was simultaneously the condition of *possibility* for the two Chechen Wars as well as military conflicts in Transdniestria, South Ossetia and Abkhazia in the early 1990s.

It is important to emphasize that this settlement was not founded on law, national or international, but was rather nomological in the Schmittian sense. There were no legal reasons why the post-Soviet space should be structured the way it was. Alternative options, from forced reintegration of parts of the USSR within Russia along the lines of Solzhenitsyn's proposal to the continuation of fragmentation within the republics, were neither more nor less legal than the spatial order established in December 1991. Allison's (2009: 1160) invocation of an 'international norm that accompanied the collapse of the multi-ethnic USSR – that the only territories that merited recognition would be those corresponding to first-level administrative subdivisions of the old Soviet state,' illustrates the problem by the ambiguity of its formulation. The 'norm' in question did not regulate the collapse of the USSR but was rather the effect of the process of this collapse and could only be construed as a norm *ex post facto*. The post-Soviet nomos is therefore a good example of the Schmittian 'act of legitimacy', which retroactively posited its own normative presuppositions. To speak of this *nomos* as a constitutive act of legitimacy is not to suggest, however, that this legitimacy was shared universally by all the political subjects of this spatial order. Precisely insofar as it is *not* law, which operates with a clear distinction between obedience and transgression, the *nomos* is always open to contestation and only exists in the mode of actively averting its own dissolution. The example of the Westphalian order of the *Jus Publicum Europaeum*, addressed in detail by Schmitt (2003: 140–212), demonstrates that the existence of the *nomos* does not exclude contestation and resistance to it that might take violent forms of imperialist or secessionist warfare. In contrast to law, the function of the *nomos* is not to command obedience but to provide orientation. Thus, the numerous post-Soviet separatist conflicts do not refute but rather prove the existence of the post-Soviet *nomos* precisely by manifesting resistance to it.

Turning to Russia's function in this spatial order, it may be argued that from 1991 until the 2008 war in Georgia, Russia actively upheld the post-Soviet *nomos* despite the widely shared perception of its disadvantageous character. Evidently, such a strategy was motivated by a desire not to let things get even worse by preventing the complete disintegration of the Russian state, the total loss of Russia's influence in the post-Soviet space and the solidification of the unipolar world order dominated by the United States. Yet, as Russia sought to prevent its own demise, it also refrained from any attempt at a radical transformation of the post-Soviet *nomos* to its advantage. As the two Chechen wars demonstrate, post-communist Russia has not been averse to the extensive use of military force. Yet, the ferocity of the Chechen campaigns contrasted sharply with Russia's lukewarm orientation towards the claims to independence of the pro-Russian separatist forces in Georgia, Moldova, Ukraine and Kazakhstan. While it is evident that many political forces in Russia, including at the government level, tacitly supported some of these claims, Russia nonetheless refrained from official support and especially the recognition of independence of secessionist territories. In fact, such recognition would have been much simpler politically in the 1990s than it is today, since the post-Soviet *nomos* was not yet solidified and did not attain the relative self-evidence it presently possesses. This conservative orientation can be interpreted as resulting less from self-interested calculation than from the commitment to the sheer existence of the spatial order as such, which conferred on Russia the responsibilities of its management and thus permitted the continued invocation of its status as a 'great power'.

While in the Yeltsin presidency this position might be explained by Yeltsin's drive to endow with a minimal form the radical fragmentation that his policies generated, in the first term of the Putin presidency it began to resemble a purposeful policy of gradually coming to terms with the end of the USSR. Exemplary in this respect is the 2002 Law on Citizenship, which severely complicated the procedures for former Soviet citizens to obtain Russian citizenship that was previously granted almost automatically. Similarly, Russia's economic policy in the post-Soviet space during the Putin presidency was marked by the gradual abolition of subsidizing the economies of the CIS states in exchange for symbolic manifestations of loyalty – a practice that was widespread under Yeltsin. Even the infamous 'gas wars' with Ukraine and Belarus in 2005–2008, which are frequently held to exemplify the revival of imperialist tendencies in Russian foreign policy, are best grasped in terms of this logic of coming to terms with the end of the USSR (see Prozorov 2008 and Beissinger 2008 for a critical response). Indeed, these conflicts regarding energy prices and gas deliveries seem to indicate a turn not towards imperialism, but rather its very opposite, that is, nationalism in its statist form, whereby Russia abandoned its past policy of subsidizing former Soviet republics in exchange for vacuous displays of loyalty and began treating the post-Soviet states as any other participant in the energy market. Indeed, it was precisely the policy of energy subsidies for the CIS states in the 1990s that could be construed as an indicator of a half-hearted and almost benign 'imperialism', whereby Russia attempted to deal with the trauma of the dissolution of the Soviet Union by asserting, at a considerable material price, its symbolic leadership in the CIS. In contrast to this policy of self-deception, the shift to the market rationality in dealing with the CIS states may be seen, for better or worse, as a sign of getting over the imperial past, whereby the 'near abroad' becomes 'abroad' pure and simple. This symbolic dissociation of Russia from the USSR was manifested in the rhetoric of the Putin administration from the moment of its inauguration. In an influential 2000 article 'Farewell to Belovezha' Gleb Pavlovsky, a political technologist who played a key role in Putin's assent to and stay in power argued for a break with the rhetoric of the 'post-Soviet' period, which had resigned Russia to the paradox of identifying with the political order that it itself negated:

> Frequently repeating the phrase 'post-Soviet space', the Russian political elite has learned not to notice that it entails a non-substantiality of Russia. … Belovezha is no longer equivalent to the 'dissolution of the USSR', because for Russia the USSR is no longer relevant. The USSR was merely an unprofitable deal for us that only entailed bad government. Russia refuses to be a post-Soviet (or an anti-Soviet) state. Russia is simply Russia, which has to be taken into account. (Pavlovsky 2000)

This rhetorical dissociation from the USSR evidently does not entail isolation from other post-Soviet states but rather serves to solidify the borders, instituted in the post-Soviet *nomos*, as stable containers of new states, Russia included. What the 'Farewell to Belovezha' refers to here is the abandonment of any revisionist designs for the post-Soviet space and the consolidation of the Russian state within its present borders. Post-communist Russian foreign policy may thus be summed up in terms of the task of the maintenance of the post-Soviet *nomos* as the condition of the possibility of the sovereign statehood of both Russia itself and the new independent states. Both the violence of the Chechen wars and the moderation with regard to the pro-Russian separatism in the CIS states follow logically from this function, which in Schmitt's theory of the nomos is formulated with reference to the concept of the *katechon*. In the following section, a brief historical-philological excursus into this concept shall be offered and its logic in the context of the post-Soviet *nomos* will be discussed.

The Post-Soviet *Katechon*

The passage on the *katechon* in the Second Letter to the Thessalonians, whose authorship by St Paul remains disputed, is one of the most intensely political texts in the Western tradition, at stake in which is the very existence of constituted power. In this letter, Paul responds to the audience's agitation concerning the imminence of the Second Coming addressed in the First Letter, explaining the present withholding of *parousia* and elaborating the process by which it will eventually take place:

> Let no one deceive you in any way. Because it will not be unless the apostasy shall have come first, and the man of lawlessness, the son of destruction is revealed. He opposes and exalts himself above every so-called god and object

> of worship. As a result, he seats himself in the sanctuary of God and declares himself to be God. … You know what it is that is now holding him back, so that he will be revealed when the time comes. For the mystery of anomy is already at work, but only until the person now holding him back (*ho katechon*) is removed. Then the lawless one (*anomos*) will be revealed, whom the Lord will abolish with the breath of his mouth, rendering him inoperative by the manifestation of his presence (*parousia*). (2 Thessalonians 2, cited in Agamben 2005: 109)

Since the notion of the *katechon* does not occur anywhere else in the Scripture, the interpretation of this passage remains somewhat ambiguous, particularly with respect to what or who the *katechon* is and what its relation is to the Antichrist (the 'lawless one'), whose revelation and abolition would pave the way for *parousia* (see Best 1972, Jones 2005). Schmitt's interpretation of this passage in the *Nomos of the Earth* is a paradigmatic example of the hermeneutic tradition that begins with Tertullian and identifies the *katechon* with the Roman Empire, endowing it with a positive function of delaying the end of time. This interpretation unfolds in the context of Schmitt's discussion of the medieval *nomos*, out of whose dissolution the modern international law of the *Jus Publicum Europaeum* arose. The unity of this *nomos* was guaranteed by the Holy Roman Empire, which is introduced by Schmitt as the first historical figure of the *katechon* and remains the only one that he considers at length:

> The Christian empire was not eternal. It always had its own end and that of the present eon in view. Nevertheless, it was capable of being a historical power. The decisive historical concept of this continuity was that of restrainer: *katechon*. 'Empire' in this sense meant the historical power to restrain the appearance of the Antichrist and the end of the present eon; it was a power that withholds, as the Apostle Paul said in his Second Letter to the Thessalonians. … The empire of the Christian Middle Ages lasted only as long as the idea of the *katechon* was alive (Schmitt 2003, 60).

For Schmitt, the understanding of the Empire in terms of the *katechon* provides a link between the eschatological promise of Christianity and the concrete experience of history, explaining the delay of *parousia* and giving meaning to historical and political action, which the imminence of *parousia* would devalue:

> I do not believe that any historical concept other than *katechon* would have been possible for the original Christian faith. The belief that a restrainer holds back the end of the world provides the only bridge between the notion of an eschatological paralysis of all human events and a tremendous historical monolith like that of the Christian empire of the German kings. (60)

Thus, for Schmitt the idea of the *katechon* made it possible simultaneously to endow Christianity with political form and significance and incorporate the pre-Christian forms of political authority into the eschatological context of Christianity. In the absence of this idea of the *katechon*, the political authority of the empire loses its concrete spatial unity and degenerates into pure 'Caesarism' (63). While Schmitt continues to apply the concept of the *katechon* in his discussion of modern politics (1997: 8, 43; 2008: 92), these references are largely allegorical, since the concrete meaning of the concept is often difficult to recognize in them, the *katechon* itself becoming one more 'neutral generalization' (see Meier 1988: 158–66; Palaver 1996: 123–4). Even in its neutral allegorical form the concept of the *katechon* remains crucial for Schmitt in his post-Weimar 'concrete order thinking': 'I believe in the *katechon*; for me he is the sole possibility for a Christian to understand history and find it meaningful' (Schmitt in Meier 1988: 162). In this statement, Schmitt explicitly proclaims as the object of his belief not a figure of the divine but rather the secular force that restrains the ultimate advent of the divine.

What does it mean to *believe* in the *katechon* and how does this belief relate to the rather more familiar belief in God? In Giorgio Agamben's argument, the belief in the *katechon* as a neutral generalization characterizes every theory of the State, 'which thinks of it as a power destined to block or delay catastrophe' (2005b: 110). The 'neutral generalization' of the concept thus coincides with its secularization, whereby the *katechon* refers to any constituted authority, whose function is to delay the unraveling of the social bond while simultaneously withholding the advent of radical redemption. From this perspective, the notion of the *katechon* resonates with the logic of police governance, whose genealogy has been addressed by Michel Foucault (2007), and restores to the immanentist concept of police its political-theological origin.

Using the concept in this secularized state it may be proposed that from 1991 to 2008 Russia functioned as *katechon* of the post-Soviet *nomos*; the restraining force that sought to endow with minimal form and consistency the ruins of the Soviet order on the basis of the reciprocal affirmation of the territorial integrity of post-Soviet states. The logic of the *katechon* permits us to specify the intricate relationship of 'local preponderance' of the great power in its region that Bull (1977: 213–19) famously addressed in terms of three forms: domination, which involves habitual intervention and use of force without justification, mere primacy without violation of sovereignty and independence, and hegemony, in which such violations must be legitimized in terms of some overriding principle. In the case of the post-Soviet *nomos*, Russia's repeated claims to hegemony prior to August 2008 remained curiously paradoxical insofar as they were conditioned by the affirmation, rather than violation, of the territorial integrity of the post-Soviet states. To the extent that Russia intervened in the affairs of post-Soviet states, it was to restrain the dynamics of disintegration and anomie that threatened the consolidation of the *nomos* that legitimized the sovereignty of the post-Soviet states. This is precisely the function of the *katechon*, whose recourse to violence is *a priori* legitimized as the 'lesser evil', a limited breach of the *nomos* that delays its rupture into limitless anomie. Katechonic great power management does not exclude exceptional and anomic interventions by the great power as long as the latter remain oriented towards the protection of the *nomos* itself.

It is this katechonic function that appears to have been abrogated in the 2008 war which makes this event much more significant and surprising than it might have appeared at first glance. As Astrov remarks in the introduction to this volume, from the perspective of great power management the Georgian war simply 'should not have taken place' and its occurrence means either that this institution is no longer operative in the international society or it has been mishandled by one of the parties. What is surprising is neither the recourse to violence itself nor the attempt to influence political developments in another CIS state, but rather Russia's abandonment of the commitment to the territorial integrity of a CIS state in its unilateral recognition of the independence of South Ossetia and Abkhazia. The widely shared impression that a line had been crossed in August 2008 (King 2008, Allison 2009, Blank 2009) demonstrates a radical shift in the nomological dimension, whereby Russia abrogated its katechonic function and thus ceased to function as the restraining force in the post-Soviet space. This can be seen as having led to the breakdown of this spatial order.

The best indication of this breakdown has been Russia's manifest failure to persuade a single CIS state to follow its recognition of the independence of Abkhazia and South Ossetia. At the time of writing, the two provinces have only been recognized by Nicaragua, Venezuela and Nauru (Zygar 2009). Even Belarus, whose economic dependence on Russia and strong symbolic ties to it as part of the virtual 'union state' would apparently leave it little leeway for autonomous foreign policy, has so far refrained from recognition. More generally, the summit of the Shanghai Cooperation Organization (SCO), held in Moscow in the aftermath of the war, demonstrated Russia's failure to present its actions in katechonic terms as acts of violence necessary for the stabilization of the regional *nomos*. Thus, Russia's claim to be a stabilizing, ordering or organizing force in the post-Soviet space, advanced since the dissolution of the Soviet Union, no longer holds and Russia's relations with its CIS neighbours are at a historic low point. While Russia may have achieved its immediate military objectives in the war, this seems to have come at the price of the loss of its 'local preponderance' understood in katechonic terms.

The abandonment of the katechonic function was also noticeable in the rhetoric of Russia's leadership during the conflict. The statements of both Putin and Medvedev, demonstrating defiance of the Western condemnation, were marked by a tone that lacked any katechonic restraint but was rather close to apocalyptic. Medvedev's claim that Russia is not afraid of a New Cold War (Associated Press 2008) and Putin's anti-American diatribes in the CNN interview at the height of the conflict (CNN 2008) manifested, if only rhetorically, the reckless abandon that is decidedly at odds with the 'holding back' function of the *katechon* and rather belong to the repertoire of what has come to be known as a 'rogue state', the force of anomie in the international order that it is the task of great power management to restrain. Should we then conclude that after the August war Russia stopped being a *katechon* and became a rogue? This is certainly a temptation many have yielded to (King 2008: 5; see, more generally, Cornell and Starr 2009), interpreting the 2008 war as an indicator of Russia's move towards a revanchist imperialism that seeks to restore hegemony over the post-Soviet states, if not to deprive them of their independence. If this interpretation were correct, Russia's 'rogue' actions would exemplify a revisionist claim to replace the post-Soviet *nomos* of territorial integrity by a new spatial order, grounded in a different 'act of legitimacy'.

The Internationalization of *Bespredel*

Yet, it is by no means certain that the war in Georgia entailed any claim for the new *nomos* in the post-Soviet space. In fact, Russia's post-war foreign policy rhetoric shows little deviation from its previous position. Moreover, it is even difficult to imagine how such a revisionist claim for a new post-Soviet *nomos* could be articulated by contemporary Russia, given its dearth of symbolic or narrative resources, which has made it extremely difficult to legitimize its policies internationally. While Russia's claims to a great power status suffer from the delegitimization of the very discourse of great powers in contemporary international relations (Neumann 2008), its attempts at the utilization of the humanitarian or liberal interventionist discourse are weakened by a lack of credibility due to the gap between the liberal foundations of this discourse and the increasingly illiberal character of the Russian political regime (see Joenniemi in this volume).

However, the problem is not exhausted by the negative image of Russia worldwide that could be addressed by the 'political technologists' that occupy the political space left vacant since the late 1990s. What contemporary Russia lacks are not merely narrative and symbolic resources that it could draw on in enhancing its reputation but a more fundamental sense of historical orientation, which conditions the very emergence of *nomos* in a constitutive 'act of legitimacy'. This phenomenon is best grasped in terms of a critical re-engagement with the idea of the end of history that as attempted in the *Ethics of Postcommunism* (Prozorov 2009). The most famous reproduction of the Hegelo-Kojevian thesis on the end of history in the post-communist period, ventured by Francis Fukuyama, presents the demise of Soviet socialism as the final confirmation of the global triumph of liberal-democratic capitalism, leaving planetary politics within a single teleological horizon. In contrast, our reinterpretation of this thesis in the context of Giorgio Agamben's political thought asserts that the proper end of history consists not in the victory of one teleology over others, but in the collapse of the teleological dimension of social praxis as such, whereby humanity is restored to its original *inoperosity*, the absence of work or historical task, to whose fulfilment the present existence is to be subjected and in the extreme case sacrificed (see Agamben 2000: 109–11; 1998: 60–2; 2005b: 99–103).

The post-communist condition can be read as precisely this collapse of teleology as a result of the process of the societal disengagement from the terrain of the political from the 1970s onwards. This disengagement did not seek a frontal ideological confrontation with the system but rather sought to render itself inaccessible to and ungovernable by the system, rendering the latter inoperative. Thus, the demise of the Soviet system was not accompanied by the emergence of a new ideological hegemony or even a pluralistic constellation, but rather a suspension of the performative efficacy of all ideological maxims and all versions of historical tasks and missions (see Prozorov 2009: Chapter 2). While during the 1990s this suspension was manifested in the carnevalesque politics of chronic crisis, in which everything took place without attaining the slightest degree of finality, the de-politicized authoritarianism of the Putin presidency is usually interpreted as the negation of this suspension, the end *of* the end of history, if such a thing were possible. Yet such a thing is precisely impossible, since the negation of negativity from within does not bring us one step closer to positivity. What the Putin presidency achieved in its quest for stabilization is then not the cancellation of the end of history but merely the suspension of its unfolding, whereby stability as such becomes an overriding value. However, what is it that was stabilized during the Putin presidency?

The political landscape of the 1990s, presently decried in the official discourse as the era of 'chaos', was characterized by the dissolution of norms, traditions, conventions and habits – a process that in the idiom of the time was termed *bespredel* (literally, absence of limits). Originally this term emerged as part of criminal slang and referred to those practices that violated the tacit rules of conduct in the hierarchical structure of the Soviet underworld. It is highly significant that in its original meaning *bespredel* does not designate 'illegality' per se and is thus entirely distinct from the corresponding Russian term '*bezzakonie*', which is literally translated as 'without-law' and refers precisely to acts or phenomena that clearly violate the established legal norms or statutes. In contrast, *bespredel* designates not the illegality of acts (that in the context of the underworld are all *ipso facto* illegal) but rather the disappearance of the very framework, in which the legal and the illegal could be distinguished, a meta-illegality or anomie to the second degree that is characterized by the radical impossibility of adjudication. In short, *bespredel* may well be the best cross-cultural translation of Giorgio Agamben's concept of the state of exception.

Insofar as the contemporary regime does not introduce any positive ideological hegemony or new positive content to the teleological dimension, what its policy of stabilization achieves is logically nothing other than the stabilization of this ruinous scene of *bespredel* itself. What was decried, tolerated or barely survived in the 1990s as a 'transitional moment', an exceptional condition on the way to something positive or substantial, became in the Putin presidency reinscribed as the substance of contemporary Russian social life as such, as *all there is*. Thus, the Putinite negation of the negativity of the post-historical condition of the 1990s does not lead to any affirmation whatsoever, but remains squarely within the dimension of negativity, from which it must draw resources for its overcoming. The paradox of Putinism is that its attempt to negate the post-historical negativity only plunges it further into nihilism (cf. Esposito 2008: 45–76). Thus, despite its self-presentation as a positive and constructive alternative to the 'wild' and 'chaotic' 1990s, the contemporary Russian regime persists in its nihilistic paradigm, all the more so as long as it keeps negating it.

In reference to the period of accelerated capitalist development marked by revolutionary societal dislocations in late nineteenth-century Russia, the conservative philosopher Konstantin Leontiev famously suggested that 'Russia must be frozen in order not to rot'. The negation of negativity in the post-transitional regime of the Putin presidency follows precisely this logic, wagering on the survival of *nomos* in its pure form, devoid of all historical meaning. This is the true sense of the uncanny slogan of Putin's first term, 'dictatorship of the law', which supplements the 'proper' (legal) power of the law with its very opposite ('dictatorship') that reveals that the former had been rendered inoperative and required the facilitating force of the latter to maintain the semblance of the existence of the concrete *nomos* of the political order. In this manner, it is the very suspension of the law by a 'dictatorship', or, more correctly, a 'state of exception', that permits the ultimate vacuity of the law in the post-historical time to remain concealed and ensures the survival of the *nomos* in an inoperative state.

Yet, as every variant of conservatism eventually finds out to its disappointment, what 'must be frozen in order not to rot' has always *already begun* to rot, hence the anxiety about its 'conservation', which would hardly arise, were the phenomenon in question safe in its proper and authentic existence. *Reconstituting* what is already *destitute*, the contemporary regime remains as post-historical as Yeltsin's in its evacuation of all historical meaning from the sphere of politics, yet, unlike the Yeltsin presidency, ventures to order the field of post-communist *bespredel* through the proliferation of purely ritualistic manifestations of authority that maintain a semblance of *nomos* amid anomie.

This reading of post-communist Russian politics permits us to understand the rupture of the post-Soviet *nomos* in the Georgian War as neither the revisionist claim for an alternative *nomos* nor a purely anomic act of 'rogue' violence. Instead, it must be grasped as a belated adaptation of foreign policy in the post-Soviet space to the strategy of the *management of anomie* that has been the substance of Russian domestic politics since the beginning of the Putin presidency. Just as the domestic *nomos* of Putin's Russia is nothing other than the stabilization of the condition of *bespredel*, the freezing of the 'rotting' anomie, so the post-Soviet *nomos* after the war is wholly contaminated by *bespredel*. While we are more accustomed to think of international relations as the domain of anarchic anomie, from which we are shielded by the legal order of the state, in this case we observe an ironic reversal of this logic, whereby Russia, as it were, *exports* its domestic anomie to the post-Soviet space. This anomie is not immanent to the 'anarchical' international society, whose management can hence only be anarchical as well (cf. Chapter 1), but rather precedes and exceeds the very idea of *nomos*. To the extent that we can still speak of great power management in this context, it is no longer the management of the international society, constituted by a nomological order, however minimal. What

Russia manages, first domestically and now internationally, is anomie itself, the exception that no longer can be subsumed under any rule.

While from a Schmittian perspective this breakdown of the nomos would exemplify the catastrophic self-cancellation of the katechonic function, the argument about the post-historical character of the post-communist condition calls for a more nuanced reading of the logic of the *katechon*. As we have seen, for Schmitt the *katechon* functions as the point of articulation between the historical and the eschatological, whereby political practice is envisioned in terms of *delaying* the end of history. Yet, one may ask, what happens to the *katechon* when the end of history has *already* taken place, albeit in a radically profane mode that renders all teleology and eschatology vacuous? In order to answer this question and thus specify Russia's new function in the post-Soviet space, we must re-engage with a thesis that was advanced as an esoteric critique of Schmitt – Walter Benjamin's theory of baroque sovereignty.

Post-Communist Anomie and Baroque Sovereignty

While our analysis of the logic of *bespredel* focused specifically on post-communist Russian politics as a post-historical condition, Benjamin's point of departure in his analysis of the German *Trauerspiel* is similarly the transformation in the perception of history during the Baroque period. This transformation took the form of the weakening of the eschatological dimension and the consequent blurring of the distinction between history and nature, whereby the '[constantly] repeated drama of the rise and fall of princes appeared as the natural aspect of the course of history, essential in its permanence' (Benjamin 2003: 88). As Michel Foucault has argued in his genealogy of modern governmentality, the temporality of this period is *indefinite*, lacking both an origin and, more importantly, an endpoint: 'There is nothing like a dream of the last Empire that dominated medieval religious and historical perspectives. … We now find ourselves in a perspective in which historical time is indefinite, in a perspective of indefinite governmentality with no foreseeable term or final aim' (Foucault 2007: 260). In this indefinite time without origin or end, which resonates strongly with our phenomenology of post-communism, the eschatological dimension is blocked and the historical world is perceived as 'nature deprived of grace' (Benjamin 2003: 81). This 'state of nature' has nothing to do with a pre-historic innocence, either idyllic or savage, but is solely the effect of the decay and decomposition of eschatological historicity:

> The religious man of the baroque era clings so tightly to the world because of the feeling that is being driven with it toward a cataract. The baroque knows no eschatology, and for that very reason it possesses no mechanism by which all earthly things are gathered together and exalted before being consigned to their

> end. The hereafter is emptied of everything which contains the slightest breath of this world. (Benjamin 2003: 66)

In this world of history-as-nature, transcendence is emptied of any possible content but remains present as an 'ultimate heaven', a 'vacuum' that is capable of one day 'destroying the world with catastrophic violence' (Benjamin 2003: 66, Cf. Weber 1992: 12–13). It is from this perspective that we should understand Benjamin's minimal yet profound amendment to Schmitt's famous definition of sovereignty: 'the baroque concept emerges from a discussion of the state of emergency and makes it the most important function of the prince to exclude this' (55). While Schmitt's sovereign consummates his sovereignty by deciding on the exception and thus bringing it into being in the manner of the miracle, Benjamin's baroque sovereign is rather faced with a more prosaic yet also more difficult task of excluding the exception, which presupposes that this exception must have always *already taken place* and even 'become the rule'. Similarly, as it has been argued here, the political rationality of Putinism in contemporary Russia is only intelligible as an attempt to stabilize one's standing and authority in the general state of exception coextensive with the entire social order, the limitlessness of *bespredel*. Thus, the evacuation of the eschatological dimension ruptures the systematic analogy that Schmitt's (1985) political theology established between the sovereign and God. Similarly to the baroque sovereign, the lords of the post-communist *bespredel* no longer have any relation with divine transcendence: 'However highly he is enthroned over subject and state, his status is confined to the world of creation; he is the lord of creatures but he remains a creature' (Benjamin 2003: 85).

What does this creature do? It is clear that insofar as the eschaton is empty and we dwell in the naturalized history deprived of grace, the victory of the 'lawless one' has already taken place and takes the form of the generalized state of exception. To the extent that the sovereign is 'itself a creature', it is necessarily itself contaminated by this anomie. Hence, the only possible task of the baroque sovereign *qua katechon* is to persevere in its own being without being consumed by the very state of exception it is always already caught up in. By the same token, the post-communist regime in the Putin presidency is best grasped as the reign *of* anomie *over* anomie, whereby exceptional measures of the kind associated with the condition of *bespredel* are deployed to order and stabilize this condition itself.

Benjamin introduces three figures of power, the relations between which permit us to understand the fate of the *katechon* in the post-historical logic of baroque sovereignty. Faced with the task of self-preservation in the general state of anomie, the sovereign may seek to accumulate as much power as possible and in this manner becomes a *tyrant*, a figure distinguished from the *katechon* by the absence of anything like a restraining function, including the function of self-restraint. From the outset, the tyrant acts on the basis of hubris, as a 'deranged creation', 'erupting into madness like a volcano and destroying himself and his entire court' (70). Falling victim to the 'disproportion between the unlimited hierarchical dignity with which he is divinely invested and the humble estate of his humanity' (70), the fearful tyrant is at the permanent risk of turning into a pitiful *martyr*.

There is only one possibility to exit the endless oscillation between tyranny and martyrdom in Benjamin's conceptual constellation, which consists in the transformation of the *katechon* into the intriguer (*Intrigant*). In contrast to the tyrant, who violently tries to exclude the state of exception and falls victim to it, the intriguer, usually represented in the Baroque drama by the servant to the prince, is perfectly aware that the state of exception is all there is and rather than vainly attempt to exclude it he tries to make use of it through ceaseless *plotting* and *scheming*: 'Baroque drama knows no other historical activity than the corrupt energy of schemers' (88). While the Schmittian sovereign enacts its transcendence through the decision on the exception, the intriguer renounces all transcendence in favour of a purely immanent governance by staging plots and conspiracies, which, in accordance with the general reduction of history to nature, are grounded in the 'anthropological, even physiological knowledge' of human beings (95). 'The intriguer exploits mechanisms of human action as the result of forces over which there can be no ultimate control, but which can therefore be made the subject of probabilistic calculations' (Weber 1992: 16). Evidently, this immanentist and naturalist modality of rule is the only possible one in the post-historical condition of post-communism, which permits us to understand the process of depoliticization that began in Russia almost immediately after the demise of the Soviet order and intensified after 1993. Unwilling to risk becoming martyrs in the case of failure of their hubristic claims to tyranny, the entire Russian political elite, from President Yeltsin downwards, transformed politics into a technology of scheming, which in the Putin presidency was perfected to a degree unprecedented in modern history.

It is easy to recognize in this 'rule by intrigue' an *Urform* of what Foucault termed governmentality (2007: 87–133), whose genealogy is traced precisely to the temporality of the baroque age that gives rise to the administrative state and the doctrines of *raison d'état* and *Polizeiwissenschaft*, whose significance for the problematic of great power management is addressed by Astrov in the introduction to this volume. Foucault famously inferred from this transformation of governmental rationality the ultimate decentring and dispersion of sovereignty, summed up in his call to 'cut off the head of the king' in political theory (1990a: 89). However, Foucault did not take into account the possibility for the sovereign to adapt itself to this transformation of governmentality without becoming entirely subsumed under it. While biopolitical government deploys its knowledge of human nature for the purposes of *ordering* or policing human existence, directing and optimizing the development of biological forces and enhancing their productivity, the sovereign intriguer relies on the same knowledge for the opposite purpose of conspiratorial plotting in order to use *destabilization* in the interest of one's own self-preservation, the management of the anomic state of exception that no longer seeks to exclude it but solely to enhance one's own standing within it (Benjamin 2003: 96, see also Weber 1992: 17).

With this formulation, the logic of Russia's foreign policy orientation in the post-Soviet space in the aftermath of Georgia war can finally be identified. In its rupture of the post-Soviet *nomos* the regime wagers on its ability to maintain and fortify itself internationally by the same process of the management of anomie that has worked successfully domestically. Rather than disrupt the existing nomos of territorial integrity in the name of an alternative *nomos*, Russia simply *suspends* the existing *nomos*, reconstituting the post-Soviet space as a state of exception, akin to the domestic space of *bespredel*. While this move may be dismissed as irrational from a legalist or nomological perspective, such a dismissal ignores the particular type of rationality proper to the *intrigant*, who lives off the uncertainty and contingency that are of its own making. While Schmitt and other defenders of the *nomos* ultimately subsume the exception under the ordering function of the norm (see Agamben 2005a: 53–7), the *intrigant* knows that the exception is all there is, hence there is no longer any need to decide on it, but solely the imperative to turn it to one's advantage.

Conclusion

While the paradigm of the *intrigant* is central to understanding the domestic-political developments in Russia since the late 1990s, it is also fruitful for grasping the specificity of Russian standing in the international society. The wager on scheming has been a key component of Russian foreign policy under Putin, observable for example, in the preference for bilateral deals with individual European states over dealing with the EU, the direct participation of political leadership in international business deals and the use of foreign media and public figures to advance the regime's agenda. There is little point in criticizing this reliance on intrigue by rehearsing the worn narrative about Europe as a 'normative power' and Russia as incapable of understanding how European politics works. What is routinely posited as Russia's 'misunderstanding' is in fact a purposeful strategy whereby it is well aware of the normative orientation of its counterpart while remaining confident about its own capacity to ignore these norms or bend them to its own advantage.

Nonetheless, while the wager on the extension of *bespredel* to the post-Soviet space is understandable in the context of the political developments in and around Russia during the last decade, it is hardly unproblematic. The stabilization of *bespredel* within Russia was made possible precisely by the territorial delimitation that contained the limitlessness of anomie within determinate geographical limits. In the absence of any teleological vision of politics that could guide Russia's becoming *in time*, the post-Soviet *nomos* with its principle of the inviolability of borders at least provided the conditions for its persistence *in space* as a delimited entity. This *nomos* made it possible for the post-historical entity to maintain itself *as* an entity distinct from others and for the regime to consolidate its power by concentrating and centralizing the use of anomie.

It is therefore not a coincidence that the process of the consolidation of the state of exception under Putin was accompanied by a hypertrophied valorization of state sovereignty, from the doctrine of sovereign democracy to the anti-American invectives of the Munich Speech. Since, as it has been argued here, the contemporary Russian state carries no historical or developmental project, for which it would deploy sovereign power, this valorization must be understood as the defence of the very boundary that delimits the zone of *bespredel* from its outside and constitutes it as a delimited site of limitlessness – a paradoxical formulation that is nonetheless paradigmatic for the state of exception, concretely exemplified by the spatial order of the camp (Agamben 1998). The camp, inside which every norm is suspended and everything becomes possible, only exists by virtue of a prior delimitation that transforms it into a zone of confinement, marked by a fundamental impossibility of flight. It is only due to these limits that the camp can function as the space of the horrifying experiment with the limitless. By the same token, the existence of the contemporary Russian state of *bespredel* remains conditioned by the sovereign delimitation, whose legitimacy has been established in the post-Soviet *nomos*. Once this condition of possibility disappears, it is by no means certain that Russia will succeed in managing the anomic post-Soviet space to its advantage.

Chapter 3
Great Power Misalignment: The United States and the Russo-Georgian Conflict

Irina Papkova

The Russo-Georgian conflict has raised important questions regarding Russia's place within the world order, and more specifically about its relationship(s) with various international actors. While it may be too much to claim that the conflict has had implications for Russia's interaction with the entire rest of the world (it has had no effect whatsoever, for example, on Russo-Uruguayan or Russo-Tanzanian relations), the war has certainly brought to light tensions between the Russian Federation and the most significant global powers of our day. For the time being at least, the United States is the preponderant world power and the dynamic between these two countries influences the patterns of interaction between Russia and the other key actors examined in this book including the EU and NATO; as such it makes sense to chart the importance of the Caucasian conflict for US–Russia relations before moving on to the others.

Many commentators have interpreted the Caucasian War of August 2008 as symptomatic of the deepening conflict between a resurgent Russian Federation and the West, particularly the United States. If we accept the general deterioration of relations as a given, then the interesting question in the theoretical framework of this volume is not why a Great Power concert between Russia and the United States broke down in Georgia, and more specifically, not why the two sides were unable to prevent their respective clients from spiralling into armed conflict on the night of 7 August. Instead, what is interesting is the dynamic behind the general breakdown in the relationship between Russia and the United States over the second half of the younger Bush's presidency that led to this outcome. Indeed, most explanations of the Russo-Georgian war have privileged the deroulement of the Russian–American relationship over the past decade, with one narrative emerging as particularly central to our understanding of the problem. For all their differences, most authors writing on the subject contribute to the following general picture: The Russian Federation has increasingly tended to chart out its own course in international politics, a tendency driven by the two interrelated factors of perceived humiliations at the hands of the West and creeping domestic authoritarianism. These developments, it is claimed, made the relationship between an authoritarian Russia and democratic West increasingly difficult to sustain, leading in the end to the Georgian crisis (Blank 2008, Cornell 2008a, Shevtsova 2008, Trenin 2009). This explanation, though, is only partially adequate, as it assumes that the United States cannot have a functional and productive relationship with non-democratic powers, which is an empirically unsustainable claim. At the same time, the aspect of the above explanation regarding perceptions does merit further exploration, as it points to those characteristics of American policy towards Russia that may have contributed to the outcome where 'the Kremlin ... can now imagine a world in which [it does not] have to care' about the consequences of a foreign policy that distances it from the United States (King 2008: 11). This chapter takes the position that the breakdown in US–Russian relations evolved out of an accumulation of mutual misunderstandings regarding the international order that can be, in the framework of this volume, addressed through insights from the International Society school of international relations, specifically, through Hedley Bull's understanding of Great Powers and their role in international affairs.

Based on insights from Bull's relevant chapter in *The Anarchical Society*, this chapter contends that the disintegration of US–Russian relations in the later years of the G.W. Bush administration stemmed from a fundamental misalignment in the way the two states understood themselves (or not) as Great Powers and their attendant responsibilities in the post-Cold War order. I further argue that, from the American side, the misalignment was compounded by a particular approach towards the Russian Federation prevalent within the relevant US policy establishment that prevented the development of alternative policies towards Russia that might have led to a different outcome.[1] The chapter ends by sketching some preliminary conclusions regarding the concrete implications of the preceding analysis for our understanding of the Russo-Georgian confrontation of 2008.

Bull's Conceptualization of the Great Powers and the US–Russia Relationship

In Chapter 9 of his seminal work *The Anarchical Society*, 'The Great Powers and International Order,' Hedley Bull begins by considering three questions: 'What are the great powers? What role do great powers play in relations to international order? What is the role of the great powers in relation to international order at the present time?' (1977: 200). Notably, Bull worked and thought about these issues in the context of the Cold War; his answer to the third question is of particular relevance to the section of this chapter that deals with the characteristics of American policy towards Russia and as such will be returned to later in the present text. For now, it is pertinent to focus on Bull's treatment of the first and second questions, as they can be used to identify some roots of the breakdown

1 I use the past tense here deliberately, on the assumption (naive, perhaps) that the Obama administration is substantively different from the previous one in two key respects: one, in the way the administration understands the American role/position in world affairs and two, in the philosophy driving the policies towards Russia. As of writing, this assumption seems to be holding.

in the US–Russia relationship. It should be noted that the analysis here does not treat Bull's understanding of the Great Powers as the benchmark against which Russian and American behaviour is measured in any normative sense; rather, it is understood simply that, in the author's view, Bull's theory usefully illuminates the situation this chapter is interested in, even if the illumination arises precisely from the theory's apparent failure to accurately map on to real-world developments in the post-Cold War era.[2]

For Bull, three criteria are indispensable for the existence of an objective group of Great Powers. First, 'there are two or more powers that are comparable in status.' In other words, there 'is a club with a rule of membership,' meaning that there 'cannot be only one Great Power' (201). Second, the members of this club are all 'in the front rank in terms of military strength.' Finally, 'the great powers are recognized by the others to have, and conceived by their own leaders and peoples to have, certain special rights and duties' (202). If we take the first and third of these postulates, certain tensions in the US–Russian relationship in the post-Cold War era become immediately evident (The second criterion, military strength, is not of immediate relevance, since neither side has, since 1990, pretended that there is any military parity between the two countries; on this point there is no misunderstanding).

From the point of view of the first criterion – the existence of a group of states comparable in status – the problem is easily seen. From Washington's perspective, the collapse of the USSR left the United States as the sole remaining super power, with a status that differed in quality from that of any other state. Initial fears of competition from Japan subsided in the early 1990s as that country faced increasing economic problems that prevented it from mounting a serious challenge to American global dominance. As the driving engine bringing Francis Fukuyama's 'End of History' liberal democracy and capitalism to the rest of the world, the United States could dismiss, at least for that moment, rumblings about multipolarity coming from its own intellectuals and from Europe and China: neither of those regional powers looked likely to attain comparable status, either

2 I am certainly not arguing that the chapter by Hedley Bull under discussion in this paper contains all the wisdom about the Russian–American relationship: there are many other factors that have contributed to its development in the direction it took in the last years of the Bush administration. (Another argument might privilege deep seated cultural differences, for example). However, with this caveat I still believe that Bull's chapter contains important insights that have not been dealt with elsewhere and as such are deserving of careful attention. Furthermore, the use of Bull's categories here should not be taken as an *a priori* claim that the world works exactly according to the model he presents in *The Anarchical Society*. Rather, Bull's categories here are used in the Weberian understanding of 'ideal types,' filtered through the reading of Zygmunt Bauman, who wrote in 2008 that 'Ideal types ... are useful and also indispensable cognitive tools even if (or perhaps because) they deliberately throw light on certain aspects of described social reality while leaving in the shade some other aspects ... Ideal types are not descriptions of reality: they are the tools used to analyze it' (Bauman 2008).

in military or economic terms, except in the remote future. Russia, for its part, was prostrate for the large part of the decade of the 1990s, and did not merit serious consideration as a potential rival. Post-9/11, the situation seemed to change in favour of a period (brief, as it turned out) of reliance on multilateral diplomacy and partnership with other powers including Russia and Iran. However, this tendency was reversed when, by late 2002, the influence of the neoconservatives led to the formalization, via the Bush Doctrine, of what had previously been simply implicitly assumed: The United States was the most powerful country in the world and intended to stay that way. Embodying ideas that had already been expressed a decade earlier by Dick Cheney and Paul Wolfowitz in the controversial Defense Planning Guidance draft of 1992, the Bush Doctrine achieved its succinct articulation in the 2002 National Security Strategy of the United States (updated in 2006), in which the core of the doctrine is elaborated: The United States embraced a unilateral approach towards foreign policy that intended to consolidate the position of the country not as primus inter pares, but as primus tout court (National Security Strategy 2006). Especially during the Bush Jr. administration, the United States simply placed itself outside of the Great Power framework, at least as it is understood by Bull. Specifically, in *The Anarchical Society*, a Great Power situation does not exist when there 'is simply one great power;' like the situation of the Roman empire and Imperial China, the position of the United States was certainly understood by the neoconservatives as 'unique,' to use Bull's own term (Bull 1977: 201). Such a self-understanding precluded even rhetorical appellations to a community of 'Great Powers': there were, notably, references in American foreign policy discourse through the 1990s and 2000s to the 'allies', to the 'coalition of the willing,' but never to the Great Powers as such, implying that the United States did not recognize any such club to exist, after the collapse of the USSR implicitly, and subsequently through the Bush Doctrine, openly.[3]

With this overall trend in American foreign policy in mind, the Russian Federation's almost obsessive employment of Great Power rhetoric becomes clearly problematic. The two sides were simply not looking at the world through the same ontological categories, especially through the 2000s. To be sure, pre-Putin Great Power rhetoric in Russia has often been understood merely as an attempt by the presidential administration of Boris Yeltsin to court the support of nationalist forces in the face of mounting social and economic problems – in the 1990s, the idea of Russia as a Great Power seemed difficult to sustain, even domestically. At the same time, Ted Hopf (2002) has notably argued that historically, due to social constraints on foreign policy decision making, it has been impossible for Russian elites to construct an identity that is not premised on the country being a Great

3 To clarify: obviously the United States recognized a group of states (the G8, at least) that are of greater importance in international relations than the rest; however, it is argued here that they did so without, in the post-Cold War era, acknowledging their equality with themselves, which (drawing on Bull) means that the US did not accept Great Power arrangements as a legitimate form of world order.

Power. Whatever the case may be, by the turn of the millennium, two factors had coalesced to cement the Great Power idea as a determining element of Russian foreign policy.

The first circumstance had to do with Bull's third criterion for a Great Power, that is, recognition. Through the 1990s, the international community seemed to progressively extend recognition of Russia's membership in just such a club of Powers with a special role in world affairs, through Russia's inclusion in the United Nations Security Council, the G8, and the development of a strained but nonetheless working relationship with NATO. Of these, membership in the G8 and the relationship with NATO in particular implied recognition by the United States of Russia's Great Power status : a problematic assumption that will be considered below in more detail. At the same time, in the 2000s, the strengthening of Russia's relationship with India and China, both self-styled Great Powers with a manifest interest in the realization of a multi-polar world, reinforced the understanding within the Russian foreign policy establishment that the country was an acknowledged Great Power. The second circumstance had to do with the increased capabilities of the Russian Federation itself as it entered the 2000s buoyed by the combined positive economic effects of the 1998 default and skyrocketing energy prices: instead of 'Who Lost Russia,' by 2001 analysts both in Russia and in the West were writing about 'Russia Resurgent,' a sobriquet the country would hold onto through the following decade. The central point here is that by the time of the Georgian crisis, for Russia being a Great Power was no longer an aspiration: the country's foreign policy elite was behaving according to a cognitive map in which Russia was already a power with special status recognized by others.[4]

Moreover, in the immediate aftermath of 9/11, the United States did, for a moment, appear to be seriously ready to treat Russia as an equal partner in the war on terror, implying an equality of status that was central to this Russian conception (and which would, in fact, make Russia a Great Power in Bull's sense). Indeed, according to Stephen Sestanovich (2008), within a year of 9/11, the Bush administration had offered Russia 'a new strategic arms treaty ... shifted US policy on Chechnya from condemnation of Russia to understanding, recognized Russia as a market economy ..., supported Russia's accession to the World Trade Organization, agreed to have Russia chair the G8 ... initiated a multibillion-dollar international version of the Nunn-Lugar program ... and upgraded Russia's ties to

4 There are many examples of this in the discourse of the Russian foreign policy elite from the mid 1990s to the present; here, it is sufficient to refer to the *Foreign Policy Concept of the Russian Federation* (adopted in July 2008 (!)). While the document does not specifically use the term "Great Power" (*velikaia derzhava*), the text is replete with references to Russia's membership in a group of particularly important states, with special responsibilities in the forming and managing the direction of international affairs, that is, an understanding of Russia's position in the world very much close to Bull's conceptualization of Great Powers and their roles (see especially the second section of the document, 'The Contemporary World and the Foreign Policy of the Russian Federation').

NATO so that Russia's representatives could participate on a more equal footing in deliberations on European security'. From these American actions, the Russian side could – and did – interpret the immediate post 9/11 situation as one in which the United States finally recognized not just the multipolar nature of the world but Russia's membership in the club of Great Powers, as a valuable and what is more important, equal partner (Black 2002, Legvold 2002, Blank 2003, Voskopoulis 2003).

However, several problematic issues would conjoin to upset this momentary equilibrium. First, for the United States, the initial multilateral response to 9/11 was replaced by 2003 with the above mentioned Bush Doctrine, as the American administration decided to go ahead with the invasion of Iraq without the support of much of the international community, Russia included. It was Iraq, in fact, that marked the moment of the radical worsening of relations between Russia and the United States, precisely because it was here that the US demonstrated their unwillingness to go beyond symbolism in treating Russia as an equal partner.

The other problems were related to the first, and can be usefully approached through Bull's second major question in Chapter 9 of *The Anarchical Society*, that is, what do the Great Powers actually do, assuming they do exist? Bull specifies two main ways in which Great Powers contribute to international order: 'by managing their relations with one another; and by exploiting their preponderance in such a way as to impart a degree of central direction to the affairs of international society as a whole.' These two Great Power roles have themselves a number of corollaries, of which three seem particularly relevant to the case at hand. Namely, Great Powers 'manage their relations with each other ... by [first] preserving the general balance of power … [second,] agreeing to respect one another's spheres of influence and [third] joint action, as is implied by the idea of a great power concert or condominium' (Bull 1977: 207). A brief consideration of these three issues is in order, as they all represent nodes at which the American–Russian relationship broke down in the run-up to the Georgian war in fairly obvious ways.

In terms of preserving the general balance of power, the problem is related to the above discussion of the misalignment in how the two countries understood their own place in the international order, particularly during the Bush–Putin years. Indeed, if, as has been argued here, the Russian Federation understood itself as a Great Power in Bull's terms, then it should not be surprising that balance of power considerations would be central to Russian foreign policy; the pursuit of multipolarity and a balanced relationship with both 'the West' and 'East' that characterized Russian foreign policy through the 2000s can be understood in this context. For the United States, in the meantime, the full implications of the Bush Doctrine and the generally neoconservative foreign policy meant something completely different: the firm establishment of the American empire, Pax Americana, through the spread of liberal democracy and capitalism in a way that presupposes, at its core, the upsetting of existing power configurations. In other words, the United States completely rejected a Great Power condominium as a relevant model for international affairs: in the post-Cold War years, American foreign policy, at least prior to the Obama administration, has been directed towards changing the existing balance in favour of unquestioned American predominance. In both Afghanistan and Iraq the (attempted) extension of American values arrived on the coattails of American military power and, at least initially in the case of Iraq, increased American economic power through the acquisition of de facto control over the Iraqi oil supply. The question of the ultimate drain of the Iraqi and Afghan adventures on real American capabilities is certainly important but not relevant to the central point, which is that, in a way bound eventually to collide with the weight assigned by the Russian side to balance of power concerns, the neoconserative ideology at the heart of American foreign policy from at least late 2002 onward precluded such considerations.

Two other attributes of Bull's ideal type of Great Power behaviour highlight tensions in the Russian–American relationship in the run-up to the Caucasus conflict for the same reason. There was a misalignment between a Russian policy neatly following Bull's notion that Great Powers respect each other's spheres of influence and an American foreign policy driven by the Bush Doctrine. Quite simply, one cannot have a functional respect for spheres of influence if one side is intent on transforming the globe in its own image. Thus, while from the Russian Federation's perspective claims of preponderance in the former CIS made perfect sense through the Great Power mirror in which Russian policy makers saw themselves, from the point of view of the second Bush administration, Russia's actions aimed at securing this sphere of influence would be naturally seen as hampering the spread of the Pax Americana and therefore as unfriendly, disruptive actions. Compounding the problem, to be sure, was the belief on the Russian side that the country had, as discussed above, been recognized as a Great Power, with the attendant prerogative of spheres of influence. From this point of view, the extension of NATO membership to the Baltic states and interference in the Ukrainian elections, both occurring in 2004 on the heels of the 2003 Iraq invasion, upset the equilibrium that seemed to have been reached in the immediate aftermath of 9/11; indeed, in examining the rhetoric within the Russian foreign policy community at the time, one comes away with a sense that the Russia side saw Iraq and Ukraine as explicit betrayals. Finally, and most briefly, based on the same fundamental misalignment in self-understanding, a concert or condominium between Russia and the United States in the Caucasus, or anywhere else, for that matter, simply could not function.

At this point, then, the argument can be summarized as follows: the Russian–American relationship broke down at least in part over a misalignment in the way the two sides understand the international order and their own position within it. From this misalignment in self-perceptions, stemmed a misalignment in behaviour that was bound to eventually lead to collisions, as the Russian Federation, particularly under Putin, increasingly acted on the assumption that not only was the country a recognized Great Power but that being so recognized brought with it a particular sphere of influence. The American side, for its part, contributed to this perception in the immediate aftermath of 9/11; however, the subsequent definitive adoption of the Bush Doctrine as the guiding ideology of American foreign policy cemented the tendency of the United States to act outside of any framework that would resemble a Great Power arrangement, heightening the likelihood of misunderstandings between the Russian Federation and the United States, as through the 2000s, they pursued their respective interests in the same geographic area. Once these interests began to collide – the securing of a sphere of influence on the one side and the spread of democracy/capitalism and thereby American global preponderance on the other – nodes at which crisis might occur began to accumulate. In August 2008, the crisis finally violently erupted over Georgia.

Narrating Russia: The Cold War that Never Ended?

The conclusion that the Russian–American relationship broke down at least partially as a result of the two countries' diverging conceptions of the global order and their respective places within it raises another interesting question worth briefly examining in this chapter. If Russia – for reasons competently explored by other authors – acts as a textbook Great Power in Bull's sense, why is the same not true for the United States, especially as regards their policy towards Russia? It is, certainly, impossible to provide a comprehensive answer to this question here. However, we can at least sketch one possible explanation: this section of the present chapter argues that the persistence of the Cold War trope in American academic and policy rhetoric reinforces the refusal of the United States to act in accordance with the Great Power model in structuring their relations with the Russian Federation. In the specific case of the Georgia crisis, this contributed both to Georgia's choice to attack Tskhinvali and to the style of the immediate American response. The discussion here begins with an empirical exposition and concludes by drawing on Bull's own understanding of US–Russian relations in the post war period to theoretically support the overall point.

The Cold War in the New World Order

Since the early 1990s, references to a 'New Cold War' have cropped up with curious frequency among relevant American think tank publications and in that part of the printed press that may be thought of as potentially having some influence on policy (for example, the editorial pages of *The New York Times*, *The Washington Post*, *The Washington Times*).[5] Historically speaking, the first identifiable references to a 'New Cold War' appeared even before the formal collapse of the USSR, in the

5 The usefulness of looking at think-tank and editorial publications is supported by the fact that many relevant authors spend their careers moving seamlessly from the policy making world into the world of analysis, whether it is at teaching or research institutions; in the cases of such authors as Zbigniew Brzezinski, among others, the link to actual policy is at its most obvious.

context of Gorbachev's attempt to reestablish control over the Baltic States; these events sparked editorial speculations about 'the Cold war ... shifting to colder climes,' with political commentator William Safire even declaring in The New York Times that 'Cold War II has begun' (Bitzinger 1991, Safire 1991). Almost at the same time, disagreements between the United States and the Soviet Union about how to handle the Iraqi invasion of Kuwait exacerbated the tendency to evaluate relations through a 'Back to the Future' model (Talbott 1991). Later, while an undeniable euphoria characterized the analysis of Russian–American relations over 1992 as the Russian Federation appeared on the international scene as the heir to the Soviet Union, the first attempts of the new state to fashion a coherent foreign policy doctrine were interpreted by some American analysts as signifying a return to the dark days of the recent past. In 1992 these voices were marginal; a year later, after the December 1993 elections seemed to sweep anti-democratic forces into power, the imagery of the 'Russian bear' and an inevitable deterioration of Russian–American relations permeated both American media coverage and the writings of academic observers (S. Cohen 1992, Covault 1992, Krauthammer 1993, Brzezinski 1994, Almond 1994).

Once it became clear that the electoral results were counterbalanced by the circumstance that the Yeltsin government had engineered a constitutional revolution of its own earlier the same year – in favour, ironically enough, of a heavily presidential system that would facilitate the slide into authoritarianism ten years later – the discourse surrounding a 'New Cold War' temporarily subsided. Partly, this was conditioned by the fact that as the 1990s wore on it became clear that the leadership of the Russian Federation was so occupied with domestic problems that foreign policy was in a state of general disarray, if not outright neglect, negating the prospect of any serious restorationist project that might menace the security interests of the United States. The Cold War spectre did not disappear entirely, however, cropping up periodically as the unfolding wars of the Yugoslav succession revealed differences in American and Russian approaches to the Balkan imbroglio stark enough to evoke images of at least a 'cool war' if not a full-blown return to the Cold War paradigm (Schorr 1994). Even so, the original model did not have to wait long for its rehabilitation, which occurred when the 1995 Russian parliamentary elections brought the newly reconstituted Communist Party of the Russian Federation (KPRF) squarely into the limelight of Russian politics (Belin et al. 1997). The concern over the direction Russian foreign policy might have taken had the KPRF leader Gennadii Zyuganov defeated Boris Yeltsin in the 1996 presidential campaign inspired massive Western financial and technical support for the Yeltsin team during that election year; with Yeltsin's victory, the looming East–West confrontation seemed averted once more.

It reappeared quite soon, however, as Boris Yeltsin took stock of the domestic situation and, in a gesture meant to placate the communist-nationalist opposition, abandoned the more or less pro-Western course of his first foreign minister, Andrei Kozyrev. Although Kozyrev's successor, Evgenii Primakov, took a pragmatic rather than overtly anti-American approach, his pragmatism led him to reformulate Russian foreign policy as being multi-vectored, with a preference for multipolarity and the restoration of Russia's role at least as a Great, if not 'super,' Power (Erlanger 1996). During Primakov's tenure relations with the West took on a decidedly sour tone due to NATO's continued expansion to the east; when Yeltsin named Primakov Prime Minister in 1998, this was interpreted by many western observers as a clear indication of a new East-West confrontation, a sentiment magnified by the stridently anti-American rhetoric emanating from Moscow during the Kosovo crisis of 1998–1999 (Donaldson and Nogee 2005).

In contrast to the final year of the millennium, the transfer of power from Yeltsin to Putin in 1999/2000 was marked by what was, in retrospect, a softening of the discourse: once more, the 'New Cold War' appeared stillborn (Graham 2000). This swing away from Cold War imagery was conditioned by the internal situation in the Russian Federation: at the end of the Yeltsin era, the economic collapse of the Federation in 1998 and the accompanying political instability led a number of prominent American authors to write the country off as a failing state that was certainly too weak to act as a significant rival to the United States (Goble 1998). Two years later, the Russian Federation seemed less of a threat than ever, as Vladimir Putin was the first to phone US president George W. Bush on the occasion of the 9/11 attacks and, indeed, proposed a serious strategic alliance in the joint fight against terrorism. To recall from the first section of this chapter, at this moment peer-reviewed American scholarship pointed in the direction of a consensus that the long-elusive Russian–American partnership was finally a reality. Even at this point, however, the 'New Cold War' imagery did not disappear entirely from American analysis, as Russia's deepening engagement with China and India was regarded by some observers as indicative of Russian plans to reactivate a policy of global rivalry with the United States (Rahm 2001). Overall, though, the solidarity around 9/11 seemed to augur a truly new Warm Peace, a situation that lasted for exactly two years before domestic events in the Russian Federation (in particular, the Khodorkovsky affair) and the row over the invasion of Iraq and the Ukrainian elections resurrected the 'New Cold War' yet again.

This time, however, Russia's newly found assertiveness on the world scene meant that Russian and American interests found themselves clashing in increasing ways, particularly in the former Soviet space; if one carefully reads the analytical publications for the period of 2003 to 2008 one comes away with the distinct impression that actually for five years prior to the Georgian conflict, the United States and the Russian Federation had been constantly on the brink of neo-Cold War hostilities. There were occasional voices to the contrary, for example, the writings of Stephen Kotkin (2008) and Andrew Kuchins (2007) from this time period decry the 'myth of the new cold war;' Kuchins in particular commenting that 'If I had a dollar for every time in the last 15 years or so that I have been asked about the imminence of a "new Cold War," I would have retired long ago'. But these criticisms of the prevailing mood remained at the margins. Far more typical were the writings of the Heritage Foundation's resident Russia analyst, Ariel Cohen (2008), who went as far as to view the Sochi Bush-Putin summit in

April of 2008 as 'the last chance to improve relations' before a potential descent into Cold War-style hostilities. Two publications are paradigmatic of the trend assessed here: Stephen Cohen's 2006 article 'The New American Cold War' (2006) and Edward Lucas's much discussed 2008 tome *The New Cold War: The Future of Putin's Russia and the Threat to the West* (2008). Lucas's book especially strikingly exemplifies the increasingly pessimistic attitude among Russia analysts, a pessimism that clearly intensified over the years 2007–2008, setting the stage for a widespread interpretation of the August war through the 'New Cold War' lens.

At this point a qualification should be made. The above discussion has focused on the Cold War trope based on a description of typical American rhetoric in which the words 'Cold War' appear in analysis of Russia's international behaviour. It might be pointed out that such reductionism is not characteristic of the writings of serious scholars of Russian foreign policy, but is rather typical either of foreign policy pundits speaking and writing outside the context of academia or of journalists with little direct experience of Russian realities. The response to this must be, first, that many of the authors referenced in the analysis so far have, at various points in their career, acted as academics and (especially) policy makers themselves; the fact that their thoughts regarding the 'New Cold War' appear outside the pages of scholarly journals does not lessen the importance of their thought for forming the appropriate policies towards the Russian Federation in the post-Soviet years (for example, Zbigniew Brzezinski, William Safire and Charles Krauthammer). Furthermore, while Edward Lucas does not, to his credit, claim academic affiliation, his book has made it to the syllabuses of graduate courses in Russian foreign policy in American universities and has been promoted at international academic conferences as 'the new Bible on Russia'.[6]

Furthermore, while it is true that the 'serious' literature on Russian foreign policy does not usually employ the 'New Cold War' as a category of analysis, it does, however, very often come to conclusions that are permeated with ideas that the 'New Cold War' phrase evokes: that Russia is a country driven by imperialistic ambitions, these ambitions preconditioned by a propensity towards authoritarianism and reinforced by perennial corruption and nationalism. This is not to say that assessment of Russia's international actions in the peer-reviewed American literature has been uniformly negative, nor that negative assessment has never been warranted by the empirical evidence. The point is, rather, even when scholars based in the American academia have found something good to say about the balance sheet of Russian foreign policy, they have uniformly done so with qualifications, usually according to the following formula: There are positive trends, but given Russia's past behaviour and the ongoing tensions between pro-Western and pro-authoritarian factions, we cannot guarantee that the picture will

6 The author witnessed a scene at the International Studies Association 2009 annual convention in New York, during a panel on Russian foreign policy, during which one of the presenters literally thumped *The New Cold War* on the table (shades of Khruschev?) and pronounced it to be the new Bible on Russia.

not turn dark again sometime in the near future (Pipes 1997, Richter 1996, Dunlop 2004, Averre 2007, Aslund 2008). There is, of course, something to be said for hedging bets, particularly in a field as volatile as foreign policy analysis, where predictions are constantly being overturned in the face of new factual developments. Thus, on the one hand, we do not have to agree categorically with criticism claiming that 'casual or routine equating of the historical Russian expansionism with imperialism, and persistent attention to the post-Soviet ambitions … actually reflect not the complex content of the real [Russian foreign] policy but the specific interests and concerns of the observers' (Kassianova 2001: 823). On the other hand, in the case of American scholarship on Russian foreign policy, hedging is ritualistic and formulaic to the degree that it suggests a deeply ingrained skepticism regarding Russia's ability to accept Western norms of behaviour (that is, domestic democracy and rejection of aggression and imperialism abroad), a skepticism that parallels the 'New Cold War' trope in the non-scholarly literature on the subject (Thomas 2009).

At the end of the day, long before the Russia–Georgia conflict, a 'New Cold War' (or the brink thereof) supposedly characterized the Russian–American relationship at least five times, appearing with a frequency of about every two to three years, to the extent that one might even be tempted to claim that the original Cold War never ended, but simply mutated into some kind of post-modern, virtual version of itself. Given these tendencies within the commentary on Russian–American relations in the years and, indeed, months before the August war, it comes as little surprise that the South Ossetian conflict set off a veritable barrage of 'New Cold War' style reactions from the relevant Washington policy circles. For example, on August 25, 2008 Zbigniew Brzezinski wrote, 'The end of the Cold War was supposed to usher in a new age in which the major powers would no longer dictate to their neighbours how to run their affairs. That's why Russia's invasion of Georgia is so tragic and so potentially ominous.' He then asks a rhetorical question: 'Will [Russia] continue to rely on coercion to achieve its imperial aims, or is it willing to work within the emerging international system that values cooperation and consensus?' From the very next sentence, however, it is clear that Brzezinski already has the answer to this question, that is, that Russia has reverted to its Cold War posturing: 'Moscow's ruthless attempt to suborn, subdue and subordinate this tiny, independent democracy is reminiscent of Stalin's times. The assault on Georgia is similar to what Stalin's Soviet Union did to Finland in 1939 … ' James Traub, in an 10 August article for the *The New York Times* (2008), evokes similar images: Georgia as Czechoslovakia in 1938, 'Trusting the West to save it from a ravenous neighbour;' even though 'Georgians are a melodramatic people … they have good reasons to fear the ambitions, and the wrath, of a rejuvenated Russia seeking to regain lost power. Indeed, a renascent and increasingly bellicose Russia is an ominous spectacle for the West too'. As a result, 'the border where Georgia faces Russia … has become a new cold war frontier'.

The next day, in the *The Washington Post*, Ronald D. Asmus and Richard Holbrooke, both seasoned members of the Washington policy community, proclaimed that 'no one wants a return to Cold War-style confrontations'; however, the rhetorical style of their op-ed, despite the policy recommendations it contains conveys the opposite message. Among other things, the authors (2008) draw parallels between Russian policy in South Ossetia and that of Nazi Germany in the run-up to World War II. Furthermore, 'By trying to destroy a democratic, pro-Western Georgia, Moscow is sending a message ... that being close to Washington and the West does not pay'; in reading this sentence one cannot avoid the impression that a Cold War is already implicitly in play. The policy recommendations that Asmus and Holbrooke put forward are also familiar: containment and pushback. On August 12th, the *The New York Times* carried an editorial by Svante E. Cornell (2008b) that paralleled both Asmus and Holbrooke's imagery of a bipolar world with Russia on the one side and the West on the other, and offered the same policy prescriptions. In the meantime, the same issue of *The Washington Post* contained an editorial by neoconservative thinker Robert Kagan, who also (2008a) described the conflict in terms reminiscent of a bipolar world familiar before the fall of the Berlin wall: 'From the Baltics in the north through Central Europe and the Balkans to the Caucasus and Central Asia, a geopolitical power struggle has emerged between a resurgent and revanchist Russia on the one side and the European Union and the United States on the other.' Also on 12 August, Ariel Cohen was quoted as saying that 'It is a Cold War-type scenario already and pretending otherwise is misreading the writing on the wall;' at the time, he spoke in his capacity as an informal advisor to the McCain presidential campaign (Karnish 2008). These examples must suffice here, but the overall tone of most policy-relevant writings on the Russia–Georgia war as it progressed in August 2008 closely follows the pattern discussed here (de Borchgrave 2008, Will 2008).

The 'Cold War' trope and the US aversion to great power politics

This odd refusal of the 'Cold War' imagery to fade away has two implications for the specific case of the Georgia crisis, one direct and one indirect. Most obviously, the dominant narrative about Russia emanating from the American policy community, particularly after 2003, constituted the backdrop against which the government of Mikheil Saakashvili would have been calculating whether or not to risk the forced reintegration of South Ossetia into Georgia. The strength of the neo Cold War trope may have rendered believable the direct message Saakashvili had been receiving from the camp of presidential candidate John McCain as early as April 2008: that the United States would 'not allow Russia to believe it has a free hand to engage in policies that undermine Georgian sovereignty' (Associate Press 2008). The role of McCain's senior foreign policy advisor, Randy Scheunemann, in leading the Georgian president to believe that American blessing and support for the move on Tskhinvali would be forthcoming has been addressed by others; it is, however, in the context of the general scenario outlined here an important detail, specifically, that the expressions of support from McCain made a particular kind of sense to Saakashvili because of the predominant American narrative regarding Russia.

In a less direct – but more important – way, the persistence of the Cold War imagery in relation to Russia says something about why the Untied States has refused to go along with the Russian (and incidentally European and Chinese) preference for multi-polarity in the post-Cold War era. Here, it is useful to turn once again to Hedley Bull, specifically, to his assessment of the postwar era: for Chapter 9 of *The Anarchical Society* is concerned not just with any Great Powers; it is only peripherally interested in the nineteenth-century European configuration that is customarily invoked when the 'Great Powers' are spoken of. Bull is interested explicitly in his own contemporary situation, which he understands (with caveats) to be one of Great Power condominium between the USSR and the United States (Bull 1977: 194–9). Yet, even while Bull treats the US and the Soviet Union as Great Powers, he is never fully comfortable with his own characterization. On the contrary, he stresses that the two countries do not necessarily act according to the ideal type of Great Power behaviour as he has developed it, writing, for instance, that 'if, then, the special rights and duties of a great power are accepted not only by the United States, but by the Soviet Union …, this acceptance is tentative only, and not acknowledged explicitly' (199). The extent to which Bull sees the precariousness of treating the bipolar world in Great Power terms is particularly evident in his discussion of the spheres of influence after World War II: for one thing, he admits that even though both sides act as though the spheres of influence exist, the areas of mutual non-interference have never been formally agreed upon (223). Furthermore, he stresses that 'it is one thing for the United States and the Soviet Union to recognize the fact that certain parts of the world are within each other's spheres of influence; it is another to treat such spheres of influence as legitimate.' From the American point of view, which is of particular interest here, the United States never accepted the spheres of influence as legitimate, even if it did deal with the division as an uncomfortable fact; yet it always remained a fact to be changed, a point Bull explicitly makes in his discussion of active US policies aimed at undermining Soviet rule in Eastern Europe (224).

Centrally important for the present analysis, what emerges from Bull's assessment of the postwar situation is a picture in which the apparent Great Power division of the globe obscured the ideological confrontation between the two sides; the tendency to think of the US and the Soviet Union as balancing each other turned attention away from the reality that, at the end of the day, the two powers regarded each other as antithetical systems of governance and, more importantly, morality. As such, the eventual goal of one side overcoming the other never disappeared. To briefly capture the point, behind this reluctance of the United States to accept the division of the world into spheres of Soviet and American influence, we can glimpse the American refusal to accept as fully legitimate the Great Power arrangement that, in Bull's analysis at least, was at the heart of the postwar order. Bull first published *The Anarchical Society* in 1977; the events of the following decade bear out his analysis of American reluctance to accept the status quo, as the Reagan administration shifted the confrontation with the 'Evil Empire' into high gear. The collapse of the USSR was accompanied by that rousing chorus 'The United States Won the Cold War;' the demise of the arrangement between the two Great (super) Powers was, from the American point of view, a universal good, and heralded the dawn of the legitimate world order: the US led End of History hymned by Francis Fukuyama.

How does the above discussion help understand the breakdown in US–Russian relations that led to the Georgian crisis? It suggests that for the United States, the Cold War 'Great Power' arrangement represents a negative model of international relations: it is how things should not be. Russia, in insisting on the Great Power model, becomes automatically guilty of wanting to return to the bad old days. Thus, in the aftermath of the Georgian war, the discussion of Russia's interest in Great Power status was noted not only in the analytical American press; it also appeared – and was explicitly rejected – in a speech given by Secretary of State Condoleezza Rice to the US Marshall Fund in September 2008. The way in which Rice (2008) refers to Russia's desire for 'spheres of influence' in the speech is significant, as she couches it in terms that leave no doubt that in her understanding, accepting spheres of influence means ceding swathes of territory to domination by authoritarian Russia – it would mean the retreat of freedom, the loss of worldwide democratic gains made possible by the end of the Cold War.

Finally, the Cold War phantom has affected the analysis even of those American authors who perceive – in contrast to Rice – the Russian–American relationship in terms of Great Power politics. Immediately after the war, Robert Kagan published an iconoclastic article (2008b) in which he claimed that Russia had succeeded in redefining the rules of the game away from American unilateralism towards a more traditional Great Power arrangement as it would be familiar from the nineteenth century. Yet, his other writings reveal that Kagan is unable to conceive of the nineteenth-century balance of power without referencing the Cold War – in his view, the nineteenth century itself saw an ideological confrontation between authoritarian and democratic nations (Kagan 2007). The logical implication of Kagan's argument is that, even if we grant that, post-Georgia, the world is governed by a Great Powers arrangement, this is not an ideal situation, as it represents the crisis-prone confrontation between the normatively positive American-led bloc of free nations and the negatively authoritarian rest (with Russia chief among them).

At the end of the day, if we follow Bull's description of the postwar situation as one in which the Soviet Union and the United States acted (even unwillingly) as Great Powers, we may look at the Georgian crisis as partially a result of entrapment in the Cold War mode of thinking. To wit, the fact that Russia continuously insisted on Great Power status over the course of the 1990s–2000s may have had the paradoxical effect of reinforcing American concerns about a return to the negatively remembered Cold War. In turn, these concerns contributed the formulation of policies meant to contain Russian ambitions; in the meantime, Russia itself took on ever more authoritarian contours, in part as a response to a perceived menace from the United States in the wake of the Iraq invasion –

thereby justifying further American concerns about Russia's desire for a 'Back to the Future' scenario. The discussion above highlighted the constantly rising tensions – framed in familiar Cold War terms – that characterized the second half of the 2000s in particular, as the vicious cycle fed on itself and multiplied the mutual misunderstandings, reinforcing the misalignment already identified in the first section of this chapter.

Conclusion

To summarize, then, *The Anarchical Society* provides several useful tools for identifying the nodes at which the Russian–American relationship broke down in August 2008, resulting in the Georgian conflict. While not claiming to a definitive account of this breakdown, the paper proposes several lines along which it might be explored through Bull's conceptualization of what Great Powers are and the role they play in the maintenance of international order. In terms of the first question, it is clear that there occurred a fundamental misalignment in the ways in which Russia and the United States view themselves in relation to the international order: while Russia, since the mid 1990s, sought recognition as a Great Power in Bull's terms and, by 2001, started to act increasingly as though the country believed itself to be one, the United States, especially after the adoption of the Bush Doctrine, acted as though there were no Great Power club of equal status but rather one, American superpower. Based on this misalignment of self-perception, the game could not proceed without serious breakdowns as the two sides were playing by completely different rules: following Bull's conceptualization of how Great Powers act, both Russia and the United States' actions in the international sphere diverged along the lines implied by the difference in their understanding of themselves. Namely, while for Russia the balance of power, spheres of influence and Great Power concerts made sense as the guiding rules in an increasingly multi-polar world, for the United States these concepts simply did not figure in the Bush-era foreign policy considerations. Finally, Bull's discussion of the US-Soviet relationship in the postwar era is helpful in understanding why the United States did not respond positively to Russia's vision of the post-Cold War world as one of a concert between Great Powers; to the contrary, the memory of the negative experience of the Cold War only reinforced the American aversion to the Great Power idea, and led to a hardening of anti–Russian attitudes within the relevant policy establishment. Once the identified incompatibilities came to the fore in Georgia, where both sides were pursuing interests defined in terms of their conflicting self-understanding in an atmosphere already heavily tinged with the negative legacy of the Cold War, armed conflict was perhaps the inevitable outcome.

Chapter 4
Russia and NATO After the Georgia War: Re-Actualizing the Great Power Management Prospects

Andrey Makarychev

This chapter seeks to analyse the consequences of Russia's military operation against Georgia in August 2008 within the wider context of Russia–NATO relations. The research puzzle I address, concerns the high volatility of these relations. Indeed, the Georgia war not only became possible because of the failure of both parties to jointly manage the conflicting effects of separatism in South Ossetia and Abkhazia, but also marked the lowest point in bilateral Moscow–Brussels relations in decades. Some Russian analysts, such as Dmitry Trenin (2009: 24), have been quick to compare the situation in the Caucasus in August 2008 with the Cuban Missile Crisis, and have argued that Russia was potentially on the brink of military confrontation with the most powerful NATO state. Yet, the subsequent improvement in these relations has not taken much time: only a couple of years after the Georgia war, Russia has admitted the validity of cooperation with NATO in such issues as Afghanistan, international piracy and nuclear non-proliferation. The Institute for Contemporary Development (INSOR), a think tank patronized by President Medvedev, issued a report in Autumn 2010, advocating Russia's eventual closer association with NATO.

The degeneration of Russia–NATO relations in August 2008 and their subsequent improvement can be examined using the old idea of great power management as a valuable conceptual tool to shed more light on the dynamics of Russia–NATO (mis)communications and (dis)connections. I will argue that these fluctuations can be explained, by and large, by two variables. One of them is conflation of both political and de-politicized practices of the two sides, and in this paper I will try to uncover the correlation between them. The second factor is the inconsistency within the subject positions and, therefore, discourses of both parties under consideration. It is the dislocations within Russian discourse that I will examine more closely in this paper.

As for the first factor, it is within the legacy of the English school that one may find some interest in the two possible patterns of great power management, namely political and de-politicized. Hedley Bull's theory contains some – though rather modest – prompts for reflections in this vein. His sympathies for *law*-based (as opposed to *justice*-based) order explain why, in Andrew Hurrell's (2002: XX) judgement, much of Bull's 'writings has been rationalist in method and technocratic in character'. Bull (1977: 305) himself related de-politicization to universalization and described different elements of a de-politicized type of international society, including ideological homogeneity (presupposing the absorption of non-Western identities into the alleged cosmopolitan culture), world government and the technological unification of the world. It is exactly this logic that sustains the making of 'world international society', which, according to Bull, presupposes the elaboration of global norms and rules to be observed by all its members. Therefore, great power management in a solidarist/universalist type of international society is a mechanism fostering a collective (consensual) code/set of rules of conduct that prioritizes technical crisis management over ideology; refrains from making loud politically loaded accusations; and criminalizes violence through the application of law-based procedures of persecuting war criminals.

Along these lines, de-politicization can be understood as a shift to universal forms of organizing and stabilizing social relations through the usage of legal and institutional mechanisms to regulate and administer the policies of major powers. De-politicization entails de-legitimation of those actors that may foment political conflicts. In terms of English school analysis, this perspective corresponds to the solidarist version of international society that may be regarded as a de-politicized social milieu unified by common norms facing no viable alternatives. The domination of universalism in its various forms is conducive to totalization of social milieu which ultimately defies politics, leaves no place for political articulations (including the axiological good-evil distinction) and requires mostly administrative and managerial techniques of governance rather than political instruments.

As for the second – discursive – dimension of the puzzle noted above, it may be tackled from two angles. One of them is derived from Foucault's tradition of focusing on inconsistencies within discursive formations that make each of them fluid and controversial if not self-destructing, on the one hand, and dependent upon other – external – discourses, on the other. What may stem from Foucauldian reflection is that it is the discursive fluctuations that may explain the fuzziness of Russian international identity. In my analysis I will use the Foucauldian departures as an important methodological tool for unpacking Russian discourse on NATO and elucidating its intrinsic contradictions and both its political and epistemic borderlines.

Another method comes from Laclau's idea of chains of equivalences that will be applied for comprehending the Kremlin's logic of constructing the relations of enmity. As I will argue, it is through the chain-of-equivalence mechanism that Russian foreign policy imagery works to shape Russian identity in a series of oppositions to a rather elastic group of inter-related 'negative others'. Yet again, very similar to the logic of Foucault, these oppositions are neither stable nor complete, which definitely complicates Russia's search for international identity.

Therefore, as one may see, the research puzzle I address will be placed in a theoretical domain whose contours are shaped by the English school in general and one of its key protagonists Hedley Bull in particular. Yet this theoretical platform will be complemented by a more radical – though still to a large extent compatible with the English school – stream of political thought known as critical theory. This paradoxical, from the first sight, mix is far from being conventional in today's academic research, yet it may open potentially innovative pathways for thinking about the nature of great power management, a concept used by Bull but still requiring deeper elucidation from different viewpoints, including those situated rather far away from the English school traditions. There are quite a few important meeting points between the English school and critical theory, including the analysis of politicization and de-politicization and the effects of war on international society.

I will start my analysis by dwelling on Bull's discussion of great power management and adding to it critical theory approaches. Then I will touch upon the prospects of using two different techniques of discourse analysis – those based upon the methodological departures of Michel Foucault and Ernesto Laclau – for the sake of studying the Russia–NATO discursive imbalances. In the final section, I will address how the uncovered trends may influence the search for a model of great power management with Russia and NATO as its constitutive cores.

Great Power Management and War: Unpacking the Concepts

What has to be explicated from the very beginning is why NATO's security actorship can be considered in the framework of the great power management concept. In their contribution to the development of the English school ideas, Barry Buzan and Ole Wæver (2003: 33) rightfully address the question of whether a great power can only be a state, or whether it would be more appropriate to view great powers as system-level poles, or a 'group of independent political communities'. In line with this argument, Buzan and Wæver justify the ascription of the great power qualities to the EU, and by this logic how they may arguably be extended to NATO as well. Indeed, under the conditions of complex multipolarity, power should not be stringently equated with states, since it becomes a more complex phenomenon including structural characteristics based upon alliance formation and collective action. It is exactly in this sense that Buzan (2004: 187) refers to NATO as a specific example of the great power management institution. Perhaps, the concept of 'great power regional security complex' developed by Buzan and Wæver (2003: 59) is a more sophisticated description of NATO's status in international society structures, which adds one more feature to the great power portrait – each of these powers is supposed to have its own regional sphere of influence, interest and responsibility.

Yet it is more important to underline that in Bull's reasoning, the institution of great power management can only exist in the framework of international society. Accordingly, when the great power management fails to work, this may be an indication of some problems with international society itself. While these problems may be rectified by the functioning of other key institutions, such as balance of power, international law or diplomacy, they may also, conversely, increase the likelihood of war as another institution in Bull's list. The importance of war experiences is a point of overlay between the English school and critical theories. For Bull, war is an institution of international society, but – one may add – an institution of a special kind: it is located *both* within and beyond its structures. It is within, since it inaugurates the whole set of both political and managerial relations; yet it is simultaneously outside the international society since it symbolizes extreme disorder and the breakdown of its other institutions, which include diplomacy and international law. It seems that for Bull, the inclusion of war into international society is more meaningful than exclusion from it. This is because he considers war not as a mere political phenomenon but 'organized violence carried on political units against each other' (Bull 1977: 178); and more essentially, 'it is war or the threat of war that helps' shape the international society. War is for this reason so 'basic that even the terms we use to describe the system – great powers and small powers, alliances and spheres of influence, balances of power and hegemony – are scarcely intelligible except in relation to war' (181). Besides, 'the international order is notoriously lacking in mechanisms of peaceful change, notoriously dependent on war as the agent of just change' (183).

A similar argument is shared by a number of critical thinkers (from Michel Foucault to Antonio Negri) who opine that war is the constitutive ground for power relations. In other words, it is war that predetermines political constellations and 'becomes the general matrix of all relations of power and techniques of domination' (Hardt and Negri 2004: 13). In clear opposition to Clausewitz, critical theorists argue that 'war is not conditional upon politics but it becomes itself the condition for authentic political practice and identity' (Huysmans 2006: 20). Mikhail Remizov, a Russian author, takes up this topic, stating 'the energy of war and of distinction between 'self' and 'other' in each culture is a colossal meaning-making resource' (2000: 29). This, to a large extent, may be applicable to the August 2008 war between Russia and Georgia. Arguably, the war was conducive to the emergence of a new power relationship involving – along with other key actors – Russia and NATO. According to the official Russian interpretation, the war was a landmark event that split the time to what was 'before' and what is 'after'. In the Kremlin's triumphalist narrative, the war was, thus, of paramount importance for the entire structure of international society, a Russian equivalent of September 11; that is, an event symbolized as a 'moment of truth' and touching upon the deepest strings of national identity. This justifies the choice of the Georgia war as a crucial point in remolding Russia's relations with Western powers, including NATO which is not only one of Russia's key international interlocutors but also constitutes a major reference point for its discursive construction of its own identity.

Yet it is not only political relations between international agents that war institutes; we may also speak of war as a basis for reconfiguration of power mechanisms that are not reducible to politics but also include managerial instruments. Bull has explicitly focused his analysis on the nature of order in international society, drawing a contrast between order (a predominantly de-politicized concept) and justice (a more explicitly politically oriented idea). Great power management is evidently about establishing order, not pursuing justice which, as the Georgia war illuminated, is always divisive and short of consensus. This implies that this managerial model may contain a great deal of injustice, including the maintenance of regional systems of hegemony based on the imposition of great powers' joint will on second-rank actors. Bull (1977: 282) makes it quite clear that 'the model of a great power concert ignores, where it does not actually seek to repress, the demands of weaker countries and peoples for change'.

Against this background, it becomes clear that what Bull advocates under the guise of great power management is a police-type of, and thus politically sterile, security order. It is at this point that the English school arguments coincide with those of critical theory that, as Slavoj Žižek (2004: 72) claims, postulates 'the reduction of the state to police agent servicing the (consensually established) needs of the market forces and multiculturalist tolerant humanitarianism'. Obviously, de-politicization by no means purports the effacement of power argument as constitutive for international order. Arguably, it is the so called de-politicized 'governmental technologies' that 'may lead to a state of domination' (Lemke 2000) worldwide. As one Russian political commentator puts it, 'in contemporary society power has merged with engineering and stubbornly claims to be of a technical background ... Politics confined to omnipresence of the virtual imaginary and technical assignments turns out to be the most radical and genuinely irreplaceable form of exercising power' (Maliavin 2004). Possibly, Žižek's (2005: 115) supposition, which evidently points to the United States, that 'de-politicized politics of human rights is the ideology of military interventionism' can also be applicable to Russia's policy towards Georgia.

The interplay between politicization and de-politicization can be better examined using discourse analysis in the next section. I will argue that while Russia's NATO discourse is shaped by mostly political articulations, some room for non-political approaches is left.

NATO in Russian Foreign Policy Discourse: Points of Communication and Discord

I will continue by analysing NATO's role in Russian foreign policy discourse. I will start this section by pointing to the NATO-centrism of this discourse. Following this, I will turn to identifying the most significant areas of discursive discordance between Russia and NATO, before elucidating a discursive mechanism that reproduces the relations of enmity as far as Russia's communications with a group of significant others are concerned. The discourse analysis approach applied in this paper requires determinacy in the selection of significant speakers, that is, those who may be considered as the most important and valuable sources of knowledge and information. In our case, there are four figures whose speech acts are of primordial importance for the state of the Russia–NATO relations:

- President Dmitry Medvedev, as the chief foreign policy maker in Russia,
- Prime Minister Vladimir Putin, who laid the foundations for what is dubbed the more nationalist foreign policy after 2000,
- Foreign Minister Sergey Lavrov, whose role in Russian foreign policy discourse consists of 'unpacking' and commenting on presidential statements and giving more food for thought for foreign audiences,
- Russia's ambassador to NATO, Dmitry Rogozin who as a former party politician with a national patriotic profile, plays a more public – and sometimes carnivalesque – role aimed at challenging and dethroning NATO's legitimacy.

NATO as a reference object of Russia's discourse

Despite all the habitual criticism of NATO, it was this alliance that on many occasions Russia regarded as an important source of international legitimacy of its policy in the North Caucasus. In the words of Rogozin, the main proposal Moscow put forward to the Alliance was that NATO should 'invite the representatives of South Ossetia and Abkhazia to our meeting so as to listen to the victim-party who actually suffered in the conflict'. The same approach to NATO as a meaningful source of legitimacy was traceable in Russia's demand addressed 'to NATO top officials to abstain from visiting Georgia because this kind of visits are interpreted by the Georgian leadership as full political and moral support of personally Mr. Saakashvili' (Rogozin 2009: 21).

The overt references to the previous experiences of NATO member states is an indispensable discursive tool that Russia applied for justifying its military operation in Georgia. In Rogozin's words, Russia faces the 'temptation of chain reaction': 'if NATO can, why can't we?'. The same logic goes for the substantiation of the Russian argument aimed at the right to defend compatriots outside the country. In Rogozin's enunciation:

> Russia keeps in mind the interventions by the US and its allies in Yugoslavia, Iraq and Afghanistan. Further, the last three cases are examples of American interventions when its own citizens did not need direct protection. But in spite of those countries' massive civilian losses at the hands of American soldiers, no one blamed Washington for a disproportionate use of force. (Rogozin 2008)

In fact, this statement sounds like a hidden appeal to exchange Russia's abstention from criticism of the US in Yugoslavia, Iraq and Afghanistan for a more explicit American understanding of Russian moves in the North Caucasus.

This situation only reinvigorates the reasoning of those in NATO who, as follows from Rogozin's (2009: 43) words, claim that Russia pretends to be a good guy, whereas it is 'just like us'. Despite Russian reluctance to admit the truth of this phrase, it seems quite fair to speak of Russia and NATO as being much closer to each other than it would appear on the surface. This explains why Russia not only recognizes NATO as its partner but deems that relations between the two actors constitute the basis of global security. As an example, Russia praises cooperation with NATO in anti-terrorist research and in anti-missile projects. The Russian Foreign Minister has even claimed that the Russia–NATO Council, where each country is represented in its own capacity, is institutionally more accommodating to Russian interests than the existing mechanisms of Russia–EU cooperation.

Russia's pro-NATO rhetoric is based on two arguments. One is of pragmatic background: it is in Russia's interest, for example, to support NATO's operation in Afghanistan where Russia shares a number of important interests with the Alliance, including the eradication of narcotics and countering Islamic radicalism. Another argument contains a greater deal of identity flavor: Russia sees itself as a constitutive part of European civilization, which puts it in some sort of cultural opposition to the Orient, including India and China. Rogozin's (2009: 10) statement that the idea of strategic cooperation between Moscow, Peking and Delhi could be conceived only by an 'insane mind', contains implicit criticism of such organizations as BRIC or the Shanghai Cooperation Organization that very often are depicted as either alternatives or counter-balances to the Western integrative institutions, including NATO. He goes as far as to assume that both Russia and NATO face a threat from the modern version of the Asiatic Tatar-Mongol hordes (Rogozin 2009: 120).

These gestures of reverence demonstrate Russia's readiness to leave the door open for negotiations with NATO and help discern some logical correlation between Russia's anti-NATO and pro-NATO discourses. Indeed, by artificially sharpening the othering of NATO by means of accentuating normative gaps that seemingly split Moscow and Brussels or by trying to expose NATO's inadequacy, Russia arguably wishes to underline – in a peculiar way though – its own importance for security arrangements in Europe and its high status as a prospective security partner to NATO.

The Foucauldian perspective

Along the lines of Foucauldian vocabulary, one may call the totality of Russia's speech acts pointing to NATO a discursive formation which appears to be a variegated and intrinsically incoherent body of texts. This discursive formation contains mechanisms that challenge its cohesion from inside; besides, as I will demonstrate, it discloses deep perceptional gaps between Russia and NATO. In doing this, I will put these gaps into five groups.

Mutual (mis)perceptions Russia definitely faces some meaningful problems in reaching a proper understanding of what NATO is as an international actor. The

Kremlin challenges the key foundational principles of NATO – its collective potential as a bloc, as well as its democratic identity.

As far as the first principle is concerned, the problem here is that Russia's foreign policy philosophy is grounded in the modernist understanding of sovereignty, while the NATO members' discourses are predicated upon trans-/cross-/supra-national integration in the security domain. This is why Russia, which believes in its self-sufficiency in the security realm, is such a reluctant security partner for NATO.

This viewpoint has some practical effects for Russia's approach to NATO: the Kremlin prefers to deal with it not as a bloc, but as a loose group of nation states where pluralism prevails over solidarism. This attitude is visible in Russia's claim that the Russia–NATO Council appears to be ineffective due to NATO members' preference for taking consolidated positions vis-à-vis Russia. In its place, the Kremlin certainly wishes for each of them to act individually. Rogozin's insistence on the 'supra-national' character of NATO sustains the vision of the Alliance as a hegemonic institution that encroaches upon sovereignties of its member states and makes them go to war regardless and in spite of their own wishes.

Yet even more consequential is Russia's denial of NATO's claim to be an alliance of democratic states. NATO places strong emphasis on the shared values that cement security integration, and is keen to present itself to the world as a 'values-based politico-military alliance' that 'provided a framework for democratic consolidation in Europe' (Highlights from the First Strategic Seminar 2009). But in Russia's view, NATO as a military alliance has nothing to do with democracy at all. Rogozin is quite explicit in this regard: 'NATO is not a union of democracies; it is a union of militaries. When the NATO Secretary General criticizes parliamentary elections in my country, he oversteps his mandate. The combination of his (negative – Andrey Makarychev) evaluation of Russian democracy with the thesis that NATO does not fight democracies – and conversely does fight non-democracies – could be interpreted as a threat to Russia' (Global Security and Propaganda Dogmas 2009).

As Medvedev's 'architectural' proposal suggests, Russia prefers to verbalize its message addressed to the West as an interest-based speech act with obvious pragmatic overtones, while most European members of NATO are inclined to formulate their worldviews in a more normative (identity and value-based) language register that inevitably contains mechanisms of othering Russia. It is obvious that NATO – as well as the EU – is interested not in *any* type of security order but in that one grounded in 'a set of fundamentally liberal values – democracy, the rule of law and individual freedom' (Rynning 2003: 481).

The repudiation of security-democracy nexus as exemplified by NATO serves a number of practical functions, two of which are of utmost importance. By doing so, Russia wishes, first of all, to challenge NATO's self-description as a democracy promoter across the world; besides, what stands behind this discursive strategy is that even without a convincing record of democratic credentials, Russia may still qualify for being accepted as NATO's security partner.

In its turn, NATO is unlikely to sustain any of the roles that Russia ascribes to itself in the world – be it 'energy superpower', the 'locomotive' of post-Soviet integration, or the architect of a new security edifice in Europe. Furthermore, the alliance often treats Russia as a troublesome partner and a source of security concerns, which explains why Russia's place in NATO's 'ring' of partners is by no means guaranteed.

Temporal othering Both parties accuse each other of being stuck in old approaches dating back to the Cold War. NATO thinks that Russia clutches to old-fashioned ideas of the Westphalian world of national sovereignties and balance-of-power type of conduct. In its turn, Russian officials are keen to draw imaginary – and seemingly artificial – parallels between NATO and the Soviet Union: thus, Rogozin (2009: 156) compares new members of the Alliance with Young Communist League ('komsomol') zealots that ultimately challenged the authority of the 'old party elite' (meaning the so called 'Old Europe'). This reasoning is consistent with the accusation of NATO in putting ideological imprints into its policy towards Russia.

Against this background, it is comprehensible that instead of the rather traditional description of NATO as a dangerously strong (even omnipotent) and unfriendly military bloc that threatens Russian interests, the North Atlantic Alliance is often said to be a relic of the Cold War, incapable of providing security in today's altered international environment in which security challenges are not bound to specific territories. Of course, Russia's portrayal of NATO as a deplorable remnant of the Cold War is questionable; yet the key problem with such labeling is that Russia itself from time to time reactualizes the Cold War legacy in quite positive contexts. Thus, Rogozin (2009: 123) has explicitly declared that Moscow is an upholder of the Cold War system of international relations – a statement that is quite illustrative of the lack of conceptual precision in the Kremlin's attempts to use the Cold War as a significant reference point in its identity discourse.

NATO's relations with other international organizations As an effect of NATO's stand taken during the Georgia war, the Alliance, according to Moscow's vision, finds itself in opposition to other key international institutions. As Lavrov (2009a) puts it, it is due to ideological considerations that NATO refuses to take seriously the prospects of cooperation with the Collective Security Treaty Organization. Even the EU, in the Russian interpretation, is not absolutely immune from possible disputes with NATO: 'By October 1 (2008 – Andrey Makarychev) EU peace-keepers and OSCE military monitors are expected to arrive at the buffer zone ... In these circumstances NATO can find itself in a situation of confrontation with the EU because of NATO's alleged intention to restore Saakashvili's military capabilities' (Rogozin 2009: 57).

On a different occasion, Rogozin (2009: 54) was keen to present the EU–Russia security agreements reached by Presidents Medvedev and Sarkozy in August 2008 as leaving NATO far behind and thus questioning the Alliance's relevance. Within this logic, NATO's role in the North Caucasus is only marginal, which partly explains why in the aftermath of the Georgia war the Russian–EU relations achieved momentum. The Russian President underlined that 'it is exactly the EU that became a resourceful, responsible and, what is of utmost importance, pragmatic partner for us' (Medvedev 2008). 'Is Europe for NATO or NATO for Europe?', the Russian Foreign Minister asked, before stressing that it is up to the EU to find 'a European solution' to the Caucasian problems, instead of 'heeding the advices from far-away'. The United States, in this logic, was called to 'come back to Europe, this is to say to share European worldview', as Lavrov (2008b) provocatively puts it.

On a more general note, one may assume that Russia wishes to present NATO not as a separate institutional pole in security terrain but rather as an instrument of American foreign policy establishment that presumably intends to spite Europe and force it to act against its own interests (Rogozin 2009: 92). Referring to the proclamation of Kosovan independence, Rogozin (2009: 102) goes as far as to claim that 'there certainly is an external manipulator that wishes to splinter Europe into small pea-like fragments.'

Of course, NATO ignores this conjecture and firmly considers itself the core of the trans-Atlantic security community and believes its functioning does not necessarily require Russia's equal participation. It is quite telling that most NATO countries prefer to speak of trans-Atlantic (not of Euro-Atlantic) security community (not of 'space' as Russia does) which only underlines the special role of the US in the Alliance and the utmost importance of a common normative agenda.

Normative cleavages In comparing the normative standpoints of NATO and Russia, I will distinguish between two understandings of norms – as values and as procedures. As far as *values* are concerned, the platforms of the two parties look rather different. The NATO standpoint is explicitly value-oriented, which is manifested in two ways. *Firstly*, NATO claims to play the role of the key security institution representing the West in general (supposedly, against the alleged non-West). *Secondly*, NATO shares the approach to security as a value-ridden concept. In other words, security protection should not be restricted to the technical maintenance of order and avoidance of atrocities; it is always about such universal values as human rights and civil freedoms.

Against this background, the Russian viewpoint looks much more ambiguous. On the one hand, the Kremlin seems to share much of NATO's normative appeal. Russian leaders have repeatedly referred to the allegedly common values on the eve of and during the Georgia war (they dubbed the Saakashvili regime undemocratic, un-European, uncivilized, etc.) and its aftermath (in Dmitry Medvedev's (2008) vision, what Russia seeks is the construction of 'genuinely democratic world order'). Yet this type of discourse does not resonate well in the West where many are convinced that Russia pragmatically is eager to join the dominating – that is, democracy-grounded discourse, and in the meantime to change the meanings of its key signifiers (in particular, the way human security is understood in the Kremlin differs a lot from the European reading of this concept). Having faced this reaction, Russia started to implicitly deny the practicability of common values, and instead turned to treating norms predominantly from the procedural viewpoint, as exemplified, in particular, by Medvedev's proposals on new security architecture in the Euro-Atlantic region.

In terms of *procedures*, the positions taken by NATO and Russia look different as well. Russia re-energized its efforts to propose a set of codified and formalized rules of behaviour in the (mostly hard) security sphere. One may argue that Medvedev's common Euro-Atlantic security space proposal is predicated upon procedural unification – universalization of the guiding principles – that constrain conflicting parties and seek to avoid bloodshed. It is not only the evident mistrust of NATO that fuels Russia's interest in the rule-based management of security issues; what is of even greater importance is that Russia's insistence on 'common security rules' reveals the Kremlin's disbelief in the prospects of unilateral actions in the future. As a weaker – in comparison to NATO – security actor, Russia prefers to rely upon institutionally de-politicized mechanisms of conflict prevention.

Yet Medvedev's universalizing logic begs two big and still unanswered questions that challenge its de-politicized background. *Firstly*, how 'common' is the presumable security architecture that Russia is eager to design? In particular, if Russia is serious about giving to Abkhazia and South Ossetia equal footing with countries like the United States or Great Britain, the whole idea will prove to be based on a pretty shaky ground and meet political resistance. *Secondly*, the alleged unification of security procedures all over the Euro-Atlantic area conceptually clashes with Sergey Lavrov's insistence on 'looking for regional solutions for regional problems' to prevent the hegemonic interventions from 'extra-regional power(s)' (first of all, the United States). The formula of 'regional solutions' – certainly reinforced by the decreasing interest from the part of the US to countries like Georgia – leads to particularization of international society and thus conflicts with the explicitly solidarist platform of the Medvedev proposal.

The competing concepts of security Russia clearly sympathizes with the hard security concept that evidently limits the gamut of security relations to the issues of military strategy and geopolitics. Yet Russia does not feel this approach to be outdated; on the contrary, the Russian discourse is full of allusions to NATO's obsolescence. In clear reference to the negativity of the Cold War experience of bipolar rivalry, NATO's enlargement is treated as the re-imposition of old-fashioned dividing lines in Europe. This is a typical reflection by Rogozin (2009: 90): 'These kinds of organizations are very long-living, because they are like old apartments – it has all the furniture in it, everything becomes dear to the heart, you don't even want to throw away an old broken ash-tray. The same is with NATO. There are bureaucrats who say if NATO disappears one day, where would we go? Where would we get our pay-checks?'.

NATO, for its part, prefers an extended security agenda that stretches far beyond what is dubbed traditional risks and dangers. NATO concentration on a soft security agenda may lead to the further marginalization of Russia that cannot justifiably expect to become a soft security partner unless it undertakes robust measures to improve its democracy record and starts effectively protecting its population against such problems as corruption, environmental decay and drug use. It is through this broader security vision that NATO seeks to rewrite its strategic concept and redefine its role in the global security scene. This process proceeds in four interlinked directions.

Firstly, NATO's conception of security gradually extends to include such seemingly non-military matters as democratic consolidation, stabilization of weak and fragile states, strengthening good governance along NATO's periphery, fighting corruption, preventing genocide, safeguarding energy flows and sea lines (in particularly, in the High North), dealing with humanitarian disasters, climate change, cyber attacks and drug trafficking. *Secondly*, NATO officials explicitly admit that the Alliance has to more intensely engage with different types of actors, including host governments, a plethora of local players, contractors, international financial bodies and non-governmental organizations. *Thirdly,* facing the necessity to deal with a growing number of different (non-state) actors and (non-Western) cultures, NATO heavily invests in soft power instruments that are needed for developing an effective strategy of global expansion. *Fourthly*, NATO is keen to geographically extend its areas of operation to regions that may include, apart from the Caucasus, such remote areas as the Middle East and South West Asia.

Re-conceptualizing Discursive Chain of Equivalences

There is another way to apply discourse analysis techniques for this research. Foreign policy imageries of Russia (as well as of NATO) may be analysed through the prism of Laclau's idea of 'chains of equivalences' which is a powerful discursive tool used for constructing the relations of enmity through identifying constellations of external others. In Laclau's (2007: 14) reasoning, each political subject faces 'equivalent threats' to its identity. It is by means of the relations of equivalence that the discursive construction of inimical otherness is effectuated. 'In a relation of equivalence, each element of the chain functions as a symbol of negativity as such' (Laclau 2007: 14), and thus can under certain circumstances be 'relatively universalized', that is, represent the entire chain.

Relations of equivalence and enmity

The Russian chain of 'antagonistic forces' is predicated upon linking Georgia to the US/NATO-centric world order that in 2008 basically looked as follows: United States–NATO–Ukraine–Georgia. This chain reflects an explicitly US-centred worldview; consequently, the 'systemic centre' against which this chain is constituted is Russia itself. The portrayal of the Georgia war as the direct challenge to the global hegemon (Rogozin 2009: 204) only confirms this US-centric posture of Russian diplomacy. The meanings attached to this scheme are interpreted as deliberate attempts to debilitate Russia through encircling it by unfriendly states.

This scheme is typical for Russian foreign policy thinking which tends to regard NATO as a security instrument of the United States. Thus, Russia complains that in August 2008 when the war with Georgia erupted, the Russia's demand for convening the Russia–NATO Council was blocked by the US. It also considers Georgia as a junior ally of the United States: in fact, 'the North Atlantic Alliance has taken Mikhail Saakashvili under its protection' (Lavrov 2008a), the Russian Foreign Minister stated. This stance justifies Russia's accusations of the US administration in fueling conflict in the Caucasus and in failing to support Russia in its confrontation with Georgia.

It is the Georgia–Ukraine nexus that seems to be of special importance for understanding the Russian logic of equivalence and its securitization. Since both countries were homes to what is dubbed 'colour revolutions' and candidates for NATO membership, Russia has tended to see their foreign policies before and immediately after the Georgia war not only as correlating to each other but also as coordinated from overseas. Both Presidents Yuschenko and Saakashvili have been portrayed as founders of undemocratic regimes that domestically provoke disintegrative splits within their countries, and externally are dependent on foreign aid.

Not incidentally, Russia applied similar discursive tools to prevent Kiev and Tbilisi from joining NATO. Russia's strategy boiled down to forcing both countries to make an unpalatable choice between territorial integrity and NATO membership – a controversial strategy, to say the least, especially in light of Russia's continued opposition to Kosovo's independence. Even before the August 2008 war, Russia claimed that Ukrainian and Georgian applications to NATO were a justification for the possible secession of Crimea from Ukraine and the permanent separation of the breakaway autonomies of Abkhazia and South Ossetia from Georgia. Rogozin mentioned that it was unlikely that Ukraine would be able to maintain its current borders if it joined the Alliance. The same argument was made with regard to Georgia: that since neither Abkhazia nor South Ossetia voted for NATO membership, they had the right to refrain from going with Georgia into NATO (Russian Newsweek 2008: 23).

Indeed, what makes the two countries similar is that neither Georgia nor Ukraine had full domestic support for the accession of their countries to NATO. In Georgia, residents of Abkhazia and South Ossetia did not take part in the referendum on NATO membership. And as far as Ukraine is concerned, only a minority of its population, concentrated mainly in the Western provinces, unequivocally embraced the idea of joining NATO.

The Ukraine–Georgia nexus was reinforced by the political and symbolic support that the government in Kiev rendered to the Saakashvili regime during the August 2008 war. In particular, former President Yuschenko issued an order that instructed the Ukrainian naval forces to inspect all Russian Black Sea vessels returning to the Russian base in Sebastopol after military duties. According to Dmitry Trenin, the practical implementation of this instruction could not only fuel military tensions between Moscow and Kiev, but also involve the most powerful elements of this chain – the US and NATO.

The discursive parallels between Ukraine and Georgia are also grounded in the Russian interpretation of historical similarities between them. The Saakashvili regime – as well as the Yuschenko presidency in Ukraine – were accused of provocatively longing for revision of the World War II glorious narrative. The Russian media lambasted Mikhail Saakashvili for purposefully insulting Second World War veterans by ordering the demolition of the war monument in the town of Gori. In the same vein, the Yuschenko administration was ostracized for the rehabilitation of Stepan Bendera who is known in Russia as both a Ukrainian radical nationalist and as a fascist collaborator. These invectives allowed Russia to portray itself as an unalienable part of 'true Europe' whose identity is largely derived from the glorification of the experience of anti-fascist resistance.

Besides, Russia treats the military confrontation between Georgia, on the one hand, and Abkhazia and South Ossetia, on the other, as well as the debate on Crimea, as the effects and consequences of the times of the spontaneous dissolution of the Soviet Union. Thus, not only Saakashvili was negatively dubbed 'a heritor of Stalin and Beria'; according to Putin, 'those who insist that Abkhazia and Southern Ossetia are to belong to Georgia are Stalinists, since they sustain the decision taken by Stalin' (Putin 2008). The same type of historical analogies, being extrapolated to Ukraine, can only strengthen the anti-communist narrative, since it is widely known that it was Khrushchev who took the voluntarist decision to transfer the Crimea – a Black Sea peninsula mostly populated by Russian-speakers and being in conflict with the central authorities in Kiev – to the formal possession of Ukraine.

Extending the chain

As a discursive tool, this chain seems to be rather elastic and flexible. For example, separatist *Chechnya* could be added to it due to Russia's frequent claim that for some years Tbilisi turned a blind eye to the infiltration of Chechen terrorists to Pankisi Gorge located in Georgia. Therefore, the logic goes, the Georgian regime is sympathetic to and supportive of Chechen terrorism. Russia insists that it is not the idea of freedom that connects Chechen separatists, Ukrainian and Georgian nationalists and their American inspirers, but the strategy of weakening Russia through encircling it by unfriendly regimes eager to challenge Russian supremacy in its near abroad.

In certain contexts, other countries can be incorporated into the chain. One example is *Estonia,* that was accused by Rogozin (2009: 41) of having sent volunteers to militarily support the Georgian attack on South Ossetia. In other situations, *Poland* may be added in its capacity of being both the US's closest ally in Central Europe and the initiator of the Eastern Dimension project that presupposes some kind of EU patronage over both Ukraine and Georgia. Paradoxically, even the closest – at least, in accordance to the official viewpoint espoused by the Kremlin – Russian ally, *Belarus,* can be inscribed into the chain of negative equivalences: Alexander Lukashenko's interview with the Georgian media in July 2010 that contained critical appraisals of Russia's foreign policy was considered in Moscow as deliberate support for the Saakashvili regime and a challenge to Russia. Another post-Soviet country, *Moldova,* where some groups within the policy elites consider NATO membership as a feasible policy option for the future, can be possibly imagined as part of the enlarged chain as well.

By the same token, the extended version of the chain may include some historical analogies: thus, Rogozin (2009: 46) provocatively characterized 'Drang nach Osten' as an equivalent of NATO's expansionist strategy. This dubious parallel did not prevent Rogozin from finding another historical analogy to NATO's enlargement – namely, Leon Trotsky with his idea of geopolitical expansion based upon radical changes of political regimes in the neighbourhood of the expanding core (Rogozin 2009: 61). In this semantic context it is hardly surprising that Rogozin (2009: 79) discovers some similarities between NATO and the bygone Soviet-era *kolkhoz,* having in mind the practice of unanimous decisions taken under the pressure of an almighty hegemon.

Yet the inscription of historical arguments in the chain of equivalences may lead one astray and produce opposite effects to initial expectations. One example is the simultaneous identification of Mikhail Saakashvili with two historical figures – Hitler and Stalin (Rogozin 2009: 43) – that play the role of 'symbols of negativity' for Russia. The very equation of the Georgian President with both of these figures, logically speaking, presupposes that in this semantic context the principal difference between Stalin and Hitler is erased, which contradicts to one of the tenets of the official Russian standpoint. This example shows that chains of equivalence is an ambiguous tool that may only complicate the discursive construction of negative otherness.

Interpreting the chain effects

The key structural feature of the entire chain is its America-centrism in all its negativity which, nevertheless, allows Russia to use the references to US policies as a perfect justification for symmetric actions of its own. Thus, in the words of Russia's deputy foreign minister, Grigory Karasin, Russian military bases in South Ossetia and Abkhazia were deployed on the same grounds that the Americans deployed theirs in Romania and Bulgaria (Vremia novostei 2009: 2). Therefore, in August 2008 and its aftermath, the Kremlin implicitly – and perhaps reluctantly – accepted the US foreign policy philosophy it had previously lambasted.

What stems from this discursive chain analysis is that each specific conflict – like the one between Russia and Georgia – is seen in Moscow through the prism of wider issues, such as the boundaries of international society, the criteria for membership and the (re)distribution of roles in it, and the positions of agents that operate on or beyond its margins. It is from here that Russia's attempts to generalize particular situations. In the official Kremlin discourse, the Georgia war was interpreted as aimed against the universalizing effects of the alleged unipolarity. Russia wished to take advantage of the South Ossetian case in order to raise a number of politically broader issues pertaining to Russia's repeated claims to be recognized as a pivotal member of the international society able to take a normative stand of its own. It is in this sense that one may understand Lavrov's characterization of the Georgia war not as a separate episode but as an event that 'uncovered the genuine situation in the world' (Lavrov 2008b) – more specifically, the discontinuation of a unipolar moment.

Yet the chain of equivalence introduced above does not seem to be a well fixed tool in Russia's discursive arsenal. Russia itself, sometimes breaks this logic of equivalence by dissociating both Ukraine and Georgia from the West. Against this background, one may identify several discursive moves that challenge the inscription of Georgia in the US/NATO-sponsored/centred hegemonic relations.

Firstly, Russian foreign policy speakers decouple Georgia from the Western normative order by portraying the Tbilisi regime as a deplorable exception, as something external and even alien to the alleged 'civilized mankind'.[1] Russia asserts that Georgia does not meet Western standards of democracy and should therefore be unwelcome as a hypothetical NATO member. The Kremlin expected from NATO the – at least verbal – repudiation of the Saakashvili regime as undemocratic (this is to say, challenging the universally accepted norms).

Secondly, in contradiction to the dominating view of Georgia as a marionette of the United States, Rogozin (2009: 227) presumed that it was the Georgian leaders that managed to draw NATO into the conflict. This interpretation evidently reverses the logic that inscribes Georgia in a US dominated group of junior allies.

Whither Great Power Management?

There are two main conclusions to be drawn from the sections above. Firstly, the security language that Russia speaks drastically differs from that one of NATO and there are no grounds to expect that the perceptional gap between the two parties may easily be bridged. Secondly, discursive construction of negative otherness, as a constitutive element of Russia's own identity, takes the form of a chain of equivalences, yet this chain is neither stable nor well articulated but rather mobile and reversible.

1 A Russian movie, 'Olympius Inferno', shot immediately after the Georgia war depicts the Georgian authorities not only as aggressors against South Ossetia but also as trouble-makers for the United States. According to the movie narrative, in staging the conflict, the Georgian military temporarily succeeded in deceiving the West into falling victim to Tbilisi's intentional misrepresentation of the situation on the ground.

In fact, the two approaches to discourse analysis that I have used above, uncover two mechanisms of politicization inherent in Russia's NATO discourse. As I have shown, there are five issues that constitute the Russia–NATO communicative terrain, and each of them is differently treated and tackled by the parties in communication. It is these interpretative gaps that fuel discursive disconnections between Russia and NATO that render political effects, since the filling of commonly used concepts or matters of common interests by particular content may be considered as one of the founding gestures of politics. Another important facet of the politicization of the Russian discourse boils down to pinpointing the mechanism of chains of equivalences that explicates the social construction of relations of enmity and the politically loaded Self–Other distinctions.

Accordingly, one may argue that Russia's NATO discourse revolves around explicitly political articulations. It is very much about sovereignty and political will that define the distinctions between friends and enemies, as well as between normal and extraordinary situations that necessitate political appraisals. In the judgement of Rogozin (2009: 31), all suggestions of unimportance of the question of who invaded whom in August 2008 are unacceptable to Russia due to their 'extreme cynicism'.

Russia not only is inclined to espouse political attitudes itself, but also seems to expect political feedback from its partners. After the Georgian war, Russia desperately hoped to gain the recognition of Russia's special rights in the post-Soviet area, which constitute, in the Kremlin's eyes, a group of countries (perhaps, another imaginary chain of equivalences) that Russia is supposed to represent. At the same time, Russia ascribes to NATO political intentions, as exemplified by the identification of countries like Ukraine and Georgia as key elements of a chain of equivalence sponsored by the United States to narrow Russia's sphere of influence. What sustains the political logic here is that each specific security incident is tackled not as a separate case of its own, but as an element inscribed in a certain explanatory logic and thus ultimately serving as a proof of alleged 'NATO expansionism'.

Against this background, what are the chances for great power management as a hypothetical framework for Russia–NATO relations, and – more specifically – in which form is the great power model achievable? It is unlikely that a Russia that gives priority to politically loaded articulations can become a good partner in great power management as understood by Bull. Yet fortunately, on a deeper level of inquiry one may uncover a more complicated picture which contains many evidences of Russia's – though much less pronounced – espousal of a different, de-politicized way of thinking about its role in the international society.

In the Georgian war and its aftermath, Russia, along with the politically loaded discourse that I have demonstrated above, to some extent experimented with a counter-discourse premised upon an opposite, that is, de-politicized logic. It seems symptomatic that the Kremlin made some – perhaps, rather modest and far from convincing – efforts to deny the existence of any (geo) political plans towards Georgia, and explained the military operation by 'two fundamental cornerstones – common sense and the supremacy of international law' (Lavrov 2008b). Such seemingly universal concepts as human security and responsibility to protect were also – though marginally and unconvincingly to the West – mentioned among justifications for Russia's military operation. Lavrov's (2010) claim that 'we did not have any choice' did not go well with the logic of sovereign decisionism and thus only strengthened the de-politicized dimension of the Kremlin narrative.

Another indication of Russia's leaning to de-politicized approaches is Medvedev's appeal to the establishment of common regulations in the security field, known as proposals of new security architecture in Europe. In the Kremlin's view, the Georgia war has made clear that international society is unfortunately defined not by the shared rules of the game but rather by sovereign decisions of the dominating actors, and this is the crux of the problem. Medvedev's proposal seems to develop Putin's belief in the global applicability of international norms, which hypothetically can be, by the same token, reversed by the acts of sovereign will and then reinterpreted.

Thus, Russia tries to reinstall its power through the partial effacement of the political content from its self-positioning in international society; to some extent imitating other power centres, including NATO, which, arguably, perceives the structural foundations of international society as moving towards greater unification and, therefore, de-politicization. It is telling that NATO sees its own security role as mostly managerial, while its eastward enlargement – as a technical procedure. Within this predominantly managerial logic, even what is dubbed 'long-term, strategic decisions' (on Ukraine's and Georgia's NATO membership) turn into non-decisions which may suit Russia – at least, in the short term.

War, Politics and Management of International Conflicts (instead of Conclusion)

The key question of my analysis concerns the nature of great power management that is arguably underway as one of most significant institutions shaping international society. There are three scenarios that are imaginable as possible pathways of Russia–NATO security relations.

Firstly, both parties – Russia and NATO – may eventually stick to de-politicized approaches. There are two basic conditions for the implementation of this option. Moscow and Brussels should avoid identity-charged discourses involving such terms as 'friends' and 'enemies', 'victims' and 'aggressors'. Next, they should ground their postures in potentially universalizable concepts that are politically neutral (like human security, democracy, transparency and sustainable development). This can make possible the elaboration of more or less standard procedures of managing conflicts based upon institutions and expertise. This type of de-politicized rationalism is grounded in the recognition of the rule of law – as opposed to political will – and paves the way for the allegedly universal international legal order, which gives Russia a chance to position itself as a 'normal' international subject that needs neither external legitimization nor foreign assistance.

The *second scenario* also presupposes symmetric actions of both parties (NATO and Russia), yet this time based upon the political type of bargaining. It is the conceptual figure of the Other – and thus the immanent possibility of a conflict with the Other – that makes the structure of international society political and, therefore, open, heterogeneous and immune to attempts to unify it on the basis of a single set of values or procedures. In terms of great power management prospects, this option presupposes the pragmatic division of spheres of influence between NATO's and Russia's regional security orders – a perspective that by now seems rather questionable and unattainable without meaningful concessions from either of the two parties or both of them.

The *third scenario* is the most complicated, since it implies that the great powers lack consensus in interpreting the nature of great power management: some of them may act in a political way, while others, vice versa, adhere to de-politicized approaches. This dissonance is conducive to miscommunications between the power centres. As the analysis of Russian discourse suggests, it is Russia that most likely ought to play a more politicized role in tackling security relations, while NATO, vice versa, should stick to a more order-based and police-type of policy stand. Yet a role reversal is also imaginable: Medvedev's new security architecture proposals, reinvigorated by the effects of the Georgia war, are evidently shaped in legalistic and, therefore, politically neutral terms, while the Western response to the Russian initiative is by now articulated in more pronounced political tones. For example, an attempt of the EU-sponsored Human Security Study Group to make Russia accept the wider concept of security that embraces its soft and human dimensions represents a political move of filling the concept of security with specific – and not uncontested – content (Helsinki Plus 2010). Besides this, Medvedev's proposals, in spite of their de-politicized bias, may face at least two types of political challenges. One of them deals with the dynamics of inclusion and exclusion: Russia can hardly win support from NATO in accepting Abkhazia and South Ossetia as legitimate participants of the Euro-Atlantic security space, while NATO, in its turn, can hardly expect Russia to recognize Kosovo in this status. The second big political issue is whether, according to the Russian vision, special (exceptional) political agreements are acceptable in a new 'security architecture'. Medvedev seems to call for more equality in the security terrain, a standpoint that logically has to deny all kind of bilateral deals such as, the Kharkiv agreement signed by the Russian and Ukrainian presidents and known as the 'gas-for-fleet' deal.

Thus, we see that what complicates the search for the great power management-type of NATO–Russian relations is the perceptional and communicative gaps between the two parties, on the one hand, and deep dislocations within the Russian discourse itself, on the other. It is the complex interplay of these two discursive mechanisms that has to be closely monitored for properly comprehending the dynamics of the NATO–Russia relationship. From the practical viewpoint, it is the de-politicized trend in the Russian discourse which has to be supported by the adherents of the great power management model, with the full understanding of the prospects of eventual re-politicization of the entire gamut of the security agenda.

Yet what if the great power management ultimately fails? Arguably, there are two options in this case: either the reinvigoration of compensatory functions of diplomacy, international law, and balance of power institutional mechanisms, or the intensification of the possibility of new wars. Among these institutions, traditional *diplomacy* seems to be the least helpful remedy: as the protracted negotiations on Nagorno Karabakh and Transdniestria make clear, they do not bring quick results. Likewise, a purely diplomatic solution of the whole gamut of effects of secession of the two break-away territories of Georgia also seems to be rather uncertain.

Yet reliance on *international law* does not open much brighter perspectives either, due to the fact that it is differently interpreted and operationalized by great powers. The Georgian war seemed to confirm Bull's (1977: 132) assumption that 'the distinction between violation of a rule and conformity to it is not always a sharp one.' In particular, there is no international consensus about the legitimacy of the recognition of Kosovo, and even much less perspectives for finding a common legal platform for the recognition of South Ossetia and Abkhazia as fully-fledged members of international society. References to international law may be politically divisive, while Medvedev's attempts to come up with a comprehensive set of legally binding rules to regulate the sphere of security in the Euro-Atlantic region look more like wishful thinking rather than a well versed blueprint capable of cementing the fabric of international society.

The *balance of power* institution is also a rather dubious mechanism in this particular situation, mostly because the major countries involved in the Caucasian affairs possess different types of power resources which cannot be easily balanced. In particular, Russia mostly relies on hard power (material, physical, military) resources, while the United States and the EU are likely to apply much more variegated soft power tools as well. Besides, as Bull (1977: 104) rightly notes, longing for a balance of power may often contradict the policy of establishing common rules that regulate security relations, which seems to be the case with Russia's claims to special interests and rights in its near abroad, in spite of the otherwise promoted idea of equal and indivisible 'security architecture' in the wider Euro-Atlantic region.

Against this background, the inability of other institutions to compensate for the lack of great power management (or its weak quality) increases the eventuality of new *wars* or threats of war in which both Russia and NATO member states might be ultimately implicated. This perspective can be deduced from the general instability in the North Caucasus, with rampant terrorism in Russia's regions closely related – both geographically and in ethnic and religious terms – to South Ossetia. It is in this sense that great power mismanagement – or 'cacophony' instead of a 'concert' – may be regarded as a symptom of the international society dysfunctions conducive to the militarization of post-Soviet security conflicts.

Chapter 5
Russia and EU's Competitive Neighbourhood

Jana Kobzova, Nicu Popescu and Andrew Wilson

The August 2008 war in the South Caucasus pitted against each other more than just the Russian and Georgian armies. It was also a clash of ambition and vision between Russia, the US and the EU. Looking at the conflict through the lenses of Hedley Bull's perspective on power in the international society and the role of great powers to manage international affairs (Bull 1977),[1] all three main actors in the region failed to achieve their policy objectives and prevent the escalation of the conflict, despite the huge amount of resources previously invested into the management of the post-Soviet space. In Russia's case, no end of diplomatic, economic, political, financial or intelligence efforts managed to alter Georgia's foreign policy course aimed at moving closer to NATO and the EU and its desire to reintegrate Abkhazia and South Ossetia. The war also exposed the limited power of the US to restrain a regional ally – Georgia – when Tbilisi decided to pursue reintegration of its territory, even through military means if deemed necessary. Importantly, the 2008 war also constituted a failure for EU's declared ambition to prevent or solve secessionist conflicts in its eastern neighbourhood. The Russo-Georgian conflict has thus become the greatest manifestation of the clash of alternative regional projects: that of Russia's would-be sphere of influence with that of an ever enlarging sphere of democracy, security and prosperity as promoted by the EU and US.[2]

Brussels and Moscow have pursued diverging goals vis-à-vis Tbilisi, relying on a different mix of what Bull called *influence* and *coercion* and what Joseph Nye later referred to as *soft* and *hard power* (Nye 1990): Russia aimed at achieving mainly 'possession goals' (that is, ownership or control) while the EU seemed to pursue mainly 'milieu goals', that is, shaping the environment (Wolfers 1966). If judged against the powerful prescription of the great powers' role in international

1 Bull proposes that the main tasks for the great powers in the international society are the following: i. Preservation of general balance; ii. Avoidance and control of crises; iii. Limitation of war; iv. The unilateral exercise of local preponderance; and v. [establishment of] spheres of influence, interest or responsibility.

2 The chapter focuses on the influence of the European Union and Russia in the region. The role of the US policy on Georgia and Washington's influence on the Georgian leadership is discussed in greater detail in other chapters of the book.

affairs by Bull, the war was not simply an example of 'mismanagement' of the great powers but was also a failure of everyone's ability to project their power. Nevertheless, the fact that the war in Georgia eventually took place raises important questions about the role of the great powers in the region, about Russia's real ability to re-assert its control over the post-Soviet space as well as about the EU's ability to shape the environment in which this space operates. This chapter therefore deals with key features of Russian and EU hard and soft power in the region and explores how Moscow and Brussels exercise their power in the post-Soviet space. It concludes with a discussion on the extent to which both the EU and Russia are genuinely able to influence the developments in their shared neighbourhood.

Powers in the South Caucasus: Russia and the European Union

Russia has tried to re-assert its influence in the region since the collapse of the Soviet Union through a variety of different means. The establishment of the Commonwealth of Independent States (CIS), while to some extent aimed at managing the post 1991 disintegration of the Soviet Union, has also become one of the main frameworks for the newly-emerged Russia to control the former Union republics, either through direct intervention (as during 1996 constitutional crisis in Belarus or via deployment of Russian 'peacekeepers' on disputed territories in the Southern Caucasus or Transnistria) or indirectly through lending political support to Moscow's protégés in CIS republics. The Orange revolution in Ukraine in 2004 forced Russia to change its tactics and turn to less visible means to back those whom the Russian leadership believed would best serve their interests. Nevertheless, Moscow's main objective – control of its post-Soviet neighbours – has remained unchanged. One of President Medvedev's five foreign policy tenets announced after the war in August 2008, in an interview to Russian television stations, is the claim that 'there are regions in which Russia has privileged interests. These regions are home to countries with which we share special historical relations and are bound together as friends and good neighbours.' Even though a sphere of influence in its 'near abroad' has been a key foreign policy objective of Russia since 1991, it was only under the Putin presidency (2000–2008) that Russia accumulated both more determination and more resources to pursue its objectives.

This view has clashed with that of the European Union's, which has advocated equal status of all states and their right to freely choose their foreign policy partners, alliances and international frameworks for co-operation. It may be argued that the EU's status as a great power is far from being self-evident: the EU was founded on the rejection of war and other forms of force. The EU portrays itself as a 'civilian power' or a 'normative' power that bases its power on co-operation and use of non-military means. However, as Karen E. Smith demonstrates (2008), the EU's foreign policy often uses the same tools used by other powers including sanctions, conditionality and coercion. These tools, while not always effective, demonstrate that there are certain great power ambitions present in the EU's narrative of a 'civilian' or 'normative' model. Nowhere are these ambitions more present than in the EU's own neighbourhood, as demonstrated in the following passage.

Russia's dominance in its 'near abroad' has also sharply contradicted the European Union's vision of an integrated and interdependent Europe where the EU model of security, democracy, prosperity and peace is increasingly replicated not just inside the EU, but also along its borders. To promote its model of security, democracy and peace and foster good neighbourly relations, in 2003, the EU launched a neighbourhood policy which Brussels offered to the EU's eastern and southern neighbourhood. In its eastern strand, the neighbourhood policy has become the EU's main tool in dealings with the post-Soviet states of Ukraine, Moldova, Belarus, Georgia, Armenia and Azerbaijan. While becoming increasingly interventionist in the region, the EU objectives, unlike those of Moscow, have not been purely geopolitical: Brussels does not aim to control its eastern neighbours nor invite these states to join the European Union. At the same time, the EU, well aware that more stable and prosperous neighbours are key for its own future growth, has gradually become one of the most important actors in the region. As a result, steps taken by the EU to further its own vision for the European continent have led to a challenge of Moscow's dominance in the region.

The 'coloured revolutions' in 2003–2004 and the war in Georgia in 2008 forced Russia to rethink its strategy, and work proactively to re-assert its influence in the region. Moscow cannot count on the 'post-Soviet' space remaining passively and permanently post-Soviet. Many in the West see Russia's hand everywhere, but many in Russia fear that Russian influence is declining. Russia therefore sees itself as still at the early stages of the consolidation of its pole (Trenin 2008), having wasted the 1990s. According to Modest Kolerov, speaking to the authors in October 2008, 'in the 1990s and early 2000s not only did Russia not control these countries, it [didn't even] control itself. Russia was a field for other peoples' geopolitical struggles. Now a united Russian will is beginning to appear and present a bill for resources which used to be free'. This is mainly a reference to the rising price of Russian gas, but Russia has used a variety of other forms of coercion: from economic blockades to the use of military force against Georgia in 2008. Since the onset of the global economic crisis, Russia has shown a very different side to its policy. In times of recession, Western states revert to utilitarian cost-cutting; but Russia thinks geopolitically. It is prepared to invest to win friends. In December 2008, Russia announced a $10 billion Anti-Crisis Fund for the post-Soviet states in the Eurasian Economic Community and during 2009 offered (though did not necessarily deliver) $500 million to Armenia, $300 million to Kyrgyzstan, $500 million to Moldova before the July elections and $2 billion to Ukraine before the January election. The runaway winner was Belarus, with $3 billion. Such sums may be dwarfed by the tasks ahead, but Russia considers them to be worthwhile investments.

The European Union, on the other hand, has not been militarily involved in the South Caucasus and until the neighbourhood policy, its influence was projected mainly through the TACIS programme which aimed at assisting the transition of the post-Soviet countries. Nevertheless, even after its enlargement, the EU remained hesitant to employ substantial hard power and continued to rely heavily on projecting its soft power in the region.

Russia 'Playing Hard'

The August war in Georgia marked an obvious culmination of Russia's use of hard power in the neighbourhood and its ultimate demonstration in the region. Tanks rolled in and the Georgian army was not as much defeated as simply evaporated. It collapsed in a couple of days under low-morale, bad communications and lack of satisfactory air defence systems. It also showed that hard power has never really gone away. Russia tends to believe in power as spectacle; and that a constant demonstration of decisiveness and ruthlessness increases its leverage elsewhere. On the other hand, Russia today is not the USSR of the Cold War. It has no broad-based military posture and no explicit aggressive strategic doctrine. However, its hard power integrates military, economic, security and financial tools and has been applied all across Eastern Europe and the South Caucasus on a number of occasions since the collapse of the Soviet Union to further Russia's ambitions in the region.

Military presence

Particularly worrying is the correlation between the Russian military presence and secessionist problems in Transnistria, Abkhazia, South Ossetia and Nagorno-Karabakh. Russia has maintained a military presence in various forms in all the countries of the EU's eastern neighbourhood even after the collapse of the Soviet Union. Belarus and Armenia are close Russian allies that rely on Russian military bases to ensure their security; Belarus against the West and potential domestic threats, and Armenia against Azerbaijan, a country with which it is still formally at war over Nagorno-Karabakh, another 'not so frozen conflict'. Russia is also involved in border management in Armenia. Not only does it help patrol the Armenia-Turkey border, it even has a presence at Yerevan airport.

Azerbaijan and Ukraine are less content with Russian military presence on their territories, but have consented to it. Azerbaijan is host to a radio location station in Gabala until 2012 at least, which allows Russia to monitor the airspace across much of the Middle East. Likewise, Russia's lease agreement for its Black Sea Fleet in Crimea was due to expire in 2017, but in April 2010, Ukraine's President Yanukovich and Russia's President Medvedev reached an agreement, whereby the Russian lease on naval facilities in Crimea would be extended beyond 2017 by 25 years, with an additional five year renewal option.

In Moldova and Georgia, the Russian military presence is ensured under the banner of 'peacekeepers' in conflict zones, stationed without the consent of the

Table 5.1 Russian troops in the six states of Eastern Europe and South Caucasus

	Number of troops	Deadline for withdrawal
Armenia	5000	2021
Azerbaijan	900	2012
Belarus	850	2020
Georgia	3702–7600	2001
Moldova	1200–1500	2003
Ukraine	13000–15000	2042–2047

Note: Data as of 2008, except for Ukraine (data as of June 2010).

Source: Popescu, N. and Wilson, A. 2009. *The Limits of Enlargement-lite: European and Russian Power in the Troubled Neighbourhood.* London: European Council on Foreign Relations.

host states and against its own commitments for a 'complete, unconditional and ordered' withdrawal undertaken at the OSCE summit in Istanbul in 1999.[3] In Moldova the military presence is used to push for a settlement of the Transnistrian conflict on Russian terms. In contrast, Azerbaijan is now glad it resisted pressure to install Russian 'peacekeepers' in 1993–4.

Territorial conflicts

Less evident are the territorial tensions that have yet to erupt into open conflict. Azerbaijan fears that Russia might support Lezgin separatism in Northern Azerbaijan (Melikishvili 2008). In Moldova, Russia has been increasingly active in the autonomous region of Gagauzia. In September 2009, the regional assembly even passed a resolution calling on the Moldovan government to recognise the independence of Abkhazia and South Ossetia.

But the most challenging territorial tensions may arise in Ukraine's Crimea, the one Ukrainian region that has an ethnic Russian majority (58.3 per cent in 2001). The local economy, in Sevastopol at least, is to a large extent dependent on the Russian military presence. And Russia has implicitly threatened that it will undermine Ukraine's territorial integrity if Ukraine moves towards NATO or tries to push Russia to withdraw its military base by 2017.[4] In September 2008 the Crimean assembly passed a near-identical resolution to Gagauzia on

3 The Istanbul documents specify orderly and complete withdrawal.

4 Putin lost his temper with Bush on the final day of the Bucharest summit, telling him: 'Do you understand, George, that Ukraine is not even a state'. Claiming that most of Ukraine's territory was 'given away' by Russia, Putin supposedly also said that if the country joined NATO it would 'cease to exist'.

the independence of Abkhazia and South Ossetia, challenging the central state's exclusive prerogative to conduct foreign policy and siding with Moscow rather than its own country in an international crisis.

Economic coercion

Hard power is not confined only to raw military power and security challenges. Russia increasingly uses economic levers, first and foremost energy, to influence its neighbours. Throughout the 1990s, Russia supplied gas at discount rates to try and keep the post-Soviet economy as a whole relatively integrated. Ukraine and Belarus are the most dependent on Russian gas. Ukraine's economy consumes enormous amounts of energy and Belarus' dependence on gas under the authoritarian Lukashenka regime depends partly on cheap gas and electricity for its political legitimacy and survival. Similarly, Moldova faces the potential additional burden of Transnistria's debt to Gazprom, which stood at around $1.5 billion by mid 2008, and has been deliberately allowed to accumulate as a future bargaining chip (a reunified Moldova might need to cede assets to Gazprom to repay Transnistria's debt). The countries of the South Caucasus are least dependent. Their economies are less industrial and they have a milder climate. Azerbaijan produces enough gas for its own needs, and Georgia switched from Russian to Azeri gas in 2007 (Russian imports now account for only 5–7 per cent of the total). Armenia receives some gas from Iran, even though Russia owns the local infrastructure and has so far prevented Georgia from buying any Iranian gas via Armenia.

Since 2000, Russia has gradually but forcibly adopted the opposite approach: using expensive gas as an instrument for infrastructure takeover and the punishment of 'unfriendly' states. While Moscow's desire to sell gas at market prices cannot be disputed, the timing and pace of gas price increases has been clearly political. In Ukraine, under president Leonid Kuchma, Russia agreed to sell gas for $50 per $1000m^3$ until 2010, but immediately after the Orange Revolution pushed for an increase to $240 (Stern 2009). When the parties could not agree, Russia drastically reduced supplies to Ukraine for a few days in January 2006 – simultaneously with a cut in supplies to Moldova at a moment of increased tensions over Transnistria.

Russia's goals have never been entirely commercial. Every time Russia has pushed for higher prices, it has also offered the target countries a political way out: either by ceding energy infrastructure or by fulfilling non-economic Russian objectives. As a result, Gazprom now controls majority stakes in the gas distribution companies in Moldova and Armenia and 50 per cent of Beltransgaz in Belarus; while non-transparent intermediaries, shell companies and corrupt schemes have penetrated deeply into the Ukrainian gas infrastructure to an extent that is not obvious even to insiders.

Trade embargoes have accompanied energy pressures. For example, Russia has banned Georgian (from 2005) and Moldovan (2005–2007) wine. It has also imposed bans at various stages on Moldovan, Ukrainian and Georgian vegetables, meat and dairy products. Even Armenia, a close ally, saw its brandy exports to

Table 5.2 Russian gas prices for the 'near' and 'far abroad'

	2005	2006	2007	2008	2009
Belarus	$46.68	$46.68	$100	$119 (Jan) – $128 (April)	$210
Ukraine	$50	$95	$130	$179.5	$360*
Moldova	$80	$110/$160 July	$170	$213 (Jan) – $253 (July) – $287.6 (Oct)	$316/$317
Georgia	$60	$110	$235 (Dec 2006)	$280	$350
Armenia	$54	$110 (April)	$110	$110	$154
Azerbaijan		$110	$230	Imports stopped in Jan 2007	n/a
Europe	$170	$257	$293	$378 (Jan) $410 (June) over $500 (Oct)	$390.5 (Jan–March)

* This was the initial headline figure after the January 2009 gas dispute. By the third quarter, the price had fallen to around $210.

Source: Popescu, N. and Wilson, A. 2009. *The Limits of Enlargement-lite: European and Russian Power in the Troubled Neighbourhood.* London: European Council on Foreign Relations.

Russia locked out of the market between March–September 2006. The most comprehensive economic pressures were applied on Georgia after Tbilisi arrested four Russian spies in September 2006. Russia introduced a transport and postal blockade, expelled several hundred Georgians and closed Verkhnii Lars, the only land-border crossing between Georgia and Russia (two other land passages are controlled by Abkhazia and South Ossetia).

EU Hard Power

The EU was founded on the rejection of most forms of force and their replacement by interdependence, the rule of law and supranational governance. The EU sees itself mainly as a post-modern power that bases its policies on cooperation and the use of non-military (predominantly economic) means (Maull 1990). This does not mean that the EU does not use coercion in its foreign policy; or that it entirely avoids getting involved in conflict settlement efforts. Still, unlike Russia, the EU has adopted a largely self-limiting approach in the security realm. The EU also tends to be much more tentative in its application of hard power. For example, most of the visa bans on Belarusian officials were lifted in October 2008 (for six months in the first instance), despite Belarus making only limited improvements in the conduct of parliamentary elections the previous September. One of the means the EU continues to project its hard power is through crisis management.

EU crisis management

Commenting on the war in Georgia, one senior EU politician claimed in an interview with the authors in November 2008 that 'the EU can't save Saakashvili from his own stupidity'. Such claims miss the point – the EU did not get involved in the Balkans conflicts because it liked or disliked Slobodan Milošević or Hashim Thaçi, but because of the broader threat of destabilization.

Despite regular statements relating to the resolution of frozen conflicts, the EU has more often than not stepped back from acting in Abkhazia, South Ossetia, Transnistria and Nagorno-Karabakh, while the Union keeps some 7000 peacekeepers from EU member states in Lebanon alone. In Eastern Europe and the South Caucasus, Russia was quick to fill this void. While Moscow thinks about its neighbours all the time, and plays them with skill, the EU, according to one EU official interviewed in 2008 by the authors, thinks about its neighbours only in times of crises. This contrast is voiced in another interview with the authors by one senior Moldovan official, who claimed: 'When we discuss Transnistria with Russia we speak at the highest political level, with the Russian president. There is no similar level of interest in the EU. There is no senior European politician – from the EU or the EU presidency – that would support advancing the conflict resolution agenda at a political level.'

Until the Georgian war, the EU was mainly involved in conflict settlement efforts in Transnistria, especially after the EU started to take a more pro-active stance in 2003; introducing a travel ban against Transnistrian leaders, appointing a EU Special Representative on Moldova, joining the 5+2 negotiating format, and launching a hundred-strong EU Border Assistance Mission to curb the smuggling networks that helped sustain Transnistria. However, the EU shied away from directly challenging the presence of the dysfunctional Russian-dominated peacekeeping force or pushing Russia to respect its commitments on troop withdrawal. A possible EU contribution to a peacekeeping mission was discussed in 2003 and 2006. The first time, the idea was rejected by Russia; the second time by EU member states' own refusal to consider sending peacekeepers. In 2006, the then EU Special Representative on Moldova, Adriaan Jacobovits de Szeged, lobbied member states to press Russia to accept a change in the peacekeeping format; but was opposed by Cyprus, Germany, Greece, Finland, France, Italy, Portugal, Spain and Slovakia. Jacobovits was almost fired for pushing the issue.

Since the Rose Revolution in 2003, it is Georgia that has been a persistent *demandeur* for greater EU involvement in conflict resolution; but the EU has been reluctant to get involved, in order to avoid tensions with Russia whom it considers to be its strategic partner (Lynch 2006). On the one hand, the EU has appointed a Special Representative, launched an EU Rule of Law Mission, and a Border Support Team. In 2006 the European Commission became the biggest international donor supporting post-conflict rehabilitation in Abkhazia and South Ossetia (excluding Russia's non-transparent financial and military support), with a total of €33 million in 1997–2005 (Emerson 2009). On the other hand, when Russia vetoed a 150-person OSCE Border Monitoring Operation and Georgia invited the EU to take over, the EU sent three experts (later extended to twelve) to help Georgia write a border-reform strategy. EU institutions never raised the prospect of sending peacekeepers to Georgia until the Russia–Georgia war in August 2008. Furthermore, EU member states have persistently delayed low level measures proposed by EU institutions, as when they tried to deploy two experts in Georgia to develop a dialogue on customs management with the secessionist authorities in 2008. The EU, fearing upsetting relations with Moscow and the regional balance, refused to invest politically in the resolution of Georgia's conflicts. Today, however, the Union has ended up investing a billion Euros and sending 300 peacekeepers just to try to re-freeze the situation.

The EU's apparent reluctance to play a bigger role in conflict management in Georgia and increase its role in the region was at least partly responsible for the escalation of the conflict by both sides, and may also have contributed to the Georgian leadership's conviction that the only means to regain Abkhazia and South Ossetia were military. If there had been international peacekeepers in South Ossetia before August 2008, the chances of war would have been drastically reduced. But the EU's non-involvement helped turn Georgia from a marginal irritant for EU–Russia relations before the war into a major stumbling-block for the development of the EU–Russia partnership. The EU can count on the insertion of the EUMM as a relative success, but has not been able to prevent the departure of both the OSCE and UN (UNOMIG).

As one EU official stated to the authors, 'after the war in Georgia, it would be stupid to pretend that the Russian military in Transnistria are just peacekeepers', but the EU remains unwilling to get involved, despite Russia pressing for a new settlement on its own terms. The EU has also been reluctant to act on Nagorno-Karabakh. It has not disbursed any funds to help with reconstruction (unlike South Ossetia and Abkhazia), partly because France, which is a co-chair of the OSCE Minsk Group and a conflict settlement mediator, prefers to keep EU institutions out of the process. The EU has expressed its readiness to send peacekeepers if Azerbaijan and Armenia agree on a solution to the conflict; but many Azeris have become more sceptical of the EU in the aftermath of the Georgian war.

Competing Soft Powers?

Russian soft power is only partly residual – such as the continuing importance of the Russian language outside Russia, the dominance of the Russian Orthodox Church in Ukraine, Belarus and Moldova,[5] and post-Soviet nostalgia. Ukraine's Orange Revolution in 2004 added an extra element. Despite much initial bluster, Russia took its reverse to heart, sat down and effectively rethought the way it operated in the region. According to Gleb Pavlovsky, 'this was a very useful catastrophe for Russia. We learnt a lot ... it very quickly became clear that they [the West] would try to export this [type of soft power revolution] to us and that we should prepare for this, and very quickly strengthen our political system. In a year we had stopped the wave of Coloured Revolutions and turned it back' (2008). Thus, the 'near abroad' has become one of the main targets for projection of Russia's 'new' soft power.

Ideology for export

The Kremlin's new ideology of 'sovereign democracy' is often dismissed as mere window-dressing. Certainly, Putin's Russia is highly eclectic ideologically (Morozov 2008). But the concept fulfils certain core needs: it helps legitimize the idea of a 'national path' towards democracy; it disguises local authoritarian features; and it establishes a link between domestic and foreign policy – countries have to be strong at home to be strong abroad. And it is available for export. The message to other post-Soviet elites is to be a ruthless survivor like Putin or Lukashenka rather than a loser like Kuchma or Shevardnadze.

Political technology

While not all of the neighbours have embraced the full ideological package of 'sovereign democracy', they all have been corrupted to varying degrees by the practices of 'political technology' – the peculiarly local term for the 'art' of manipulating elections through a wide array of cynical and often illegal instruments. Russia sends and pays its political advisors to help friendly parties throughout the region, but can rapidly change its favourites. For example, in the 2005 Moldovan elections, Russian 'technologists' worked against the ruling Communists and then in 2009 on their behalf. Many semi-authoritarian local regimes have copied techniques first developed in Russia: such as manipulating 'administrative resources' at election time and using the power of TV to set up 'virtual parties' (Wilson 2005).

After the Orange Revolution, Russia opened a new 'NGO front', setting up a series of umbrella organizations to project its 'soft power' abroad, such as Vyacheslav Nikonov's Russian World, set up in June 2007. In September 2008, Putin even suggested that Russia support civil society in Georgia, saying 'it would

5 In all three states the Russian Orthodox Church has branches which operate under different names, but are still part of the Moscow parent church. In Belarus, an estimated 80 per cent belong to the Belarusian Orthodox Church, in Ukraine 37 per cent to Ukrainian Orthodox Church (Moscow Patriarchate), and in Moldova 75 per cent to the Moldovan Orthodox Church.

Table 5.3 Attitudes to the Russian leadership in the Eastern Neighbourhood

Azerbaijan	66%
Moldova	62%
Ukraine	53%
Belarus	51%
Armenia	30%
Georgia	22%

Note: Data as of 2008. Percentage expressing approval.

Source: Popescu, N. and Wilson, A. 2009. *The Limits of Enlargement-lite: European and Russian Power in the Troubled Neighbourhood.* London: European Council on Foreign Relations.

be incorrect to leave Georgia to nationalists and irresponsible people, allowing them to tear it to pieces'.

Following the 'matryoshka nationalism' principle of the late Soviet era,[6] Russia has also played divide and rule by backing parties that represent minority nationalisms, like the Rusyns in Ukraine or Gagauz in Moldova (or Latgalians in Latvia). This can even be faked if necessary, as with the 'appeal' by the Crimean Tatar party Milli Firka for Russian support in September 2008.

Media

Most Eastern European states have nationalised their media markets since 1991. Some even block Russian press broadcasts. Azerbaijan stopped the rebroadcast of ORT in July 2007 and RTR-Planeta in January 2008. De facto, however, Russia is still a key player in local media markets, via cable or nominally national editions like 'Komsomolskaya pravda' in Ukraine and in Belarus, and by selling content to local channels. Russian production dominates local DVD and CD markets. Russia is also strong in new media. Russia mediates access to international debates through websites such as www.inosmi.ru, where selective articles from the West are translated into Russian. Russian bloggers are popular throughout the CIS. Moscow-based discussion hubs such as Pavlovsky's Russia Journal at www.russ.ru use plenty of non-Russian CIS authors. Russia has also used the internet for more nefarious purposes, including so-called 'web-brigades' and organized cyber-attacks on Estonia, Lithuania and Georgia.

Message is as important as medium. Most international events, from NATO enlargement, relations with the US to local CIS affairs are perceived through the

6 Smaller nationalisms appearing inside one another, like Russian dolls.

prism of Russian interpretations projected through tightly controlled Russian TV. The media coverage of the August war in Georgia in the neighbourhood normally either took the Russian line or blamed both sides.

Passportization policy

The war in Georgia led to allegations that Russia has deliberately handed out passports in order to create or bolster minorities that it then claims the right to protect. Information on numbers of Russian passport holders is difficult to obtain, as dual citizenship is nearly always banned in the region. Russian policy after 1991 was to offer passports to all former Soviet citizens, but most who took up this opportunity moved to Russian soil. Between 80,000 and 100,000 passport holders are estimated to be in Transnistria (but only 20,000 elsewhere in Moldova). Estimates for Crimea range from 2,000 to 100,000, with maybe 10,000 in Sevastopol. Armenia has some 15,000. In September 2008 the Russian Duma amended the 2002 citizenship law, easing the five year residency requirement; although passports could still not be handed out in situ – applicants would have to move to Russia. Russia also pays pensions in some regions, like Abkhazia.

Russia's economic role

Access to Russia's fast expanding economy has been of key importance, at least during the boom years of 1999–2008. Moldova and west Ukraine are the only parts of the region where most migrants or seasonal workers head west. Elsewhere huge numbers benefit from visa-free travel to Russia, taking pressure off local labour markets and making remittances a powerful new economic factor and potential political tool throughout the region. Russia's expulsion of Georgian workers in 2006 was therefore particularly worrying for states with similar numbers working in Russia, like Armenia and Azerbaijan. From 2001 to 2006, recorded remittances from Russia to the rest of the CIS grew tenfold from $836 million to $8,868 million. Even in Moldova, 43 per cent of remittances were from Russia, compared to 56 per cent from Europe (Shelburne 2007). Remittances out of Russia are also ten times bigger than the flows in the other direction.

Fast GDP growth before 2008 meant that Russia remained a key market for goods and services, despite the gradual realignment of trade to the West (see below). Belarus (26.7 per cent of total sales in 2007), Ukraine (22.5 per cent) and Moldova (17.3 per cent) export most to the Russian market; the South Caucasus three surprisingly little (all less than 13 per cent) (Popescu and Wilson 2009), as they have the strongest third party relationships (Turkey, the Middle East) and partially reoriented their trade after the trade wars of Putin's second term (Georgia most obviously, but Azerbaijan stopped importing Russian gas in 2007; Armenia's transport links run through Georgia). Even after the global economic crisis, Russia's relative importance will remain.

Russian FDI is hard to track, as much is routed from offshore holdings in countries like Cyprus, or via local subsidiaries or front companies so that it does

Table 5.4 Workers from the six EaP states in Russia and the EU

	Russia	EU	Total remittances (estimated annual in $)
Armenia	2.5 million	150,000	1.5–2 billion
Azerbaijan	2 million	100,000	1–1.5 billion
Belarus	300,000–700,000	60,000–70,000	2-3 billion
Georgia	1 million	50,000	1 billion
Moldova	344,000	350,000–500,000	1.6 billion
Ukraine	2 million	3 million	8.4 billion

Source: Popescu, N. and Wilson, A. 2009. *The Limits of Enlargement-lite: European and Russian Power in the Troubled Neighbourhood.* London: European Council on Foreign Relations.

not count as FDI at all. But even on official figures (see below) it is high throughout the region, even in Georgia, which arguably acted as a constraint in August 2008. Russian businesses still have other Georgian acquisitions in mind, including the local railways, electricity export and the gas pipeline to Armenia.

The global economic crisis has allowed Russia to pick up some assets relatively cheaply. In January 2009 VEB (Vneshekonombank), where none other than Vladimir Putin is chair of the supervisory board, bought Ukraine's troubled Prominvestbank for a knock-down $150 million – and promptly injected $900 million. At the end of 2009, the same bank facilitated the financing of the acquisition of the one of Ukraine's largest steel groups Industrial Union of Donbass by a group led by a Russian businessman Alexander Katunin. Additionally, Russia is targeting power plants in Chişinău and Balti, Moldova and German Gorbuntsov's Incredbank bought 53 per cent of Moldova's Universalbank in early 2009 for $4.4 million. There are also some examples of the opposite, however, including how, Oleg Deripaska's Russkie mashiny was forced to shelve its plans for a joint venture with the Belarusian MAZ truck factory in February 2009 and that the only Russian-owned mobile operator in Moldova Eventis was considering selling its business to either a Swedish or German company.

But conventional indicators give a misleading impression of Russian economic power, which is often concentrated in hard power areas, such as infrastructure and energy. Russia finds pressure points and uses them for political influence in a way that the EU does not. Countries can do without IKEA, but not without gas. According to one Ukrainian official, speaking to the authors in May 2008, '80% of Russian engagement is economic … real politics in Ukraine is gas. All the rest is for TV news and so on. If you control gas, you control the main political groups in Ukraine'.

Table 5.5 Foreign direct investment in the Neighbourhood: the biggest Russian deals

Belarus	• Gazprom for 50% of Beltransgaz 2007–11, $5 billion. • Russkie Mashiny proposal for joint venture with MAZ truck factory, 2008, $1.5 billion. • Vneshtorgbank for Slavneftbank, 2007, $25 million.
Ukraine	• Four out of six oil refineries. • Ten regional energy companies. • Mobile phones (Alfa has 43.5% of Kyivstar, Golden Telecom, MTS for UMC, 2001–03, €350 million). • Rusal has the Mykolaiv and Zaporizhzhia (70%) aluminium plants. • Rosukrenergo. Banks (Mriya, Vneshtorgbank-Ukraina, Prominvestbank).
Moldova	• Gazprom for 50% + 1 shares of MoldovaGaz in 1999, plus 13.4% Transnistrian stake 2007. • Inter RAO UES for Cuciurgan power plant, 2005, $100 million. • Eventis mobile phones. Universalbank, 2008-09, $4.4 million for 53%.
Georgia	• UES and Rosenergoatom for distribution company Telasi, 2003, $26 million, plus power company Mtkvari energetika and Khrami hydroelectric power plants, (via Multiplex) Tbilisi Tskali water supply. • Inter RAO UES 30% of electroenergy, and the Enguri Power Plant. • PromInvest for Madneuli mines 2007, $51.1 million for 97.25%. Vneshtorgbank.
Armenia	• ArmRosGazprom, 1997, now 68% owned by Gazprom. • Inter for Metsamor nuclear plant, 2003, plus the Armenian Electricity Network, 2005, $75 million. • Russian Railways for South Caucasus Railways, 2008, promising to invest $570 million.

Source: Popescu, N. and Wilson, A. 2009. *The Limits of Enlargement-lite: European and Russian Power in the Troubled Neighbourhood.* London: European Council on Foreign Relations.

The 'kickback economy'

Russia and the CIS also share a common culture of 'kickback economy' (*ekonomika otkatov*), a post-Soviet business culture based on informal practice, the exchange of favours (*blat*) and outright bribery (Ledeneva 2006).[7] The last is by its very nature difficult to track. Ironically, it tends to be middle-ranking states, where the media is relatively free but the kickback economy still exists, that suffer the most damaging publicity. In Ukraine, the notorious case of Rosukrenergo was

7 *Blat* is widespread and often a means of dealing with non-market conditions. Not everything that looks like corruption from outside is actually corrupt.

eventually exposed by a persistent media – but corrupt practices in the energy sphere have hardly ended. It has been argued that the sheer amount of corruption involved, with the company's gas worth an estimated $4.35 billion a year at 2007 prices, was the biggest single factor in forcing the Orange Revolution off track after 2004 (Chov and Elkind 2009).

The limits of Russian soft power

It is an open question whether some types of Russian soft power are soft enough to be effective. Covert action, political technology and the kickback economy could all just as easily be classed as hard power. Russian soft power also suffers from its opaqueness. According to Masha Lipman, 'Russian foreign policy has big holes. We haven't decided what our "privileged interests" are. Russia wants Ukraine to be dominated by Russian business, but you can't put this on paper'. Often enough, in fact, policy 'is not just not put on paper, it's not put in words'. It is also an open question, especially after the war in Georgia, as to 'whether fear of Russia reinforces Russian soft power or undermines it'. In many cases, the impact of soft power is 'small compared to Russia's image as a country which uses force to promote its interests'(Lipman 2008).

Many types of Russian power are double-edged. Local regimes have learnt how to deploy the methodologies of political technology and sovereign democracy themselves. Azerbaijan has used its abundant oil money to co-opt parties and NGOs. In 2005, it set up *Ireli*, the Azeri equivalent of Nashi. Moreover, the same methods can be used to keep the Russians out. Any given election or political event may end up a contest between covert Russian moves and counter-moves by the home side.

Fake democracy can also easily stay fake. Western organizations like the Konrad-Adenauer-Stiftung or America's NED or IRI seek to build political parties and civil societies long-term. The Russians arrive late, often on election eve, and seek to *buy* influence, resulting in too many firefly parties and politicians. Political parties might use their Russian connections for an electoral campaign, but are very opportunistic allies. 'Russia-friendly' NGOs lack transparency, leading to corruption and, ironically (as this is normally the key point in the Russian critique of Western-funded NGOs), Potemkin 'grant-eaterism' taking hold. Many therefore die an early death, such as the 'Caucasus Institute of Democracy', set up after the Rose Revolution.

EU Soft Power

The EU's most important soft power resides in its attraction as a model of peace, prosperity and a rule of law. However, pro-EU sentiment in the neighbourhood is often broad but shallow, hedged with more ifs and buts than in the candidate states of the 1990s. In all six states there are pro-EU sentiments, some strong (Moldova and Ukraine) and some apparently weak (Belarus), and some strong pluralities

Table 5.6 Opinion polls in the six Eastern partnership countries on support for EU versus Russia/CIS integration (2008)

	EU integration	Russia/CIS integration
Armenia	25%	29%
Azerbaijan	37%	17%
Belarus	33%	45%
Georgia	82%	8%
Moldova	72%	52%
Ukraine	34%	42%

Source: Popescu, N. and Wilson, A. 2009. *The Limits of Enlargement-lite: European and Russian Power in the Troubled Neighbourhood*. London: European Council on Foreign Relations

(Georgia): but none have the pro-EU 'national consensus' that accession states normally had in the 1990s.

Nevertheless, this is still a powerful starting-point. Many EU member states also serve as individual exemplars, like Poland for Ukraine and Romania for Moldova. Pro-Russian sentiment is also multi-faceted and often shallow, based more on historical legacy, common cultural ground and practical economic benefits than the attractiveness of the 'Russian model' as whole, which appeals mainly to elites.

The accession perspective

In such a fungible climate, neighbourhood public opinion is strongly affected by the feasibility of the accession perspective. For years, the EU and the neighbourhood states played Catch-22. Neighbourhood governments argued that a clearer accession perspective would help them break the domestic logjam of reform; Brussels insisted that any membership perspective must be conditional on practical membership prospects, via fulfilment of the Copenhagen criteria. The game changed radically in 2005. EU rhetoric may not have changed substantially after the twin 'no' vote in France and the Netherlands, but neighbourhood states are sufficiently well-attuned to internal EU politics to know that practical deliverables certainly had. Ireland's rejection of the Lisbon Treaty in 2008 was depicted as a second existential crisis for the EU in the Russian media, and the message was relayed to most of the neighbourhood states.

Neglecting the Eastern neighbours

The ENP has been effective in broadening the relationships between the EU and its neighbours and led to thick and regular contact between administrative bureaucracies across a wide spectrum of issues: The ENP process has created a focus for civil society campaigns around political and judicial reform. There are many individual success stories such as the EUBAM. Visa-facilitation has been another potentially attractive offer, although the failure of individual member states properly to implement the agreement has led to complaints in the Ukrainian parliament. Ukraine and Moldova are now moving towards a visa-free status, but they do not yet have the type of road-map granted to the West Balkans in 2008. Ukraine and Moldova are moving towards Deep Free Trade. The offer may be less attractive to neo-liberal Georgia, or to energy-rich Azerbaijan. However, others can be encouraged to play catch-up.

Yet, the ENP has always been vulnerable to the dual critique of never delivering on its initial promise and remaining an essentially technocratic process. Even with an extra €350 million under the EaP, ENP's financial assistance (ENPI) has had little impact in countries like Ukraine and Azerbaijan. Ukraine, for example, currently receives an annual average of €123.5 million, which Ukrainians like to claim is at least partially offset by the amount they have foregone by lifting visa fees for EU citizens in 2005. And even where ENPI could matter (in Armenia, Moldova), Russia is ready to match or outpace the EU's financial commitments to these countries.

Even when it comes to financing governmental projects, the EU's slow and complicated funding procedures limit the EU's impact on the ground. For example, in Moldova there are four European information centres: one is funded by George Soros; two by the Eurasia Foundation with money from USAID, the Norwegian MFA and the Swedish International Development Agency (SIDA); and one by the Greek Agency for International Development. None are funded by the EU itself.

Combining the eastern and southern neighbourhoods in the ENP may not be the fatal flaw that is sometimes suggested (the launching of the Mediterranean Initiative helped smooth the path to the Eastern Partnership), but there is still a structural imbalance in the amount of political attention paid to the Southern and Eastern neighbours. The EU has a longer history of interacting with its southern neighbours, because the Eastern states have only recently become a 'neighbourhood'. Southern countries like France, Spain and Italy are natural lobbyists for the southern neighbourhood. Germany is primarily interested in Russia and views relations with most Eastern neighbours through the prism of its partnership with Russia. The new EU member states from the 2004 and 2007 entries have their own problems with the global economic crisis.

As a result, EU institutions' engagement in the neighbourhood are unbalanced. The geography of foreign trips of senior European officials is particularly telling. Between 1999 and 2008, the High Representative for CFSP made only one visit to Moldova, Azerbaijan and Armenia (in 2001, during a Troika tour of the region organized by the Swedish Presidency), five to Georgia (twice in 2008), but sixteen each to Russia and Ukraine (thanks to the Orange Revolution). In comparison, Solana made 119 visits to the Middle East and North Africa.[8]

8 Between September 1999 and November 2004, Chris Patten made thirteen visits to the Euromed, and only one to the east, to Ukraine (plus six trips to Russia). Between

Table 5.7 EU assistance to neighbours (millions EUR)

Euromed	1995–2005/6	2007–2010	Euroeast	1991–2005/6	2007–2010
Algeria	436.8	220	Armenia	380	98.4
Egypt	1000	558	Azerbaijan	400	92
Israel	–	14	Belarus	229	20
Jordan	500	265	Georgia	506	120*
Lebanon	417	187	Moldova	300	209.7
Morocco	1500	654	Ukraine	2400	494
Syria	286.5	130			
Tunisia	875	300			

*After the war the European Commission offered a reconstruction and stabilization package 2008–2010 which totals €500 million.

Source: European Union's Neighbourhood Policy website.

The European Commission's diplomatic presence in the world is similarly skewed. It has bigger delegations in some African countries than in the neighbourhood, though this is in part because they were set up at an earlier date, when more resources were available, and because poorer countries tend to have more EU officials working on aid distribution.

When delegations are small, EU member states tend to go their own way. The tiny delegation in Minsk, which only opened its doors in March 2008, is one reason why member states gave out different messages to Belarus in the run-up to the September 2008 elections as to the precise conditions for renewed dialogue.

The slow reorientation of local economies

On the other hand, the EU has had more of an economic impact in the neighbourhood, albeit mainly at an elite level. Trade patterns are more diversified than is often thought. Apart from Belarus on the import side, all six have less than 30 per cent of their overall trade with Russia.

One telling EU success story was the Moldovan Autonomous Trade Preferences (ATPs, for free trade access to EU markets). An estimated 400 Transnistrian companies registered in Chişinău in the summer of 2006 in order to receive trade

November 2004 and October 2008 Benita Ferrero-Waldner made twenty Euromed visits, fourteen to the Eastern neighbouhood and six to Russia.

Table 5.8 Visits by the EU High Representative for Common Foreign and Security Policy (October 1999–October 2008, number of diplomats in delegations)

Euroeast		Euromed		The Rest	
Armenia	3	Algeria	11	Barbados	8
Azerbaijan	1	Egypt	16	Botswana	9
Belarus	2	Israel	13	Burkina Faso	6
Georgia	13	Jordan	21	Guatemala	7
Moldova	2–3	Lebanon	14	Sierra Leone	6
Ukraine	13	Morocco	24	Zambia	7
		Syria	8		
		Tunisia	18		

Source: Data for visits were gathered from High Representative archive available at the European Union Council website.

Table 5.9 Trade patterns of the Eastern Partnership states, 2007 (%)

	Exports/EU	Imports/EU	Exports/Russia	Imports/Russia
Belarus	43.8	21.8	26.7	59.9
Ukraine	31.5	36	22.5	30.6
Moldova	50.6	45.6	17.3	13.5
Georgia	30	23	12	5
Armenia	48.9	66.9	13	13
Azerbaijan	27.6	29.3	8.7	17.6

Source: Popescu, N. and Wilson, A. 2009. *The Limits of Enlargement-lite: European and Russian Power in the Troubled Neighbourhood.* London: European Council on Foreign Relations.

certificates. Exports to the EU rose by 59 per cent over two years, twice as fast as export growth to Russia. When Transnistrian steel and cement exports were hit hard by the global economic crisis in autumn 2008, this only served to emphasise that the region's isolation was a thing of the past.

Businesses in the eastern neighbourhood do not enjoy the free ride of Russia's massive energy rents. They have to bend more towards the rules of international finance, because they need the money (albeit while trying to keep local business culture intact). Ukraine has seen the biggest changes in corporate culture, as businesses have had to change their act to sell themselves for IPOs and IFIs. That said, the six states still have different trading patterns and operate in different trading blocks. They trade less with each other than the accession states of the 1990s.

Table 5.10 Foreign direct investment in the Neighbourhood: the biggest EU deals

Belarus	• Telecom Austria for 70% of MBC (Velcom), 2007, €730 million • Heineken for Syabar brewery 2007, c. €130 million • (Commerzbank for Belinvestbank on hold)
Ukraine	• Mittal for Kryvorizhstal 2005, €4 billion • Banks – Raiffeisen for 93.5% of Aval, 2005, $1,028 million • BNP Paribas for 51% of Ukrsibbank, 2006, $500 million • Unicredit for Ukrsotsbank, 2008, $2.2 billion • Intesa for Pravex Bank, 2008, $750 million • Credit Agricole for 98% of Index Bank, 2006, $254 million • Lactalis Group bought leading dairy producer Molochniy Dom, 2007 • Groupe Danone bought Rodych Dairy Plant in Kherson, 2006
Moldova	• Orange/France Telecom for Voxtel, 1998, $8 million • Union Fenosa for three power distributors (Red Chişinău, Red Centru and Red Sud), 2000, $25.3 million • Société Générale for 70.6% of MobiasBanca, 2007, €18.5 million (plus another 24.8%) • Lafarge Cements for Rezina cement plant, 1999
Georgia	• BTC (Baku-Tbilisi-Ceyhan) pipeline finished 2005, $3.9 billion South Caucasus pipeline (Baku-Tbilisi-Erzurum) • Greenoak sold Batumi oil terminal to Kazmunaigas in February 2008, after an investment of $200 million • Société Générale for 60% of Bank Republic, 2006 • Heidelbergcement for 51% of Kartuli and Saqcementi, €150 million invested • TeliaSonera 97.5% of Geocell, 2008
Armenia	• Greek OTE for Armentel, 1998, $142 million. • Germany's Cronimet for 70% of Zangezur mine (Molybdenum and copper), 2004, $132 million • ING secured Haypost (the Armenian postal service) in trust, 2006 • Pernod-Ricard for YBC (the Yerevan Brandy factory), 1998, $30 million
Azerbaijan	• BP 30.1% of BTC (Eni/Agip, Total, 5% each) • BP 25.5% of South Caucasus Pipeline (Eni via LukAgip, 10%, TotalFinaElf, 10%)

Source: Popescu, N. and Wilson, A. 2009. *The Limits of Enlargement-lite: European and Russian Power in the Troubled Neighbourhood.* London: European Council on Foreign Relations.

The limits of EU soft power

Compared to Russia, the EU is under-utilising its considerable soft power. Even in the areas where the ENP has real traction, the EU risks undermining its own potential. It devalues the accession perspective by putting so much energy into persuading countries not to apply. It weakens the centrifugal force of an often over-assertive Russia when it pursues a 'Russia first' policy. The steady accretion of benefits from the gradual westward reorientation of the region's economies has yet to extend from elites to masses. The enormous increase in people-to-people contacts since 1991 has been slowed by the effect of the Schengen 'wall'.

Particularly damaging is the perception that the EU, a project based on the rule of law, does not keep its promises. A senior Moldovan official interviewed in 2008 states that 'Moldova has problems in the implementation of the ENP action plan, but so does the EU.' Contrary to its obligations under the Action Plan the EU does not 'continue its efforts to ensure the fulfilment by Russia of the Istanbul commitments'. Ukraine and Moldova have complained that many EU member states do not respect the visa facilitation agreement that came into force on 1 January 2008. The Ukrainian parliament even called on the government to re-introduce visas for EU citizens, because the EU was not respecting the existing agreement.

The EU is also too focused on the long-term. It tends to wait for soft power to act, and pays too little attention to the urgent problems of short-termist and fragile states – which ultimately also undermines its long term attractiveness.

Conclusion

Russia considers its readiness to use hard power to be a power resource in itself. Its actions against individual states are quite clearly often designed with demonstration effects in mind. Russia is consequently a feared but credible foreign policy actor. But the wide array of hard power used by Russia has also exposed its weaknesses. The war in Georgia was in part a demonstration that all other forms of Russian power – economic, political or ideological – had failed. Russia's military presence in the region has often undermined state building efforts, but has never been strong enough to re-assert Russian hegemony. Despite years of pressure on Moldova to accept a permanent Russian military presence in exchange for reunification with Transnistria, Moldova still insists that Russian forces should withdraw. Russia's exploitation of secessionist conflicts has encouraged greater international involvement in the post-Soviet space. Georgia and Ukraine continue to strive for closer links with the EU and even NATO. Moldova is trying to replace Russian military peacekeepers with a civilian mission with the EU as the main actor. In the aftermath of the war in Georgia, the post-Soviet states may be more likely to yield to Russian demands but are also more aware that such concessions will come at a high cost.

Modest Kolerov has stated in stark terms that neighbourhood states 'can struggle for their sovereignty, but it will cost them dear ... sovereignty in the neighbourhood of Europe is more expensive than sovereignty in the neighbourhood of Russia. This is the economic reality' (2008). But Russian economic pressures have also showed the limitations of Russian power. Embargoes, blockades, and oil and gas supply cuts have made target states more pliant to Russian interests in the short run; but their effects have often been smaller than expected. Russia's sanctions have also diminished its future economic leverage by driving the targets to diversify their economies. After Russia introduced the ban on Moldovan and Georgian wines their economies still grew by 3–5 per cent and 9–12 per cent respectively.[9] Georgia successfully reoriented most of its wine exports, while the limited effects of the Russian blockade on Moldova only underscored the fact that Russia has only 15 per cent of the country's external trade, compared to 50 per cent for the EU. Russian pressure on Georgia, strengthened rather than weakened Saakashvili in the build-up to the August 2008 war and strengthened his perceived freedom of manoeuvre. The Ukrainian economy absorbed the shock of the sudden increase in gas prices in 2006 and improved its energy efficiency – though indefinite increases are a different matter. Ukraine was likely to be much harder hit by the crisis in January 2009, as it was already in recession. Hard power and economic coercion also undermine whatever efforts Russia invests into its soft power. When Russian hard power is too hard, it touches sensitive existential issues of sovereignty and territorial integrity for the neighbourhood states and creates resistance.

The EU, on the other hand, has relied almost exclusively on soft power. Support for the region's (still un-finished) transition to fully-fledged democracies, assistance in adoption of respective parts of *acquis communitaire* and other measures have been the key means of Brussels' engagement with its eastern neighbourhood. At the same time, the EU's efforts to shape the developments in the region and further promote its own standards of democracy, rule of law and security have been undermined by a weak political strategy: too often is the EU trying to advance its goals through administrative means without investing considerable political capital in their promotion. Importantly, in its eastern neighbourhood, the EU soft power and influence face far greater challenges than in Central and Eastern Europe ten years ago. Brussels has to engage with regimes much less enthusiastic about the EU at a time when the ultimate reward the EU can offer to its partners – EU membership – is no longer a realistic option in the short and medium-term. Greater EU involvement in the region has been further prevented by the EU – Russia relations taking precedence over the Union's relations with the partners east of its borders. More often than not, while trying to manage its closest neighbours, the EU has ended up managing – and fixing – its relations with Russia. This is unlikely

9 According to World Bank figures, Moldovan GDP growth in 2006 was 4.8 per cent, and 3.0 per cent in 2007. Georgian GDP growth was 9.4 per cent in 2006 and 12.4 per cent in 2007.

to change in the near future. The EU therefore needs to think about how to make its soft power more effective and how to effectively pursue its objectives in the eastern neighbourhood even if they may clash with those of Russia.

The war in Georgia has most bluntly exposed the limits of both Russia's and the EU's power in the region: neither Brussels nor Moscow was able to advance their own objectives or prevent transformation of the conflict into a fully-fledged war. While in the region, both sides are able to project their power to a certain extent, the lesson learned from the August conflict is that both the EU and Russia need to adjust to the reality that the east European states are sovereign actors. The war in Georgia has clearly shown that for the foreseeable future, Eastern Europe and the South Caucasus are likely to remain zones of competition: neither side is likely to prevail over the other, or establish a true zone of influence in which local states act like them and in subordination to their rules.

Chapter 6
The Georgian–Russian Conflict: Acute, Frozen or Settled?

Pertti Joenniemi

The August war of 2008 did not unfold as a one-off event soon to fade into oblivion. Instead, the initial shock reverberated through the post-conflict discourses and contestations. Although many of them assert the paradigmatic nature of the event, there appears to be little agreement on what the war was actually about. Moreover, the applied frames of interpretation tend to discriminate against, and push to the periphery of attention, some potential accounts.

For a start, there has been much support for the view that the short, five-day war was of ground-breaking importance: 'the little war that shook the world' (Asmus 2010). Some observers used the conflict in order to condemn what they regard as overly optimistic efforts of grounding the European order in interdependence, dialogue and common norms. The conflict has apparently demonstrated that these aspirations were ill-founded and has raised anew the spectrum of great-power rivalry (Allison, 2008, Fedorov, 2008, Friedman, 2008). These back-to-the-past interpretations presenting Russia as demonstrating its will to secure, if not to expand, a sphere of privileged interests have dominated not only the public discourse, but also, to a considerable degree, the narratives employed in the sphere of scholarly analysis.

In such works, the conflict has been viewed as a calculated war by proxy, with the US backing and arming Georgia and/or Russia using South Ossetia as a disguise for offensive action (Cornell et al. 2008, Nichol, 2009); that is, an episode in the confrontational relations between Russia and the West (cf. Makarychev 2009: 11, Pain 2009: 16). Furthermore, successfully marketed images of Georgia as a distinctly Western and neo-liberal country (Halbach 2006) have added ideological and moral connotations to this confrontation. These images appealed to many in marking out Georgia as being well on its way to joining 'us', while at the same time presenting Russia as a threatening 'other' (Ditrych 2010; Nodia 2005) whose accelerating military presence in South Ossetia gave further credence to old fears and vulnerabilities leading ultimately, to the shelling of Tskhinvali by Georgian forces.

In other words, a rather unpredictable event which took by surprise most observers and, perhaps, even participants – including, to some degree, both Russian and American leaderships – was readily accounted for through rather unsurprising images of international relations. Hence the talk about 'Russia's return to great power status' (Friedman 2008: 4) and, more generally, references to a process of 'normalization', that is, a shift that restored the relevance of realist interpretations concerning the character of international relations. These 'classical' interpretations, including that of the English School, have thrived on the ensuing perception of 'normalcy', including war, as an 'institution of international society', being back on the agenda.

Again, Russia was seen as promoting this general view at least since the Kosovo conflict when it refused, in no uncertain terms, to abandon the traditional conceptual baggage of *Realpolitik*. This corresponded, as testified among others by Timofey Bordachev (2009: 62), to a persistent trend in Russia's policies: 'A belief in traditional Westphalian sovereignty is therefore now a central principle of Russia's foreign policy and a key point of difference with the "liberal interventionist" West'. In the language of the English School (Buzan 2004), Russia, it seemed, stood for a 'thin', traditional, conflictual form of international society.

It is noteworthy, however, that in the case of the Georgian–Russian conflict Russia broke this long-standing pattern. It undertook a *discursive jump* by suddenly signaling preparedness to abide by the dictates of the moral and ethical account of a 'thick', post-sovereign nature. Rather unexpectedly, Russia maintained that its engagement in the clash was all about 'peace enforcement' and 'humanitarian intervention'. Russia, employing such concepts as 'genocide' and 'ethnic cleansing', arguably intervened in order to protect the two break-away provinces of South Ossetia and Abkhazia along with the Russian peacekeepers and Russian citizens in the region against Georgian abuses of power.

In other words, Russia positioned itself as an actor engaging in a local conflict as a guardian of those in danger and more generally a defender of the value-based international society along the lines of the policies previously advocated in other contexts by the US and EU. It aspired against all odds for recognition as a major power by pursuing 'liberal interventionism', invoking explicitly normative arguments and advocating in general 'a European solution to the Caucasian problems' (Gorenburg and Makarychev 2009: 5). In short, it was intent on joining the hegemonic accounts supporting the very 'thick' nature of international society. Still, in line with Iver Neumann's (2008: 128–30) conclusion to his study of the historical unfolding of Russia's position in European politics, this change again did not result in the recognition Russia yearned for. The view that Russia was sincerely knocking on the door of the 'thick' liberal international society was, by and large, rejected.

Moreover, there was no such 'thick' society for Russia to join, since the discursive hegemony had actually shifted. Georgia was regarded as a small state in danger of losing its sovereignty as well as a formidable part of its territory. The event itself was not even conceptualized in a neutral fashion as a 'war' between Russia and Georgia but rather viewed as 'Russia's war in Georgia' (Sestanovich 2008: 13, Cornell et al. 2008) with Russia positioned as an unprovoked aggressor. Traditional state-related interests with emphasis on independence, sovereignty and territorial integrity were now placed above the rights of individuals or other similar normative departures.

Russia was subsequently again categorized as a 'non-us' to be denied any constitutive impact in defining what the conflict was about. Interestingly, the rejection of a normative frame as an inter-subjectively shared one took place in spite of considerable evidence indicating that Georgia actually initiated the hostilities (Amnesty International 2008, International Crisis Group 2008 and 2009, Independent International Fact-Finding Mission on the Conflict in Georgia 2009). The image of Georgia as a victim has remained so dominant that evidence to the contrary – provided also more recently by Wikileaks (Mouritzen, 2011) – has failed to have much impact.

Thus, it seems that discursive hegemony may at least occasionally change in such a way that it does not matter much whether Russia accepts the dominant, norm-based account underpinning the post-Cold War liberal order or if it instead abides by some of the key arguments of the 'classical', sovereignty-related discourse. The borders may in any case be re-drawn in a manner that will invariably present Russia as an outcast.

My contribution here focuses on these discursive shifts. The aim is not to defend the various views on offer. It is neither about passing judgement on the nature and root causes of the conflict *per se,* nor favouring and siding with a particular interpretation at the expense of another. It is instead an attempt to outline a broader interpretative frame focusing on congruence and incongruence between the various views, interpretations and subject-positions, above all those of the European Union, the United States and Russia.

The frame outlined stays within the confines of the English School in being related to the division into 'thin' and 'thick' international society as well as the role of the major actors (viewed as great powers in the vocabulary of the School) seen as the custodians of international society through their policies of conflict-mitigation. Yet, it evaluates the various discourses by reference to the weight assigned within them to security. Consequently, the various postures and changes in those are assessed in terms of four possible strategies: securitization, de-securitization, a-securitization and re-securitization.

Framing Postures

As noted by the English School, even conflictual constellations, such as war, contain within themselves some seeds of commonality. A convergence of positions may occur, for example, when actors agree in their shared *securitization* of international society, stressing threats and the need for various security-related countermeasures, such as 'balancing'. Not surprisingly, *de-securitization* as a joint attempt to reduce these security threats may become a common stance as well, signifying an effort to defend and preserve the societal, even if still conflictual, nature of international relations. The de-securitization discourse would focus on mediation and rapprochement and invite various initiatives in confidence-building and arms control, for example. Still, as with securitization, security-related arguments would stand out as the key elements of the discourse. Some form of security-speak would account for the postures adopted, determine the way the subject positions unfold and inform the probable direction of future relations between the actors in question.

In contrast, the liberal and explicitly value-based discourses rest on a different ontology, being far less geared towards security. Arguments pertaining to security decline in constitutive standing whereas values such as democracy, human rights and good governance are elevated to a key position. The discourse also allows, as security and insecurity are no longer viewed as polar opposites, for a dismissal of the whole security-based argument. It allows for stepping *beyond security* and focusing on other things such as integration and development; that is, departures that mostly unite and bring the parties together in the context of a dense international society. Notably, such a dense form amounts to more than a 'thick' international society and could be described as a 'saturated' one. It is saturated in the sense that the classical power-political dangers and the problem of anarchy; that is, issues underpinning the theorization of the English School (Bull 1977: 9–10), are seen as having been overcome and left behind. It therefore also entails a possibility that security does not always have to remain constitutive of international relations.

Yet, the theme of security may also re-enter such 'saturated' discourse. It is not categorically excluded and may, in one of its forms, enter the stage due to attempts at *re-securitization*. This would be the case once questions are raised about the need to defend an already 'saturated' sphere against various efforts aimed at bringing it back towards 'thick' or even 'thin' forms of international society.

Thus, departing from the existence of two radically separate discursive settings and the way security enters each of them as an argument, the interpretative framework employed for analysing the relevant subject positions in the debate on the August conflict unfolds as follows:

Table 6.1 Mode of security-speak

Logics of international society	Deployed discursive approach	
Sovereignty- and interest-based logic of a 'thin' international society	securitization	de-securitization
Norm-based logic of a 'saturated' international society	a-securitization	re-securitization

By placing all the major parties to the August conflict within this framework, it is possible to trace instances of either congruence or incongruence in their respective postures, depending on which mode of security-speak they adopt, either individually or in some shared manner. A shared posture may consist of the parties contributing to and engaging themselves in an intense and continued securitization. Security-speak would hence figure as a kind of common language along the lines staked out by the English School, albeit one that may, despite the shared logic, set the parties apart from each other resulting in a rather 'thin' international society. Engaging in re-securitization yields a similar result by weakening the saturation of international society, whereas de-securitization and especially a-securitization tends to be far less prone to the emergence of tensions and conflict-ridden relations thus adding considerably to the 'thickness' or 'saturation' of international society respectively.

Overall, some forms of incongruence may be the outcome of a certain *shared* discursive logic but may also result from *different* and competing discursive logics. The Russian and the Western framing of NATO's operation in Kosovo exemplify, as noted above, the latter stance and so do the approaches to the Georgian–Russian conflict, at least initially, even though the positions of the parties were for a while reversed: Russia supporting a liberal and norm-based reading, whereas the West stood for a standard sovereignty-related approach. With Russia then moving back towards an emphasis on the logic of undivided sovereignty, the prospects for congruence around a 'thin', securitized version of international society improved, albeit raising the question of whether this meeting-point would freeze on the level of *continued* securitization, escalate in the direction of *intensified* securitization or result in joint moves towards de-securitization

Individual Postures

The EU distinguishes itself from most other actors on the international scene in being explicitly driven by normative concerns and in relying on civilian rather than military means of influence. It is frequently viewed as being 'beyond' and 'after' security. It stands for a sphere of 'post-security' in the sense of having reached – through reflexive learning from its own past – a state with security-related concerns no longer dominating the agenda. The danger of war breaking out among member-states is arguably no longer present. Europe has turned into something exemplary and represents more than just a 'thick' form of international society. The state of a-security resulted from successful de-securitization, and one may, on good grounds, talk about the EU as having reached a 'saturated' form of international society.

It then also follows that the EU, having overcome its past and security dilemma generally (Joenniemi 2011), has become a 'normative power'. The Union may consequently set standards for what is considered appropriate conduct in the sphere of international relations (cf. Diez and Manners 2007). The investment into the power embedded in norms is closely connected with economic forms of power, which then points to efforts of 'domesticating' international relations above all through a strong emphasis on integration and development. In having largely stayed aloof from security-talk, the EU therefore has also stayed outside of the various European security-related institutions. Security has not figured as a constitutive argument except in the sense that securitization is something to be avoided. It was to be left behind as a relic from an utterly problematic past.

Yet, arguments pertaining to security have increasingly crept back into the EU-discourse since the end of the 1990s. Numerous voices have contributed to *re-securitization* by arguing that even normative aims have occasionally to be backed up and defended against violations by a resort to military means. The alterations within the norm-based logic then paved the way for a security strategy, initially in 2003 and then in a revised form in 2008, to be devised with the acquisition of various forms of military power as well as in EU participation in a number of humanitarian interventions. Voices insisting on the EU abandoning its 'Kantian' nature (Kagan 2003) and advocating the grounding its subjectivity in the acquisition and use of 'hard' power (Cooper 2003, van Ham 2008) have multiplied. There are, in fact, analysts arguing that a certain tipping-point has already been passed (for example, Diez 2004). They assert that the approach of re-securitization in a norm-based context has over recent years been increasingly traded for securitization in a more traditional manner.

This seems to imply that congruence on the terrain of *Realpolitik* is no longer totally off-limits and the acquisition and even use of military means are more and more seen as integral attributes of the EU. This developmental path appears to lead away from the initial emphasis of a-securitization and move through re-securitization towards more classical securitization.

In comparison, the constitutive discourses unfolded somewhat differently in the case of the United States, especially during the Bush junior administration. They were based more on Hobbesian rather than Kantian, modern rather than postmodern departures. In line with the Hobbesian emphasis, the US was far less prone than the EU to drop sovereignty-related arguments and stayed with securitization as the central mode of security-speak. This left little reason to expect that the US would engage in any re-securitization as it has not endeavoured at stepping beyond security in the first place, while the option of de-securitization remained readily available as a possible meeting-point, being an invitation for powers interested in linking up with the US through an engagement in conflict management, cooperative security, arms control or, for that matter, disarmament, that is, activities characteristic of the 'thick' international society.

Although such a version of international society presupposes certain normativity as a shared concern, its list of priorities as to the norms to be pursued is somewhat different from that of the EU. Whereas 'governance' with connotations of a-security characterizes the EU's approach, the US is much more inclined to operate in the sphere of 'high politics' with the moral zeal articulated through the employment of more abstract markers such as 'freedom' and 'democracy'. This results in preference for 'top-down' policies, rather straight-forward in style and accompanied more often than not by resort to the use of military means of influence, whereas the EU stance tends to unfold in a 'bottom-up' manner with the option of military involvement to be used only in exceptional cases and with utter caution (Kopstein 2006).

Still, the existence of a rather broad spectrum of options in the American discourse suggests that considerable changes and even jumps may occur pending political fluctuations. Thus, more recent, post-Bush, US policies have been described as pragmatic in nature with more emphasis on multilateralism, the re-ordering of global institutions and in this context involving the emerging powers and making them responsible stakeholders (Krastev et al. 2010: 56). The emphasis also seems to have shifted to some extent away from Europe towards more global concerns, although Russia appears to remain of considerable interest as a 'partner' in view of various efforts at strengthening the 'thick' features of international society and pushing for de-securitization. It is against this background that influential voices in the American debate have more recently found reasons to suggest that Russia should be invited to join NATO (Kupchan 2010).

This brings me to Russia's established postures, in all likelihood the most problematic ones. Although Russia generally displays features of waging a rather traditional discourse with much emphasis on sovereignty and security-related issues, it has on occasion also subscribed to explicitly norm-based departures. As noted by Sergei Medvedev (1999), there is, in general, a cyclical pattern to be traced here with the option of almost opposite postures alternating with each other. However, in the end, Russia's ability to follow up the various norm-based proposals and join the different initiatives aimed at firmly anchoring it in the European norm-oriented discourses has proved to be rather weak. In addition, there has been little preparedness – with sovereignty-related securitization as one of the approaches still around – on the Western side to open up and accept Russia as an actor with an equal voice and with normative departures of its own (Sakwa 2008: 267–98).

Significantly, being unable to join in a European system premised on liberal values and the enlargement of the EU and NATO, Russia has attempted instead to position itself, albeit with little success, as a kind of alternative Europe premised on more classical European values. Yet, and notwithstanding such a failure, the question of integration has remained a point of convergence and Russia has on occasions displayed considerable interest in taking part in EU-related cooperation, even if, more often than not, it has found reasons to express its dissatisfaction with the conditions on offer. The initiatives pertaining to inclusion have mainly come from the Union, although there are also cases pointing to the opposite, with Russia advancing integrationist proposals and the EU pursuing a more assertive and exclusive orientation (Prozorov 2009). Again, recently, the prospects for dialogue and a meeting of minds have seemed to improve with Russia elevating economic development and modernization into major objectives of its foreign policy and showing increasing signs of accepting the EU and its norm-based approach (Krastev and Leonard 2010: 39).

Still, in the sphere of explicitly security-related policies, Russia has consistently emphasized securitization and cautious de-securitization, rather than a-securitization. It has resumed the patrolling of strategic bombers, suspended unilaterally participation in the CFE-treaty and threatened to withdraw from the Intermediate Range Nuclear Forces Treaty (Fedorov 2008). This policy was in some cases complemented by moves of de-securitization such as the proposal of a new European security treaty presented by President Medvedev in June 2008. The Merkel-Medvedev idea of an EU–Russia security dialogue, presented in July 2010, further strengthens aspirations towards de-securitization.

To be sure, the Georgian–Russian conflict of August 2008 disrupted this tenuous balance in favour of securitization with efforts at 'mutual delimitation' as forms of de-securitization put aside as quite secondary. Russia, as argued by Yuru Fedorov (2009), set on a course of 'controlled confrontation' and did so with considerable fury and without much hesitancy. Georgia was presented not only as a post-Soviet state challenging Russia but was depicted as an aggressor not to be appeased, with 'Munich' employed as a metaphor justifying the decision to engage in war, in turn, presented as a war in defence of European civilization (Medvedev 2008a). Moreover, the Russian leadership resorted to arrogant statements meant to downplay and undermine the legitimacy of various western claims, on the one hand, and assert Russia's self-sufficiency as a great power on the other: 'Russia does not fear anything, not even a new Cold War' (Medvedev 2008b). Within this logic of securitization, Russia suspended cooperation with NATO and announced that it could very well do without WTO membership. Western criticism of Russian policies was presented as reinforcing and justifying Russia's choice of defending its dignity and interests against attempts to test its strength and endurance (Nichol 2009: 28).

Relational Postures

Given the individual postures established long before the war of August 2008, the post-war emphasis on securitization does not come as something altogether unexpected. What is more interesting is how different positions, once put together in bilateral relations result in different responses to this securitization. Thus, in the case of US–Russian relations, both parties seem to converge rather unproblematically on a shared de-securitizing stance. In the case of EU–Russian relations, this de-securitizing strategy is less open, given the EU's preference for a-securitization.

In general, incongruence between the individual postures of the EU and Russia existed for some time. Various conflicts, such as the two Chechen wars, tensions between Russia and some of the post-Soviet states, authoritarian developments in Russia as well as various 'affairs', such as the Yukos case or murders of journalists and advocates of human rights, contributed to the deterioration of relations (Kramer 2009: 62–4). Russia complained that it was constantly presented with requests to adapt to a set of ready-made and rather 'ideological' rules, rather than being offered a dialogue between equal parties. At the same time, it wondered whether legalistic, administrative and in a number of other ways 'non-political' EU had any subjectivity of its own. The EU, for its part, felt itself being betrayed and let down because of a wide discrepancy between Russia's promises and its deeds. Agreements were not respected in practical policies and the norm-based critique of authoritarian tendencies, lack of openness and deficiencies in democracy were met by Russia in a 'look at yourself' manner. All in all, despite regular meetings and an up-keeping of the cooperative rhetorics, little practical progress was achieved, with some analysts (Barber 2008) suggesting that the frequency of summits should be reduced in the future, in order to avoid disgraceful biannual demonstrations of the ineffectiveness of the EU–Russia 'strategic partnership'.

The August clash between Georgia and Russia undoubtedly fitted the contentious pattern in EU–Russia relations and pointed to a further accentuation. Their relationship reached, no doubt, its lowest point since the end of the Cold War. In general, serious doubts emerged as to Russia's credentials in an integrationist and 'saturated' context and there was instead increased disillusionment with Russia's Europeanization.

The Rose Revolution of November 2003 prompted the EU to pay increasing attention to Georgia and this trend was further accentuated by Georgia becoming a direct neighbour of the Union after the accession of Romania and Bulgaria. Yet the Union's role remained relatively modest with the relationship relying on conditionality (cf. Diez, Stetter and Albert 2006) and geared towards strengthening of the Georgian state by supporting juridical reforms and re-structuring the border guard service (Blank 2009: 112–14, Carothers 2009, Fean 2009). In general, the approach was technocratic in essence with unwillingness to cross from the technical side to the political one tackling above all the tension between democracy and a rather authoritarian as well as repressive rule of the Saakashvili government (George and Stefes 2008, Lazarus 2010). The EU also aspired to improve Georgia's dialogue with its secessionist parts, although issues pertaining to security were approached mainly indirectly (cf. Lynch 2006, Tocci 2008).

However, the establishment in 2003 of a EU Special Representative in the Southern Caucasus region – with special emphasis on Georgia – might be seen as an indication that the initial technocratic stance could be gradually complemented if not substituted by other, more openly security-related approaches. So, it hardly came as a surprise that, already after the outbreak of the conflict, the EU and its member states became actively involved both in the intense negotiations in Moscow in September 2008 (cf. Allison 2008: 1159) and in the setting up of the Geneva talks that followed (Fean 2009: 6). Yet, despite the EU being increasingly accepted as a mediating and a moderating force, Russia's abstention from the integrationist discourse left it in a rather problematic position. A considerable number of EU members sided strongly with Georgia, while Poland unequivocally translated the situation into securitizing language by deciding instantly to conclude the agreement to host parts of America's missile-defence shield (Krastev 2008).

Interestingly, soon after the initial tensions caused by the war subsided, EU–Russian relations did not move away from such extreme forms of securitization towards de-securitization. Instead, the preferred path seemed to be a-securitization, so that, rather than focusing immediately on issues of trust and confidence-building, the parties turned to economic interests and common concerns in more technical fields, as indicated by the 'modernization partnership' launched in June 2010. These steps might later be accompanied by more security-related endeavours as the joint Merkel-Medvedev proposal on the establishment of the EU–Russia Political and Security Committee and calls also for cooperation in the sphere of crisis-management operations seem to testify. France, for its part, aired the idea of a 'single EU-Russia zone of security and economic cooperation' (Gorka-Winter and Kumoch 2010). In this case, a move from securitization towards de-securitization is preceded by a discursive jump from securitization to a-securitization.

By contrast, the post-conflict development of US–Russian relations has not involved any such jumps; dramatic changes in US foreign policy under President Obama notwithstanding. This is hardly surprising given that these relations have been dominated by security-speak all along. It is because of this initial congruence that even before the Georgian war, Russia had been able to improve its standing vis-a-vis the US by joining 'the war on terror', for example. US–Russia relations have never departed from the various sovereignty-related postures, nor have they called for further steps towards saturated forms of transnational integration. Consequently, both securitization in relation to a third party and de-securitization in the sphere of their mutual relations remain readily available.

Thus, even though the US discourse on Georgia was heavily reliant on normative arguments, presenting Georgia as a democratic island 'in a sea of post-Soviet autocracies and kleptocracies' (Mitchell 2009: 88), it never abandoned its focus on sovereignty and security, so that membership in NATO was seen as an obvious solution to Georgia's numerous problems (Lynch 2006: 51–4). Georgia itself fuelled the strategy-related discourse and bolstered its position by stressing its willingness to contribute to the combating of terrorism and to take part in the Iraq war. Accordingly, there were good reasons to conclude that, in the end, Russia decided to respond to securitization in kind – by further securitization: 'the war in Georgia can thus be understood as the desire to finally make itself heard by inspiring fear' (Gomart 2009: 21). Firmly rooted in the logic of security-speak, the conflict signified for Russia a 'revenge for almost two decades of humiliation and geopolitical retreat' (Pain 2009: 16).

Here, a more conventional 'classical approach' to international relations offered counter-arguments without resorting to EU-like a-securitization (Kissinger and Schultz 2008). Whilst securitization retained its position as the key discursive posture, its conclusions increasingly moved in the direction of the recognition of Russia's importance in the broader context of US global aspirations (cf. Mitchell 2009: 93). Following this view, the Russian–Georgian conflict was seen as irrational. It broke out as something unintended, went too far and could potentially have unwelcome effects on specific security issues such as developments in North Korea or Iran but also international relations at large.

Already the Bush administration refrained in the aftermath of the conflict from any further aggravation of the US–Russian relations: rhetorics aside, 'it did little when Russia invaded its neighbour' (Shapiro and Witney 2009: 55). Measures such as depriving Russia of its place in the G8, withdrawing US support for Russia hosting the 2014 Winter Olympics in Sochi, installing ABM components in Europe or supporting Ukraine in terminating the Russian naval presence in the Crimea in 2017 (Nichol, 2009: 19) were brought up in the discourse as conceivable forms of sanctioning Russia, but all of them were rejected. Analysts, characterized US response to the Russian action in Georgia as being 'muted' (Antonenko 2008: 24) or 'tepid' (Blank 2009: 425).

The Obama administration has simply continued and gone along the path already opened up by the previous administration. The reason why, with its policy of 'reset' in US–Russian relations, it has gone much further down this path is its 'thicker' view of international society (Ikenberry 2009: 81–3). Connected to this is an explicit downgrading of an overly ideological approach and upgrading of a more pragmatic, albeit still security-related one. The resulting de-securitization has transformed Russia into a 'partner' yet again.

Subsequently, the US has backtracked on its initial plan to deploy ABM components in Poland and the Czech Republic. The opening for Georgia to enter NATO has been narrowed down, a dialogue and serious negotiations both on political and expert level concerning a new strategic arms control treaty have been initiated, and a more conciliatory stance has been adopted towards Russia's European security pact. Russia, for its part, has returned to cooperation with NATO, allowed the transit of non-lethal military supplies for US troops in Afghanistan, shelved the threat to deploy nuclear weapons in Kaliningrad and accepted more generally that there is indeed a need to 'reboot' US–Russian relations.

In general, the US and Russia increasingly position themselves within a shared discursive setting and meet each other in a rather cooperative manner. In doing so, they have also been able to achieve a far less conflictual relationship compared to the previous state of affairs of being located either within different discourses or jointly pursuing intensive securitization. Rather than aspiring for a joint interpretation of the Caucasus conflict, the parties have pushed the issue to the fringes of their dialogue and focused instead on a far less problematic agenda.

Concluding Remarks

In bringing about a vigorous if not an alarmist debate, the 2008 war has added weight to security-related arguments in the sphere of international relations. The conflict did not unfold as an isolated incident but has brought about a more general debate on whether power politics are back in town. Although initially that seems to be the case, the long-term effect may well be different. The clash has brought with it not only incongruities but also meeting-points, especially in the realm of de-securitization in US–Russia relations. De-securititazion, in turn, has eased the situation and contributed to a dialogue which has the potential of being extended towards the EU as well.

Still, differences in the potential trajectories of Russian–EU and Russian–US relations are visible through comparison of two recent proposals. Ivan Krastev and Mark Leonard (2010), scholars at the European Council on Foreign Relations (ECFR), suggest that the EU should react to Russia's initiative concerning a European security treaty by inviting Russia and Turkey to come informally together in order for this trilateral group to jointly tackle various European issues. This does not imply, however, that the settling of conflicts such as the Georgian–Russian one is bypassed altogether. As one condition for any further progress on the path of inclusive policies, the authors stress, Russia has to contribute actively to a search for solutions to local conflicts still existing on the outskirts of Europe.

On the other side of the Atlantic, Charles Kupchan (2010), a research fellow at the US Council on Foreign Relations, advocates inclusive policies by suggesting that Russia should be invited to join NATO. Notably, he too sets conditions by emphasizing that either Russia's or Georgia's membership in the Alliance can hardly be thought of if Georgian–Russian relations remain conflictual and are left without any efforts of resolution.

Kupchan's NATO-oriented proposal is obviously far more security-geared than the one advanced by Krastev and Leonard, with the latter being more focused on finding political rather than security-related remedies to the various problems plaguing relations between key European powers. Both of them are premised on the understanding that it is necessary as well as realistic to aspire for increased commonality, albeit differerent from each other in the sense that there is less emphasis on security in the one advanced by the Europeans. Their thinking is more EU-oriented and therefore more oriented towards a 'saturated', or at least 'thick', version of international society. The move proposed by Kupchan follows up on a well-established de-securititazion trajectory characteristic of both Russian and US foreign-policy discourses.

Obviously, from the standpoint of great power management, or top-down approaches preferred by both Russia and the US, the position of the EU appears to be the most problematic. It is difficult for the EU to engage in great power management premised, in turn, on de-securitization, given that the Union has distanced itself from *any* security centred discourses. Yet, it is far from being obvious that the top-down approaches are the most effective ones in dealing with local aspects of conflicts such as the Russian–Georgian war, preferring instead to put them to one side, and with them the not-so-great parties, be they small states or non-state actors. Therefore, although great power management may contribute to the maintenance of 'thin' and even 'thick' versions of international society, discarding the 'saturated' view, with its preference for a-securitization, may still be premature.

Chapter 7
Pragmatic Foreign Policy: Managing Power Differentials in the Wider European Society of States

Pami Aalto

In this chapter, I will discuss the import of 'pragmatic foreign policy' vis-à-vis great power politics. In particular, I will look at how small states can avoid triggering such wars as that between Russia and Georgia in 2008 which are not in the interests of the countries involved or any of the great powers in the wider European society of states. In the theoretical sense, I will seek to substantiate and extend Hedley Bull's (1977) idea of 'great power management' to take better into account the roles that small powers can play in the maintenance of regional order. This is especially important in the context of contemporary Europe, where small powers are more numerous and enjoy more leeway than at the time Bull was writing.

I will first discuss what can be meant by the often heard notion of 'pragmatic foreign policy'. It is a notion that we have historically associated with and continue to relate to the foreign policy practices of a number of both great and small powers. However, we have often not thought very carefully of whether our references to it have much analytical currency and what kind of practices actually can go under this category. Reviewing recent pragmatic literature in the discipline of international relations (IR), I will suggest that this situation has to do with the inherent conceptual ambiguity of the term pragmatism. Second, to round the conceptual problem, I will introduce a typology of the specific *roles* by which pragmatic foreign policy may be enacted. In this mapping exercise, I draw from empirical examples within the wider European society of states as it has evolved from the early twentieth century until present. Third, I will elaborate on the present-day applicability of the outlined pragmatic foreign policy roles by means of a case study of Finnish and Russian foreign policies, as well as their mutual relations in the context of the Northern Dimension policy, where the impacts and limitations of pragmatic action have particularly been evident.

It has to be acknowledged that pragmatic foreign policy represents only one possible means of thinking of and responding to the repercussions of the Georgian–Russian war. Its outbreak is the first instance of outright interstate war in the former Soviet territory since the early 1990s. Consequently the war shook our ideas of what type of international society prevails among the states of the wider

European area. First, we may deem the Georgian–Russian war a result of Georgian idealization of the institution of sovereignty and a denial of self-determination to its secessionist territory in South Ossetia. Second, in a game-theoretic image we may take it as an example of Georgian and Russian brinkmanship in the shifting regional balance of power. Third, we may decide to view it as a failure of diplomacy. Fourth, recognizing the special order-maintenance tasks of the region's great powers (Bull 1977: 207), we may conclude that their mutual 'management' failed to prevent the crisis, especially when thinking of what kind of secessionist precedent was set in Kosovo with the support of the US and EU in spite of Russian protests. Or, we could combine elements of all these explanations. But we would, nevertheless, be left with the fact that the wider European international society of which the warring parties were part, failed to facilitate a non-violent outcome. Instead the institution of war was re-invoked, marking the return of a more narrow pluralist society that many thought was passé. My main question here concerns the extent to which pragmatic foreign policy can help ameliorate the inherent instabilities within the wider European society of states.

At the same time, it is important to note how looking at pragmatic foreign policy can help us to move beyond the great power bias of the English school of IR theory. That the central focus of the school has been on international society where great powers hold considerable sway, has made this bias natural. A framework for extending the school's work onto the regional level has been suggested (Buzan 2004: 16–18). The study of nationalism, an institution which helped many small states enter society, is also part of the school's work (Mayall 1990). However, within the school, there is very scant analysis of the ways in which small powers can influence interstate society, in particular vis-à-vis regional security.[1] They as a rule lack access to the management mechanisms of great powers, whilst they are the ones most clearly constrained by those mechanisms. My main question here concerns the role pragmatic foreign policy practices play in facilitating small powers' conduct vis-à-vis great power management in international society, particularly for those who are badly caught out by power differentials in their own neighbourhood.

It may appear that a lot is made in this paper of pragmatic foreign policy. Some of the practices introduced do not seem to connote enough agency to warrant calling them policies. Yet, my intention is to outline a continuum of options primarily for small states whose room of manoeuvre is on average more limited than it is for bigger powers. The most active roles that would change the character of the whole society are normally not available to them. In instances where a small power appears extremely active, at issue may in fact be a supporting role alongside better resourced actors. The very passive roles determined by traditional geopolitics,

1 See for example, a recent bibliography on the English school which gives no entries on the key word 'small state' (Buzan 2010). The first English school work on this subject mainly concerns the role of small states vis-à-vis the global international society (Bergman Rosamond 2010). In this chapter the focus is more clearly on regional security in Europe.

such as mere protégée, are not of great interest here as they do not connote much of an element of choice (cf. Holsti 1970: 254). Overall, the pragmatic roles to be discussed are situated in the wide middle terrain of the active-passive continuum of foreign policy and they can only be taken on by actors possessing enough resources to make a choice between them. However, actors can enact different roles in different geographical contexts (253), whilst they also have to follow a logic of what is 'appropriate' in each of those.

It may also appear that too much is made of the illustrative case study of the Northern Dimension which from the systemic point of view may look marginal. Some may doubt if these policies represent anything inherently good or morally desirable. But this is not the point. Rather it is their beneficial consequences for the maintenance of international society. Here I side with Bull's (1977) concern with states-based order. However, this does not mean totally forgetting the basic interests of human subjects who through their mutual ties help to bind society together (Buzan 2004: 217–20). In line with the pragmatist tradition, then, what is offered here is neither a universal statement of morality nor a code of conduct in foreign policy. Rather it is an effort to outline possible strategies for situations where we think other foreign policy options may fail. With an eye on such situations we need to be aware of what may count as 'pragmatic' and in what conditions can such policies be exercised.

What is 'Pragmatic Foreign Policy'?

Any action judged to be 'pragmatic' must be understood in the context of the pragmatist tradition of thinking and acting. Following this, there are many meanings and uses of the term pragmatism that first have to be discussed before we can understand properly what pragmatic foreign policy is. First, the colloquial meaning of pragmatism refers to operating not on the basis of value-based principles. Instead, what simply 'works' in specific conditions will be more important. In other words, ends justify the means (Little 2009: xiii).

Second, the philosophical or epistemological meaning of pragmatism refers to how truth consists not of correspondence with the facts as scientific or metaphysical realists might have it, but of successful coherence with (everyday) experience (Little 2009: xiii). Although this meaning of pragmatism moves towards the domain of philosophy, it has clear implications for the field of foreign policy where general theories and big truths have not been popular. As Friedrich Kratochwil puts it, pragmatism has little time and concern for irreconcilable metatheoretical disputes. Instead it suggests a dialogue among those applying different theories. Such analytical and methodological eclecticism is warranted, as in practical contexts we cannot wait to know 'the truth', and yet we need to act (Kratochwil 2009: 11–13).

This is not to say that pragmatist considerations could not have important roles in solving theoretical problems. Pragmatism can help us to make sense of scientific debates for practical ends. This can be done by means of pointing at the simplest explanation, assessing the degree of explanatory power, or making an inference to the best available explanation. Here we confront the major pragmatist claim of how knowledge is always connected to human practice and goal-directed activity. The ability to realize practical goals, hence, becomes the ultimate test of knowledge (Chernoff 2005: 80–1). Here the social function of academic research is acknowledged, whilst its meaning in isolation from the wider social fabric is doubted.

A pragmatic idea of the centrality, grounds for and consequences of action have arrived late into IR. New influences are slowly adopted within this fairly conservative discipline, which nevertheless borrows heavily from the outside. As the origins of pragmatism are in the work of Peirce, Dewey, James and others, in this instance, we have philosophical imports into IR (Bauer and Brighi 2009: 2–6). But in this chapter these imports are not proposed as yet another addition into the highly philosophical 'fourth debate' of contemporary IR. Rather, pragmatism helps us to put into perspective some of the post-positivist perspectives within the 'fourth debate' of IR: many of them have strong normative concerns to voice, but simultaneously remain ill prepared to offer much guidance as to the policies by which their concerns could be addressed (Chernoff 2005: 9–19). Pragmatism can hence help IR return to practice, and provide an idea of the historicity of action. This can then help us to eventually see possibilities for the 'betterment' of the world, which was one of the central aims of pragmatist philosophers (Bauer and Brighi 2009: 2–6) and has been the objective of classical IR theory since the very beginning (Holsti 1985).

For the betterment of the world, alternatives are needed. Policy-makers, who bear the concrete responsibility for foreign policy choices, have an especially burning need for seeing the menu of choice and understanding the practical consequences of those choices in order to make decisions. For this end, they need to make calculations and judge on rationally justifiable beliefs about the future (Chernoff 2005: 5). This simple point is important. It makes us painfully aware of the need to decide in conditions of no perfect information, and limited time as well as human resources. Crucially, when the focus shifts to making decisions, and their grounds and consequences, we must also move beyond simple dichotomies between 'idealist' or 'realist' lines of action. Ideas and norms are realized within the confines of time and place. Sensitivity to the other and listening and knowing the 'rules of the game', assume predominance (Rytövuori-Apunen 2008a: 131–7, 2008b: 325, cf. Kratochwil 2009: 22).

The ambiguity that by now starts building into pragmatism – that many things can 'work' in foreign policy practice, subject to time and place – suggests that attempting a more precise conceptual definition is a doomed effort from the start. Hence to round the problem and develop a framework amenable for empirical analysis, I will suggest a typology of 'pragmatic foreign policy'. Helena Rytövuori-Apunen's pragmatist point that policy actors are what they regularly do (2008b: 324–8), is a helpful remark in this effort. To me, it leads to think of different *roles*, which for Dewey connoted behaviour resonating with expectations developed through interaction or which would be enacted in formal positions (see Holsti 1970: 236–7). Looking at roles can help us to understand better the range of options for pragmatic foreign policy.

Roles in Pragmatic Foreign Policy

Holsti first brought the concept of role into foreign policy analysis in order to account for the behavioural variety that existed even in the supposedly rigid conditions of the Cold War. This helped to introduce more precision into the analysis of balance-of-power politics. My use of the concept of role is the more specific one of introducing more precision into the analysis of 'pragmatic' foreign policy.

For Holsti, roles exist in relation to others. One cannot enact a role purely by oneself. Roles can only be taken on in concrete (regional and wider) self-other interactions. He further discriminates between the others' expectations or role prescriptions; one's own role conception; actual performance of the role in terms of decisions and actions; and the position in the system of prescriptions in which the action takes place. It is important to note that each actor may enact a multiplicity of roles as part of their foreign policy conduct (Holsti 1970: 238–40, 254).

Holsti's idea of role prescriptions and the position of a role in the system of role prescriptions are strongly linked. In the English school tradition, they are both part of the same social *structure* or surrounding policy environment, which is conceptualized in terms of the type of interstate society and the set of its defining institutions. The classical pluralist European society is defined by the institutions of sovereignty, balance of power, diplomacy, territoriality, great power management and war (Buzan 2004: 143, 171–2). This type of traditional society creates different conditions for role-playing than does a strongly solidarist society of the contemporary EU's type – with war being absent, and market, democracy, human rights, nationalism and popular sovereignty, as well as environmental stewardship entering the picture (Aalto 2007: 466–7). Three different perspectives can be mentioned vis-à-vis the structure. The institutional perspective implies the type of structure and types of roles that are allowed within the constraints set by that structure. A more interactionist perspective, by contrast, implies a degree of intersubjectivity, learning and socialization in the more active formation of that role. The intentional perspective adds the calculations and rationality that the foreign policy actor brings into the encounter or to the negotiating table in the process of enacting the role (Aggestam 2006: 14–18).

While Holsti is also aware of the different historical manifestations of roles, looking at them through the English school helps us to make this explicit. Roles have their *historical sources* that may include both material and social features, and are usually associated with concrete foreign policy examples and developments (cf. Aggestam 2006: 21–2). Finally, in order to capture the importance of pragmatic foreign policies for the maintenance of society, great power management and small states' place within it, it is essential to analyse what *impacts* roles have. They can occur at the level of the whole society of states or an individual state. Impacts can also be facilitative or decisive, issue-specific or general.

On this basis, I will next suggest a typology of roles that pragmatic foreign policy actors can enact in the wider European society. Five different pragmatic roles will be discerned: neutrality, non-alignment, Finlandization, bridge-builder/honest broker and multi-vector foreign policy. For each of these roles I will first give a 1) basic description and then discuss its 2) structural positioning; 3) historical sources; and 4) structural impacts. The roles to be discussed are pragmatic in the sense that they are situated in the middle of the continuum of active and passive roles given by Holsti (1970: 255). Very active roles such as Holsti's revolutionary leader/imperialist are not pragmatic in the Bullian sense of maintaining order but rather transformatory. Very passive roles such as Holsti's protectee, for their part, have more impact on the mere systemic aspect of interaction among states rather than the society among them; and I am interested in the latter.

(i) *Neutrality* is a consistent stance or a formal declaration whereby the neutral state commits not to take the side of any other power. In a conflict or war context, this means the defence of one's own territory and non-participation in any belligerent acts between two or more conflicting parties (see also the discussion of non-alignment below). Neutrality is a pragmatic role in that it strongly reflects considerations of the limitations set by time and place, often in the context of strong great power interests and notable power differentials in the neighbourhood.

Neutrality is strongly linked to the balance of power institution. In fact, neutrality becomes fairly meaningless in the absence of a strong degree of polarity. Neutrality is intended to protect territorial integrity and with it the right to exercise diplomacy is retained. It is also an effort to maintain sovereignty as it represents an effort to avoid risking it in warfare other than for the defence of one's own territory. For this reason, neutrality precludes any participation in great power management, apart from the actions that for example, the United Nations can stipulate on the basis of international law. With this Westphalian set of institutions, the most natural structural setting for exercising neutrality is a pluralist society of states. Solidarism, in contrast, erodes the relevance of neutral rights in obliging one to conform with commonly agreed practices and questioning stand-alone policies (cf. Buzan 2004: 49).

The historical sources of neutrality are in the late nineteenth and early twentieth century international law and related political practice. However, the emergence of ballistic missiles since then has questioned the application of the neutral's right or ability to defend its own territory. Other developments have had the same effect: the violations of neutrality declarations in the First and Second World Wars, the total warfare introduced in the Second World War and the globalization of national economies (Encyclopaedia Britannica 2009). The Cold War bipolarity did, however, allow for some grey zones where neutrality conceptions could be adopted – in the European context, most notably in Austria, Finland, Ireland,

Sweden and Switzerland. Amongst these, Sweden's neutrality was performed actively whereas Switzerland's was much more passive or even isolationist (Holsti 1970: 252–3).

The impact of neutrality in preventing involvement in military operations and in maintaining peace in international society is mixed. Estonia, Latvia and Lithuania, which declared themselves neutral during 1938–9, endured Soviet and German military invasions. In Finland's case, a debate prevails among historians of the extent to which its neutrality in the Cold War actually helped to maintain sovereignty. In 1944, the Soviet Union explicitly requested Finland to disarm the German troops in the country in exchange of recognizing Finland's neutrality (Apunen 2008: 192). From thereon until the 1990s, Finland practiced armed neutrality, although throughout the Cold War, Soviet confirmation of Finnish neutrality was continuously looked for. Since then, Finland has maintained an independent capacity for territorial defence in conventional warfare. Only prior to assuming EU membership, were references to neutrality dropped both in Finland and Sweden. Switzerland made some concessions to Germany during World War II but strove not to become identified as a part of the Allied front. Today, Switzerland prefers to stay outside any binding membership in entities such as the EU and NATO, clings to armed neutrality and only joined the UN by referendum in 2002. In Austria and Ireland, the domestic debate in the context of EU membership has made their original neutrality pledge ambiguous (Forsberg and Herd 2006: 87–103).

(ii) *Non-alignment* can be understood as a policy remaining free of military bloc commitments or refusal to militarily commit to any side in conditions of conflict involving bloc members. Non-alignment, hence, allows more room for manoeuvre and connotes a more specific commitment compared to neutrality. In the military sense, it provides a shield for a policy of neutrality and is therefore a strongly related concept.

The structural environment most amenable for non-alignment is pluralist society. Non-alignment, as a balance of power concept, loses its meaning in conditions of low polarity. It is designed to preserve sovereignty and territoriality. It involves active diplomacy that may also translate to a capacity for mediation but is more designed to prevent one from becoming overrun by any colonial, imperial or hegemonic aims of great powers or of any such threats ensuing from their mutual management.

Non-alignment is historically closely associated with the Cold War era Non-Aligned Movement headed by Nehru, Nkrumah, Nasser, Sukarno and Tito, which was directed against the dominance of the two superpowers. What in the wider European context remains from this organizational legacy is the membership of Belarus, two Central Asian states (Uzbekistan, Turkmenistan), and observers in the former Yugoslavia (Croatia) and former Soviet territory (Armenia, Kazakhstan, Kyrgyzstan and Ukraine). Apart from this organization dominated by developing countries, for the neutrals in Western Europe and the Nordic region, non-alignment was a natural corollary of neutrality policy – even though we know of Sweden's secret links with NATO in the Cold War (Forsberg and Vaahtoranta 2000).

The impact of non-alignment can be significant for maintaining regional balance of power. A good example is the so-called Nordic balance during the Cold War where Sweden remained outside the formal structures of NATO in order to balance Denmark and Norway's low-profile NATO membership, and Finland's Friendship, Co-operation and Mutual Assistance (FCMA) treaty with the Soviet Union (Mouritzen 2001: 297–8). On the borderlands of contemporary Russia, non-alignment functions somewhat paradoxically. On the one hand, it offers an alternative for security integration through NATO and hence effectively helps to maintain the outer echelons of what remains of Russia's historical empire. Simultaneously non-alignment remains such a vague status that Uzbekistan – a country itself often associated with regional hegemonic ambitions (Deyermond 2009) – is a member of the Russia-led Collective Security Treaty Organization, where aggression against one member is defined as aggression against all. For Finland and Sweden, holding fast to non-alignment cannot be explained without a reference to their foreign policy traditions. For Finland, it is a means of maintaining the NATO option in the context of its relationship with Russia and Europe; for Sweden, it is linked to eliminating other options and strengthening the country's international moral and developmental commitments (Karp 2007: 45–8). Non-alignment has not precluded these two countries from taking an active role in EU and NATO led crisis management operations or accepting the Union's solidarity commitments.

(iii) *Finlandization* is a pejorative term coined in German political debate, implying Finland's subservience to the Soviet Union's pressure and anticipation of any possible such pressure even before it appeared (Singleton 1978: 325). Sergei Medvedev has interpreted Finland's case as 'self-finlandization' – 'a self-fulfilling prophecy which had more to do with the subconscious complexes and traumas of Finland than with the objective reality of the Soviet threat' (Medvedev 1999: 101). Finlandization can in the more general analytical sense be defined as 'adaptive acquiescence' where in the absence of a balancing option, a regime adapts actively and purposefully to external pressure in order not to become completely dominated by a stronger power or fall into the role of being a mere puppet regime. In the process, the acquiescing state sacrifices some values whilst maintaining at least some core values (Mouritzen 1988). Thus understood, it is an extreme case of pragmatic foreign policy and, according to critics, paradoxical in that the ends may be worse than the sacrifices made in choosing the means.

As a general analytical concept, Finlandization refers to a role enacted within a structural context of pluralist society with a significant degree of imperial, superpower or great power overlay. The role connotes an effort to maintain at least a degree of sovereignty coupled with full territoriality and purposeful but constrained diplomacy. This role is suited for conditions of narrow great power management and/or little chances of influencing it.

The historical cases to which Finlandization is related as a political concept include the Finnish example. Here, foreign policy was geared towards securing the internal development of the country (cf. Holsti 1970: 269–70), including the maintenance of elements of (mixed) capitalist economy. Other examples include, Denmark's foreign policy towards Nazi Germany before the Second World War and West Germany's fears of sliding into such a policy towards the Soviet Union during the Cold War. In the post-Cold War Baltic states, the term has functioned as a warning against policies of appeasement towards Russia even though Finland's Cold War policy receives wide private acknowledgement from Baltic foreign policy makers as one suited to the then very specific structural conditions.

Among the impacts of Finlandization we can count its role in the maintenance of regional balance in the Nordic area. But it also meant over-sensitivity towards a more powerful neighbour and self-inflicted loss of sovereignty. Applying Watson's terminology to a regional context, that role could support a system somewhere between a regional hegemony whereby a stronger power is able to determine, to some extent, the external relations of a smaller state while leaving it domestically independent; or a suzerainty relationship of one country exercising political control of vaguely defined 'overlordship' over the other, whether that control is legitimate or not (Watson 1992: 15). Such hegemonic or suzerainty roles without the Finlandization reflex can be found in the ways in which some European micro-states have arranged their relations with their patrons (for example, the Vatican).

(iv) *Bridge-builder/honest broker* role is a more positively associated pragmatic role in presupposing sensitivity to the concerns and interests of several interlinked actors; unlike in the much more unidirectional case of Finlandization. Bridge-builder or honest broker roles also imply a much more active stance than neutrality, non-alignment and Finlandization which are relatively passive roles.

Discussing 'honest broker' roles in the structural context of the EU, Federica Bicchi notes that EU member states taking such roles may be more effective promoters of EU foreign policy initiatives than 'true believers'. Believing in an already formulated proposal, the latter run the risk of failing to convince the other parties to embrace their own favoured norm or practice, and may be insufficiently open for the proposal to change during the policy formation process among other states (Bicchi 2007: 29–34, 186–8). Bridge-builders can work within a wide variety of societies. The case discussed by Bicchi is the strongly solidarist 'internal' EU international society, which has an extensive set of deeply internalized institutions, and which consists of EU members and applicant states wishing to conform with the EU's society (Diez and Whitman 2002). In such a society, honest brokers in fact only coordinate the internal formation of EU foreign policy. The actual jointly agreed foreign policy can then be anything but bridge-building. But as I will imply below, extending the idea of honest brokering to actual foreign policy conduct, can have considerable relevance in the context of the more pluralist wider European society.

Being fairly generic, there is no one clear origin in political history for a bridge-builder or honest broker role. In a narrow sense, it can be related to a politically neutral or non-aligned status as in the case of the international conflict mediation services offered by Nordic elderly statesmen from the Cold War era to the present day. However, bridge-builders can range from small to big powers depending on the recognition of a sufficient degree of impartiality or equal significance to all concerned parties. In the latter case we could speak of a hegemonic broker – as for example, some US administrations have been able to act in the Arab–Israeli conflict or the way in which the US allowed and helped broker the birth of the European Community (Dinan 2004: 32–41).

An obvious impact of bridge-building is the maintenance of co-operation which in cross-border interaction across blocs can be of value (Leland and Hoel 2008). The realization of cooperation depends entirely on the broker's ability to find and articulate convincingly the existence of converging interests. Bridge-building can be a generic foreign policy role or it can be related to a specific policy issue. The impact on the society of states can also vary in these terms, from none to decisive.

(v) *Multivectoral foreign policy* is a position adopted in Putin's Russia since 1999 as well as in Ukraine (Shmelova 2008). It is also occasionally mentioned in places like Lithuania and even Kyrgyzstan. Its pragmatic nature ensues from an acknowledgement of how power differentials condition ambitions and action. In Russia's case, we find a regionally differentiated foreign policy, which balances between threats and opportunities prevalent in different directions in different moments and which takes into account Russia's limited capacities vis-à-vis the American leadership of the system/society (Oldberg 2005). Such pragmatic, multi-vector behaviour can also be conditioned by a balancing act between different schools of Russian foreign policy-making – realism, geo-economics, Eurasianism and Atlanticism (Godzimirski 2005).

Multivectoral pragmatism can take co-operative forms in a society characterized by joint threats and opportunities or competitive forms in a society seen as allowing temporary co-operation at best (see Sakwa 2004: 226–9). Active, more engaging forms of pragmatic multi-vector policy can also be dissociated from more passive forms of powerless acquiescence (Pravda 2003: 46–7).

The historical origins of this role are firmly in the Putin era perceptions of Russia's relative weakness vis-à-vis the US and, in the economic sense, also to an extent vis-à-vis the EU, Japan and the rise of China. Thus in Russia's case, the policy essentially becomes a tool of buying time in order to build more strength through stockpiling proceeds from energy trade in the medium to long term. When understood as a non-ideological or a 'common-sense' foreign policy in opposition to the more idealist promotion and protection of socialism during the Soviet era (Morozov 2008: 154), the policy also remains a pragmatic effort of realizing calculable interests and profits.

The impact of this role is that it supports regional differentiation of societies alongside the global society that for Russia will always remain the key. In the European direction, it allows an approach towards the Union's highly institutionalized society in terms of highly selective EU–Russia integration along the market institution (Aalto 2007). Regarding former Soviet territory, we witness a mixed pattern of pluralism and solidarism in the sense of divisions and partial re-integration. In Asia, by contrast, we find Russia operating within a largely pluralist society. None of these patterns necessarily represents a pragmatic policy on its own, although there is the aspect of manoeuvring within the constraints of what is possible – and in Georgia's case, war clearly was possible without dramatic immediate consequences for Russia.

The discussed five pragmatic foreign policy roles can now be summarized:

Table 7.1 Pragmatic roles in foreign policy

	Structure	Historical sources	Impact
Neutrality	Pluralist society with salient power differentials and great power interests	19th–20th century international law; Cold War	Mixed record
Non-alignment	Pluralist society with salient power differentials and great power interests	20th century Non-aligned Movement; 'grey zone' strategy in Cold War Europe	Can be significant for regional balance of power; or allow a wait-and-see policy
Finlandization	Pluralist society with a strong imperial/superpower/great power overlay	Cold War Finnish–Soviet relations; fears of German appeasement	Maintains regional hegemony/suzerainty as a partial sovereignty rescue
Bridge-builder	From pluralism to strong solidarism	Some background in the tradition of (Nordic) small-state diplomacy	Maintenance of co-operation; anything from generic to specific
Multi-vector foreign policy	Pluralism; frontiers of pluralist and solidarist societies	Putin era in Russia, Ukraine's foreign policy balancing between 'east/west'	Allows for flexible positioning and regionally differentiated societies

Pragmatic Foreign Policy in Linking Solidarist and Pluralist Societies

My discussion of pragmatic foreign policy roles suggests that some of them are suited mostly for pluralist society, some for both pluralist and solidarist societies, whilst some are particularly applicable for mediating along and negotiating over their frontiers. As already implied, the contemporary wider European society of states from the Atlantic to the Urals is a loose pluralist arrangement within which we can discern a narrower, highly institutionalized EU international society with a strongly Kantian solidarist character. Between these analytically separable societies, we find a 'grey zone' or hinterland which in the geographical sense refers to the westernmost parts of the former Soviet Union. The inherent instabilities within the wider European society – best manifested in the Georgian–Russian war, and which were my starting point for this chapter – are acutely felt in this region.[2]

The major policy processes within this grey zone of wider Europe include the EU's neighbourhood policy and its other policies, Russia's policies and its multilateral initiatives for the CIS, and the constellation of EU–Russia relations, including the strategic partnership level as well as bilateral relations between EU member states and Russia. The next question then concerns the import of pragmatic foreign policies for managing that constellation and maintaining order there (Figure 7.1).

Starting with the first option in the typology of pragmatic foreign policy, we only find remnants of neutrality within the current EU. Switzerland's posture stands largely outside the international society dynamics discussed here. Finland, Sweden, Ireland and Austria have either abandoned this status or diluted its meaning considerably. This shows how problematic this role becomes in a solidarist society (cf. Forsberg and Herd 2006: 102–3). However, in the former Soviet territory, Turkmenistan declares neutrality. While Belarus is also tied to neutrality through its constitution, its long-standing military co-operation and integration projects with Russia throughout the 1990s and 2000s have set question marks over the policy's actual content. In any case, within the eastern part of the strongly pluralist wider European society, neutrality at least in principle offers one means of managing the notable power differentials that all of the region's actors have with Russia, thus also balancing US interests over the region.

The case of non-alignment is mostly similar to that of neutrality. Non-alignment can be proposed as an order-saving and thus society-maintaining role in the context of the debate on further NATO enlargements in the vicinity of Russia's borders. The Russian political class almost unanimously interprets this prospect as a negative challenge (Mäkinen 2008: 316–20). Thinking of the whole wider European society, the institution most obviously under stress is great power management, and any NATO enlargement debates are set to strain that institution even more. For small states on the EU–Russia hinterlands, even a half-heartedly played non-alignment role can remain useful for managing in the absence of further EU or NATO enlargements.

Finlandization remains a possible strategy for several states in the former Soviet territory. However, in contradistinction to the historical case of Finland's acquiescence policy towards the Soviet Union, alternative options may yet open up in the form of 'western' and 'European' acquiescence, especially for the states in the westernmost part of the region. These include the perspectives of NATO membership and deeper ties with the EU through its neighbourhood policy even if further EU enlargements are not on the cards in the short term, due to the Union's own internal fragmentation and enlargement fatigue. In general, Finlandization is a

2 Here the Balkans are taken as a largely pacified region for which membership in the solidarist EU international society has been promised through the Stability Pact.

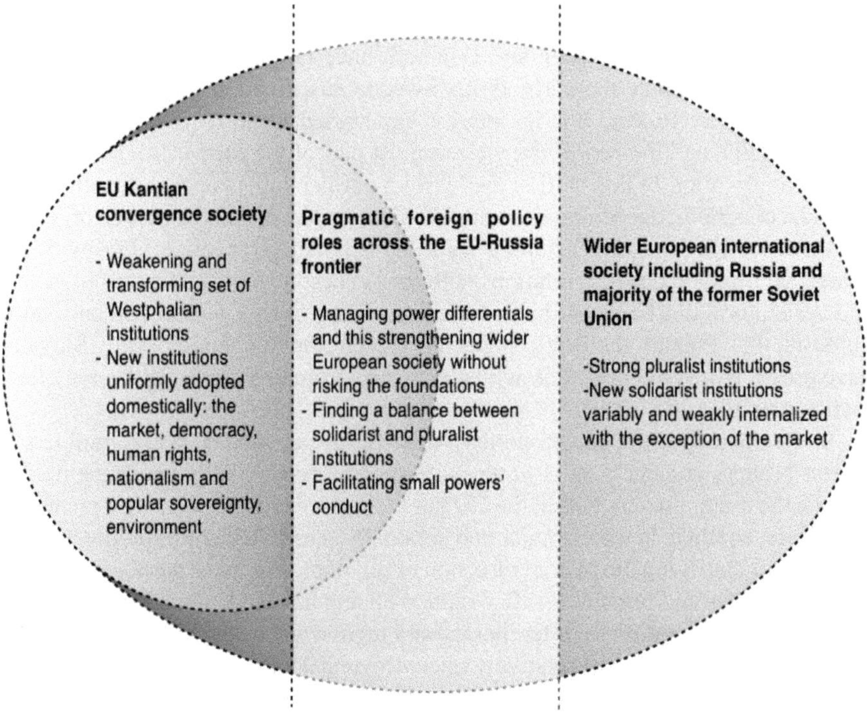

Figure 7.1 The space for pragmatic foreign policy roles across the EU–Russia frontier

policy of choosing a bias. In relation to the Kantian EU society, it would ultimately mean voluntarily becoming a member with equal, albeit proportional rights (if membership is available); in this picture Finlandization as a concept would lose its original meaning of acquiescence vis-à-vis an external power. In relation to the wider pluralist society, Finlandization would mean falling into an actual suzerainty or under-hegemony relationship vis-à-vis Russia. As Finlandization in this way, in the present context and historically, translates into a policy of acquiescence towards Russia, it cannot really mediate between the two societies. This makes its import for maintaining the wider European society marginal. At best it can provide a prospect for disadvantaged neighbours of Russia to survive in case the overall European society becomes extremely weak.[3]

3 A not so distant relative to this role appears to be what Stefano Guzzini suggested to me as 'poodle', citing the example of Italy during the Cold War. Italy first allowed the stationing of Jupiter nuclear missiles on its territory of which the use was under joint US and Italian decision. Italy authorized the withdrawal of the missiles as part of the resolution of the Cuban missile crisis in 1962.

Bridge-builders are ideally positioned to mediate between the two societies. In the present context, Sweden and Denmark have largely lost this potential role vis-à-vis Russia. Since the early 1990s Sweden has invested notably in regional cooperation with Russia, but its interest has started to shift towards the Baltic states, Ukraine and the rest of the westernmost part of the former Soviet Union. A good manifestation of this shift is the 'eastern partnership' proposal, together with Poland, concerning deepening ties with Ukraine, Armenia, Azerbaijan, Georgia and Moldova, which is mostly irritating from the Russian perspective.[4] Denmark has somewhat troubled political relations with Russia despite the fact that the economic and agricultural ties between the two are flourishing (Aalto, Blakkisrud and Smith 2008: 11–12). Poland, the Baltic states, the Czech Republic and possibly Slovakia have probably lost the potential, whilst Hungary, Romania and Bulgaria may have high potential (Aalto 2009).

In the context of the contemporary wider European society, bridge-builders or honest brokers are likely to assume issue-specific roles. This is because neither Russia, the major powers within the EU nor the Union's institutions need mediators for solving conflicts in which major and nationally sensitive institutions are touched upon, or for clarifying the overall direction of relations. For these purposes, existing summit formats and practices suffice quite well and have a demonstrable problem-solving capacity regardless of temporary and regular setbacks (Aalto 2008).

However, in the case of relatively uncontroversial and less politically sensitive institutions, such as the market and environmental stewardship, we encounter issues of a relatively concrete nature instead of abstract and highly divisive principles like sovereignty, democracy and human rights. Here the question is how such concrete policy issues are translated into successful multilateral formats on the regional level. In this context, the capacity of honest brokers becomes pivotal as will be shown below.

Finally, in the case of multi-vector foreign policy, at issue is more an effort to internally coordinate a state's foreign policy rather than a policy with a tangible impact on the actual content of relations across the two societies. That is, while multi-vector foreign policy is a pragmatic yet fairly generic choice for the state practising it, it does not necessarily connote much pragmatism *within* any of the single vectors. Its main value for the maintenance of society is realized when it is deployed as a 'realistic' policy concerned by profits in place of 'ideas'.

Out of the discussed roles, bridge-building remains the most consequential pragmatic foreign policy role for negotiating the instabilities within the wider

4 As Guzzini further points out, the role of Poland can in the more general EU context be taken as a 'spoiler' which may or may not realize its own pragmatic concerns through blocking issues, as witnessed when Poland delayed the starting of negotiations for a new EU–Russia treaty in 2006. My discussion sidelines 'spoiler' roles due to their actual effect in weakening rather than strengthening society, which may not be in the ultimate interests of the 'spoiler' (although arguably in the Danish and British cases within the EU historically, we may have seen such tendencies).

European society even if neutrality and non-alignment provide some options for small states in particular. Crucially, we must accentuate here that roles can be combined depending on the geographical direction at issue. In this meaning, we can in fact entertain a version of multi-vector policy. In a situation where the great powers in the wider European society are in disagreement over order, as best manifested in the Kosovo and South Ossetia/Georgian–Russian cases, multi-vectoring is precisely what smaller powers could do, conditioned by their resources. In the final section of this paper, I will illustrate the merits and limitations of bridge-building in these conditions, by referring to Finnish–Russian relations in the context of the Northern Dimension.

Brokering a Northern Dimension to EU–Russia and Finnish–Russian Relations

As implied above, the most obvious candidates for honest brokers mediating between the solidarist EU society and the pluralist wider European society in the Northern European context remain Finland and Norway. Of the two, Norway is the main broker in the multilateral Barents cooperation with Russia, and an equal partner together with the EU, Iceland and Russia in the new Northern Dimension policy jointly agreed by these parties in autumn 2006.[5] Finland, for its part, as an EU member state with a pragmatic tradition of relations with Russia, helped broker the new format of the policy after the problems encountered with the first version of the Northern Dimension after 1998. The biggest problems included the Russian criticism of it being too EU-centred and thus wrongly 'ordered' (Aalto 2006a).

By this time, the neutrality and non-alignment roles had started to look too minimalist and restrained in the changing structural context that now allowed for more proactive stances. The Finlandization role was also more or less becoming history in this northern part of Europe. In these conditions, brokering a new policy was a handy response that simultaneously helped to cross some of the remaining divides in the region. Thus the new policy must be understood as a partial measure of repairing some of the remaining problems in the European order; in particular finding a more equal role for Russia at least in the regional context of Northern Europe, and partially, in the wider context of the Northern Dimension's new linking with the great power level of EU–Russia relations (see below). At the same time, the Northern Dimension enhanced the European focus on Russia by supporting the development and fast-tracked European integration of Russia's northwest in a manner not compromising Russia's role in the grander practices of great power management. How this was possible and how it succeeded can be answered here.

5 See for example, *Political Declaration on the Northern Dimension Policy*, and *Northern Dimension Policy Framework Document.*

Many EU policies that are directed at or impact upon Russia are 'universalizing' in the sense that they do not acknowledge Russia's role in great power management (Aalto 2006b: 54). Unlike them, the new Northern Dimension acknowledges the need to be sensitive to Russia's needs by accepting it as an equal partner and pledging not to create new dividing lines. This is something that the Russians have repeatedly asked for since the collapse of the Soviet Union:

> The present policy framework document is a joint achievement of the partners. The Northern Dimension partners recognize that their cooperation framework can only be driven by the spirit of partnership and based on shared confidence. The Northern Dimension policy is henceforward a common project and a common responsibility. It will help to ensure that no dividing lines are established in the North of Europe. (Northern Dimension Policy Framework Document 2006)

Crucially, brokering the new Northern Dimension was a process relatively free of the problems associated with 'true believer' type role-play. The policy is declared to be founded on 'internationally recognized principles', but it does not operate on the basis of conditionality, which is otherwise typical of EU foreign policy. In this, the Northern Dimension reproduces the spirit of equality in the EU–Russia 'common spaces' project and its roadmaps (Aalto 2007):

> The Northern Dimension will be a regional expression of the Common Spaces EU/Russia. Russia and the European Union will make the Northern Dimension policy a cross-cutting topic and a tool where appropriate for the implementation of the road maps for the Common Spaces with full participation of Iceland and Norway in matters relevant to [the] Northern Dimension. (Political Declaration on the Northern Dimension Policy)

The policy 'will seek complementarity among its partners and participants' and 'will focus on areas of cooperation where a regional and sub-regional emphasis brings added value'. Priority is on 'result-oriented proposals'(Political Declaration on the Northern Dimension Policy). All this reflects the down-to-earth, practical nature of the policy that is very clearly based on concrete projects with a strong Russian focus. These concrete projects, in turn, are geared around common interests and include realistic short-term targets within a clearly defined area of policy. It is hence logical that the tried and tested Northern Dimension Environmental Partnership (NDEP) and the Northern Dimension Partnership on Health and Social Well-Being (NDPHS) remain at the policy's core. In October 2008, The Northern Dimension Partnership on Transport and Logistics and in November 2009, the Northern Dimension Partnership on Culture were established. The prospects for energy partnership were elaborated at the political and academic level (Aalto, Blakkisrud and Smith 2008), but were ultimately deemed too limited in that area of policy.

The impact vis-à-vis regional order of Finland's brokering of the new Northern Dimension is that it maintains, strengthens and multilateralizes the tradition of cooperation between Finland and Russia, and Norway and Russia, which in both bilateral cases have a history dating back to the 1970s (Hoel 2008, Tynkkynen 2008). In both historical cases the cooperation had some functions for maintaining the relatively low tension within the Nordic balance, hence helping to find avenues for overcoming the rigidities of the then prevailing great power order. The impact vis-à-vis the wider European order is that the multilateral format of the Northern Dimension (and other related regional cooperation) provides a second, albeit more limited channel for management in times when relations between the EU and Russia are strained – which they are at regular intervals. Here we can recall how both the first and the existing Northern Dimension were agreed at a time of EU–Russian confrontation in overall relations – during the 1997–8 war in Chechnya, and in late 2006 with the Polish–Russian meat trade dispute and Poland's refusal to allow the Commission to start negotiations for a new treaty with Russia. This impact in offering stable multilateral fora is not often noticed in most of the policy commentary on EU–Russia relations.

The impact on promoting development in Northwest Russia without compromising Russia's great power role is highlighted by Russia's own commitment in the form of investment into the ND. By 2010, Russia had invested 40 million euros into the NDEP's environmental window, accounting close to a third of the funds committed for that purpose thus far. The NDEP's nuclear safety window, for its part, was funded by the EU, its member states, Norway and Canada (NDEP News 2010: 3).

The limitation of Finland's brokering act is obvious: in regional multilateral cooperation only relatively non-controversial institutions free of national security considerations can be successfully dealt with directly. Thus the gravest disputes and institutions relating to great power order and their mutual management are unmoved. The negotiable institutions at play include environmental stewardship as enshrined in the NDEP. The involvement of private actors in the transport and logistics partnership in particular, relates to the functioning of the market institution. At the same time, it admittedly runs into the parties' conceptions of the territoriality and boundaries institution – which may be slightly modified but surely not revolutionized with this activity. Cooperation in health, social and cultural issues when narrowly defined stands somewhat outside the cornerstones of pluralist society. Yet it strengthens the existing thin notions of shared European identity, when understood in its widest sense, across the EU–Russia frontier. While the balance of power institution remains intact, the great power management institution is supported at the regional level by providing a second, regional track to EU–Russia relations where some more specific and practical issues of common concern can be tackled free of grand (and divisive) questions pertaining to order. The sovereignty institution is not directly challenged by the regional co-operation of today where states remain the main funders and the Russian parties are controlled by the federal government. Diplomacy is strengthened. Overall, solidarist institutions and people-to-people contacts are at best smuggled in with the rationalistic goals of the Northern Dimension cooperation. However, at the same time many of the more idealistic policies pursued by the EU and its member states have not managed to do that at all.

Conclusion

My purpose in elaborating our commonsensical notions of pragmatic foreign policy in more detail have been two-fold. With regard to ameliorating the inherent instabilities within the wider European society of states, I developed a typology of pragmatic foreign policy roles that occupy a wide middle terrain along the active-passive axis of foreign policy options. Of these roles, neutrality and non-alignment can facilitate great power management and maintain balance of power. The benefits of Finlandization only occur when the whole society weakens drastically, and its impacts are at best narrowly regional in fairly specific contexts. Honest brokering or bridge-building have wider structural impacts especially when speaking of crossing the divide between the solidarist EU society and wider European society of states by means of establishing new channels of interaction.

With regard to facilitating the conduct of small states in the current society and their prospects of contributing to great power management, alongside the order-maintaining functions of neutrality and non-alignment, we can also find some beneficial effects ensuing from pragmatic foreign policy roles for the sovereignty and territoriality institutions that these actors often hold dear. Finlandization can in principle offer shelter for small actors experiencing strong overlay. Bridge-building and brokering is a means for small states to contribute to order and great power management through regional initiatives; as was evident in the case of the Northern Dimension in EU–Russia relations. However, this option is constrained by the fact that not all of the institutions that are fundamental to the functioning of the overall society are impacted upon. The market institution and actual incorporation of market actors that are expected through some of the policy's partnerships is a special case here. This is because the market institution makes the whole wider society more solidarist owing to the nature of markets that do not follow state and regional boundaries alone. The market institution is, especially in its more interventionist or social democratic mode – as seen in the conditions of the financial and economic crisis since 2008 – the one and only solidarist institution of international society that is not severely disputed by many of the states in the wider European society.

What emerges as crucial in pragmatic role-playing is skill and an eye for the occasion and audience, just as in theatre-acting. In the language of pragmatism this is what 'works' in a given context. This returns us to Holsti's point of how different roles can and should be combined in different geographical directions, especially in conditions where great power management does not work ideally and parts of the prevailing order are contested. In this analysis, the import of pragmatic foreign policy remains just what its name implies: pragmatic managing and gradual betterment within the constraints set by time and place. Taking into account the human interests involved, this remains clearly short of the more revolutionary evolvement of society that a more principled foreign policy may, for better or worse, produce. For Georgia, the expectations raised by the revolutionary promises of US policy since 9/11 and its harder line in relation to Russia clearly led it to forget the importance of a balancing act between roles.

Chapter 8

A Society of the Weak, the Medium and the Great: Southeast Asia's Lessons in Building Soft Community among States

Alan Chong

International society is an exercise in mental and diplomatic acclimatization to power, its unequal distribution, as well as the need for sovereignties to coexist with one another. It is the central claim of the most ardent proponents of the English School of International Relations. Yet it remains unclear as to how such an anarchical society might exist in the specificity of the world of the politician and professional diplomat. Charles Manning (1975) himself raised the issue of the design of 'society' as a gregarious undertaking among human beings. Questions come to mind as to whether equality of status ought to be defined in absolute terms within sociality among states. Furthermore, there are connected questions of whether, within society, order trades off against justice; or if material gains might be obtained at the expense of normative values. The operationalization of international society becomes ever more complex when one ponders it in relation to the relative roles of weak states, medium powers and great powers. In short, the question arises in concrete terms of how any semblance of 'society' should coexist with the practice of Great Power management of international affairs.

The Russian invasion of Georgia and its military support for irredentist claims in the Georgian provinces of South Ossetia and Abkhazia in August-September 2008, manifest the nightmare scenarios for all regional weak states and medium powers. Furthermore, Russia's assertiveness under the Medvedev-Putin leadership has extended to the denial of gas supplies to its immediate neighbours to the West as part of a design for the geopolitical domination of natural resources (Kramer 2009). On the surface, this pattern fits the category of great power realist behaviour of power maximization at the expense of the weak. Closer inspection may reveal that there may be more sociopolitical issues attending to Russia's position as a great power bordering Central and Eastern Europe. Such issues may range from accommodation of Russia to issues of sustainable neighbourliness in relation to the admission of weak states within the North Atlantic Treaty Organization (Erlanger 2008).

Against this backdrop, this chapter on an Asian region that is geographically removed from Russia and Central Asia seeks to contribute some reflections on the substance of 'great power management'. Hedley Bull's leading work on the 'anarchical society' is inadequate in merely assuming that great power management ought to be perceived from the perspectives of the diplomatic offices of recognizable great powers. Bull's idea of management translates as how great powers 'contribute to international order' (1977: 199–207). This is consequently interpreted in two directions: how great powers manage relations with one another and how they provide 'a degree of central direction' to international affairs. According to Bull, there are six ways to the art of managing order by these powers: balance of power; avoiding or controlling crises among one another; limiting wars amongst themselves; 'unilaterally exploiting their local preponderance'; drawing up and adhering to 'spheres of influence'; and joint action interpreted through 'the idea of a great power concert or condominium' (200). He provides little discussion of the agency of non-great powers. This is reflective of Bull's realist inclination: the non-great powers do not seem to matter, by default, since the relatively more powerful states provide the ordering of international affairs. He does, however, concede that in the application of the above instruments, great powers may have to satisfy some of the non-great powers' demands for social justice, economic alleviation and security assurance (222). But this is achieved not out of altruism but to keep up the appearance of legitimacy as a responsible great power within the wider scheme of managing order. Consequently, it might be wondered if non-great powers could exploit this great power image of vulnerability to their advantage.

Southeast Asian states have responded to this challenge by constructing regional practices that discursively entwine great powers within a community of desirable neighbourliness. This has arisen through a conjunction of factors that favour the moderation of aggrandizing behaviour and the expression of elastic forms of cultural and normative solidarity. It will be argued that Southeast Asian states have come to join a diplomatic community largely as a result of historical accidence. Furthermore, certain facts of colonial legacies have ensured that the succeeding postcolonial states have had to resist or accommodate to their neighbours' sovereign claims. Sovereignty was in fact a western import that was inadequately socialised during the extended process of colonialism. Moreover, the question of development emerged with formal statehood and self-determination. Choices had to be between the extremes of import substitution strategies and export oriented ones. These issues coloured the interpretation of participation within regional international society.

To expedite the chapter, the argument will proceed as follows. Firstly, a brief survey shall be made of the theoretical definition of international society by its English School proponents. The elasticity and vagary of the social aspects of the concept shall be highlighted as necessary tools for understanding the *modus operandi* of Southeast Asia's regionalism. Secondly, the case of Southeast Asia will be examined in terms of its trappings as a regional international society with two broad features: accidental sovereignty, and a learning of 'regionness'. Following this background, it will be argued that the characteristics of this regional international society calls attention to the *infinite reciprocation of tolerance,* the *discursive obfuscation of threat perceptions*, the *'soft' features of diplomatic balancing*, and *open-ended confidence building*. Through these features, small/

weak states and medium powers within Southeast Asia have shaped the norms and rules for great power behaviour. Within this context of discursive moderation, great power behaviour in Southeast Asia appears to be in accord with Hedley Bull's appreciation for the nebulousness of 'the institutions of international society' in terms of 'a set of habits and practices shaped towards the realization of common goals' (1977: 71).

International Society and the Meaning of the Social

International society begins with sociological assumptions about the nature of human society. According to Charles Manning, one of the progenitors of the concept, it starts with the notion of the nation as 'something participated in, belonged to' by individuals (1975: 13). The agency of a group should only be construed as more than a sum of a number of individual wills because 'it was a plurality cohering in terms of, and by virtue of, certain assumptions' (1975: 14). Stepping this social arrangement up to the level of nation-states interacting with theoretically equal units, Manning argued that each nation-state functioned as a corporate whole – a notional person. Therefore, there is every reason to presuppose that international society can be what men in collective units make of it: 'As men behaving in the world of fact produce changes in the world of law, to be appreciated in a special professional thinking-cap developed for this purpose, so men, including men playing roles in governments, produce, by their behaviour in the world of fact, changes in the notional world of diplomatics, some of them also incidentally in the world of international law ... ' (Manning 1975: 35). Applying a comparable logic to a reading of international relations as power politics, Martin Wight argues that the latter description gained currency with the dissolution of medieval Christendom and the concomitant emergence of the modern sovereign state. On the level of the individual, it was 'a revolution in loyalties' whereby 'the common man's inner circle of loyalty expanded, his outer circle of loyalty shrank, and the two met and coincided in a doubly definite circle between, where loyalty before had been vague ... A power is a modern sovereign state in its external aspect, and it might almost be defined as the ultimate loyalty for which men today will fight' (Wight 1979: 25). In this elementary aspect, power is constructed and reconstructed as a circle of loyalties to some purpose.

And that purpose is in turn shifting according to Wight's classification of 'dominant powers', 'great powers', 'world powers' and 'minor powers'. A dominant power is one 'that can measure strength against all its rivals combined.' Yet even when pursuing straightforward aggrandizement, 'it generally also appeals to some design of international unity and solidarity' (Wight 1979: 34–6). In this manner, Wight drew parallels between the expansionism of Louis XIV's France and Hitler's Germany.

A 'great power' is so claimed because it 'is recognized as great by its contemporaries', and in its self-revelatory aspect, great power status 'is completed by war' (45–6). For Wight, the Congress of Vienna first coined the label great power through its mere act of convening a directorate of powers to settle the post-Napoleonic order among themselves. Likewise, England, Holland and France had to defeat the preeminent powers of the day in a 'splendid' war that signalled their arrival, although each had to undergo internal processes of territorial and administrative consolidation first. Similarly, Japan and the US had each defeated a major European power before they were accorded respect by the other powers as fellow 'greats'.

'World powers', according to Wight's description was a passing historical category rather than one applicable to non-western great powers. He defined a world power as 'a great power which can exert effectively *inside* Europe a strength that is derived from resources *outside* Europe' (1979: 56). Wight was taking a long rear-view mirror perspective from the European experience, and as Hedley Bull and Carsten Holbraad explained it in an editorial note to Wight's chapter, the latter set out this definition in 1959 even as European great powers were ironically finding their military and diplomatic power ebbing worldwide due to decolonization and the US-Soviet bipolar competition (Wight 1979: 60, fn. 10).

'Minor powers' were by contrast a residual category covering every type from regional great powers to middle powers and small states that do not even deserve the label of a power in international relations. Although this category is extremely important for comprehending the intellectual importance of the foregoing study of Southeast Asia, Wight did not manage to elaborate on their importance except to suggest that political size did not necessarily predetermine the size of minor powers' contributions to the international society. Citing the examples of Geneva in the sixteenth century, Weimar in the late eighteenth century and Switzerland in the nineteenth and twentieth-centuries, Wight argued that these 'have had a culturally stimulating or beneficent influence on the whole states-system' (1979: 62).

For the purposes of this chapter, it is perhaps a matter of marginal concern in redefining 'minor powers' or 'non-great powers' in specific terms. Nonetheless, some useful working elaborations might be spelt out as follows: medium powers are those whose military and diplomatic reach do not extend significantly beyond their contiguous boundaries; small states are those who possess populations of under 30 million or who do not possess any credible military reach beyond their national frontiers. However, some small states might also be 'weak states' in terms of how states, frail in one dimension of power, such as the military, mineral resources and territorial size, may compensate by building up power through vigorous economic activity, hosting foreign wealth, nurturing able diplomats, cultivating reputations for mediation and serving as models of good governance for territories and populations of their size (Handel 1981, Chong 2010).

In these early underpinnings of the concept of international society, it is evident that the social aspect of international politics operates as that intangible adhesive that brings a society into being. Such a society is likely to be hierarchical where power and prestige are in alignment in most cases, and especially where dominant and great powers are concerned. Yet such a society is potentially regulated by degrees of mechanisms operating on the rule of common consent of the participating states regardless of strategic size. Bull's *The Anarchical Society* rearticulates the social constructivist strands in Manning and Wight by arguing the anthropological fact that all societies are driven by the search for order. This order is not an end in itself, it is meant to generate the structure that supports the attainment of other more important goals of life such as physical safety, the assurance that promises are kept, and finally that property ownership will be stabilised and respected (Bull 1977: 3–4). Henceforth, it could be extrapolated that an international society 'exists when a group of states, *conscious of certain common interests and common values*, form a society in the sense that *they conceive themselves to be bound by a common set of rules in their relations* with one another, and share in the working of common institutions' (13; emphasis added).

The strength of volition in adhering to norms and international regimes is noteworthy here for it then leads one to directly understand that any society of states aims at four goals. Firstly, there is a vested interest by all states in the preservation of their society, and especially the manifestation of that social characteristic in the operation of a system of regular diplomatic interactions. Secondly, there is the goal of maintaining the 'independence or external sovereignty of individual states'. Thirdly, the international society desires peace in its basic common denominator of 'the absence of war ... as the normal condition of their relationship, to be breached only in special circumstances and according to principles that are generally accepted'. And, fourthly, the society of states desires 'limitation of violence resulting in death or bodily harm, the keeping of promises and the stabilization of possession by rules of property' (16–18). These are probably Bull's most heavily quoted passages but they deserve an airing again in the prelude to the Southeast Asian case because they lay the intellectual background for a *social* constructivist understanding of how this developing world regional project manifests a peculiar zone of peace that is short of a Deutschean security community. Southeast Asia is a relatively harmonised regional international society of weak states, medium powers and great powers in the sense that these diverse members have been able to forge a flexible regional compact that has survived four decades of infractions to its norms and even enticed its erstwhile 'enemies' and indifferent great powers to adhere to its *modus operandi*.

Southeast Asia as Regional International Society: The Emergence of ASEAN

The geopolitical region of Southeast Asia is an ideal vehicle for exploring the meaning of the social dimensions of a regional version of international society due in part to its *tabula rasa* quality following decolonization. In addition, this region is also valuable for theoretical exploration especially because it has had to construct society by rediscovering the basic facts of human sociality extrapolated onto international politics. In short, this case study is anchored by the feature of the *accidental sovereignty* of its state actors, as well as its experience with a *learning*, or self-invented socialization, process. Accidental sovereignty is of course a quality that is associated with colonialism and its legacies in the context of Southeast Asia. Learning follows from the accident of becoming a sovereign, Westphalian state: how does a newly sovereign state consolidate its national boundaries in relation to the new borders of its neighbours, who claim comparable sovereignty, without consolidating nationalism to any degree?

European colonialism essentially created the geopolitical region of Southeast Asia. It did not exist beforehand. Prior to the arrival of European power, this region was a congeries of overlapping local and transoceanic authorities. There was no equivalent of constitutionally static secular sovereignty as envisioned by Bodin and Hobbes. Instead political authority was founded upon concertina-like patterns of religiously-derived centres of virtue and majesty. Hindu and Buddhist beliefs partly explained maritime empires such as the Srivijaya and Mataram based in large swathes of present-day Malaysia and Indonesia. Likewise, the Khmer and Ayuthia empires in Indochina also claimed allegiances based on cosmo-religious beliefs. One construed relations of power according to beliefs in the circles of virtue and life merit. Commoners, and lesser princes, owed allegiance depending on the pious reputation of the rulers of existing political realms. They would also switch allegiances upon perceiving the awe of superior military prowess, but more frequently, they would venerate the sheer splendour and mastery of knowledge-cum-wisdom displayed at certain courts of authority. Into this Hindu-Buddhist conception of intra-societal relations entered the Europeans; first through the Portuguese, the Spanish and the Dutch, followed in quick succession by the British and French. Although Westphalia was still some way off when the Iberian powers first penetrated the region, their cannon-armed ships, frequent resort to armed intimidation and mercantilistic practices, represented a more secular and extractive formulation of government than what indigenous Southeast Asia was used to.

The Dutch, British and French reinforced all of the extensions of the unified Westphalian state when they too projected their gunboats into the region, but just as importantly, they actively colonised large tracts of Southeast Asian land. In doing so, they imposed western notions of rational bureaucratic authority upon the natives. Borders and allegiances had to be fixed according to the 'rule of law'. The US and Japan, being latecomer imperialists, merely repeated what their European rivals had done and more; they systematically stirred a sense of nationalism from the beginning of their imperial projects. What is pertinent from this description is that the Southeast Asian native mentality was introduced into the twentieth century through the logic of sovereign borders, economic development, and macro-identities called nation-states. International law, as an extension of domestic law, governed nascent relations between colonial states rather than cosmo-religious imaginations. The legacy of Westphalia spread in this way to Southeast Asia.

As a result, when one examines the writings of the initial prime ministers, presidents and party secretaries of Southeast Asian states, the rhetoric of modernization appeared curiously mixed with socialism, nationalism, Islam, democracy, capitalism, Christianity and Buddhism. Modernization also filtered into governance through the ideas of defending sovereign borders and mustering energies for material development, while *also* recovering lost historical territories once alienated by colonial rule. The *postcolonial condition* was an impromptu political climate of experimentation with every shade of reform, revolution and self-definition. Consider the following quixotic and fragile reasoning put forth by Indonesia's first president, Sukarno, in 1945 evoking organic defensive nationalism while also asserting that it is also a precipitate nationalism with internationalist principles that avoids the 'European errors' of Fascism:

> [M]en and place cannot be separated! Impossible to separate people from the earth under their feet. Ernest Renan and Otto Bauer only looked at men alone. They thought only about their 'Gemeinschaft' and the feeling of men, 'L'âme et le désir'. They were only thinking of character, not thinking of the earth, the earth inhabited by those people. What is that place? That place is a country. That country is one entity. God Almighty made the map of the world, created the map of the world. If we look at the map of the world, we can show where are the 'entities' there. Even a child, if he looks at the map of the world, can show that the Indonesian archipelago forms one entity. On the map can be shown an entity of a group of islands between two big oceans, the Pacific Ocean and the Indian Ocean, and between two continents, the continent of Asia and the continent of Australia. ... The National state is only Indonesia in its entirety, which was set up in the time of [the ancient kingdoms of] Sriwijaya and Modjopahit, and which now we also ought to establish together. Therefore, if you, gentlemen, are willing, let us take as the first principle of our state *Indonesian Nationalism*. Indonesian Nationalism in the fullest sense! Neither Javanese Nationalism, nor Sumatran Nationalism nor the Nationalism of Borneo, or Celebes, Bali, or any other, but the Indonesian Nationalism which at one and the same time becomes the principle of one National State ...
>
> The nationalism we advocate is not the nationalism of isolation, not chauvinism, as blazoned by people in Europe who say 'Deutschland über Alles', who say that there is none so great as Germany, whose people they say are supermen, cornhaired and blue-eyed 'Aryans', whom they consider the greatest in the world, while other nations are worthless ... do not let us say that the Indonesian nation is the noblest and most perfect, whilst belittling other people. We should aim at the unity and brotherhood of the whole world. (Sukarno 1998: 134–6)

Even the more revolutionary, Marxist-Leninist Vietnamese dressed up their nationalist accomplishments at the close of the Second Vietnam War (1964–75) with tones of pan-Asian pride coupled with intense anti-western and anti-imperialist tirades. In the words of Le Duan, the erstwhile Secretary-General of the Vietnamese Communist Party:

> The victory of our war of resistance against the US aggressors and for national salvation is the victory of the banner of *national independence*, the victory of a patriotism forged by thousands of years of glorious effort to build and defend our nation and now raised to a new height by the Party of the working class. Nothing is more precious than independence and freedom. This truth has served as the bugle-call urging our people, generation after generation, to rush forward and chase out all invaders and traitors ...
>
> This victory is the victory of *socialism*, the highest ideal of mankind and the most profound aspiration of the labouring people, which has become a reality over half of our country as well as for one-third of mankind, a system in which the people have become the real masters, free from the exploitation of man by man, a system in which everyone lives in independence and freedom, has enough food and clothing, receives proper education and enjoys a rich and healthy moral life. Such a system is indeed the source of the inexhaustible strength of the people in the North, and a great stimulus to our compatriots in the South ...
>
> We pledge to strengthen the unshakeable militant friendship between the Vietnamese people and the people in our two fraternal neighbour countries – Laos and Cambodia – on the basis of respect for each other's independence, sovereignty and territorial integrity, for the sake of the security, growth and prosperity of each people ...
>
> We will persist in our policy of strengthening solidarity and friendship with our neighbours in Southeast Asia and the countries of the Third World in the struggle to regain and maintain national independence, consolidate sovereignty and oppose all schemes and manoeuvres of imperialism and old and new colonialism ... .(Le Duan 1998: 293–4)

The inheritors of postcolonial political authority were evidently trying their best to adapt the characteristics of modern European political institutions to their new circumstances. Modern nationalism is depicted as appropriating an organic lineage that stretches into the distant past. National claims to territoriality predated the arrival of the colonisers and require either restoration or re-assertion. Moreover, there is the frequent invocation in the name of semi-literate populations at the point of independence that they have understood their predestination as clearly as their vastly superior European educated leaders. Socialism, appeals to a new community and solidarity are presented as being perfectly compatible with each other. In these ways, postcolonial sovereignty was manufactured, or cobbled together, from the myriad concepts the ideological mobilizers had picked up from the European lexicon through their imported education. This 'accident' of independent statehood compelled the new Southeast Asian postcolonial states to confront unprecedented problems attending to borders in all dimensions.

The newly independent states of Southeast Asia were staggered historically in their stages of international socialization since they obtained formal independence in different years. The Philippines were the first to be decolonized in 1946, followed by Burma in 1948 and Indonesia, following a bloody struggle, by 1950. The rest obtained independence throughout the 1950s and 1960s with Brunei being the exception in 1984. The Philippines' early foreign policy sought community with its erstwhile colonizer, the US, through a military alliance, and subsequently joined the Southeast Asia Treaty Organization (SEATO) in 1954 at Washington's behest. Burma sought community through the nascent Asian race relations conferences and the burgeoning Afro-Asian non-aligned movement. Indonesia, too, initially sought a role beyond the region and attempted to play for leadership as one of Southeast Asia's largest states within the non-aligned movement. President Sukarno, the first president of the Indonesian Republic, sought to offset domestic economic underdevelopment with demonstrations of prestige on the international stage. Not surprisingly, Sukarno secured for himself a place as one of the five founding members – along with Burma, China, India and Yugoslavia – of the non-aligned movement whose initial summit took place in the Indonesian city of Bandung. While Indonesia chose to throw its lot in with international left wing currents in the 1950s, Cambodia, Laos, Malaysia, Singapore and Thailand preferred to orientate their foreign policies either towards proximity with their former colonial rulers, or with the US, and one another. With the exception of the Philippines and later South Vietnam, most were not prepared to embrace Washington too closely due to the heightening of Cold War tensions and the aggressive tone of alliances led by the US. North Vietnam had no qualms aligning for a time with both Beijing and Moscow, since both were part of the communist fraternity that had helped secure its independence. Furthermore, Vietnam had yet to be a unified political entity being divided at the seventeenth parallel.

Thus, the Cold War rendered regional international society stillborn and cleaved into fractions that sought community along mostly ideological lines. Throughout the 1960s, several attempts were made under the labels of MAPHILINDO and the Association of Southeast Asia (ASA) to forge a genuine regional organization but these were overshadowed by Cold War considerations. Malaysia, Thailand and the Philippines deliberately excluded Indonesia from the ASA since Jakarta was seen as a stalking horse for communism and certainly, the former three wished to create a loose bulwark against the 'red tide' in tandem with the treaty-bound US military presence in the Philippines. South Vietnam, Burma, Laos and Cambodia were either too preoccupied with fighting communist insurgencies, or gained more comfort adhering to neutrality supposedly guaranteed by the Cold War superpowers. North Vietnam, of course, wanted nothing to do with an essentially non-Marxist initiative. MAPHILINDO was an attempt to play the racial card in 1963 to whittle down territorial and ideological animosities amongst the newly federated Malaysia, and its neighbours, the Philippines and Indonesia. This too was stillborn and scuttled within days of its formation due to domestic political considerations in the three countries. In fact these three states, along with Singapore, were involved in a low intensity war dubbed *Konfrontasi* (Confrontation) between 1963 and 1965 which revolved around rival nationalistic and ideological interpretations of sovereign frontiers for perpetuating neo-colonialism by ex-colonial powers. Moreover, there was an abundance of territorial disputes over land and maritime boundaries that had been originally drawn up by the erstwhile colonial powers. Through these estrangements and false starts, along with a change of leadership in most of the non-communist Southeast Asian states, the Association of Southeast Asian Nations (ASEAN) was born in 1967 in an attempt to steer a more constructive way through the postcolonial minefield of national sensitivities.

Against this backdrop of contentious diplomatic encounters, all ten states of Southeast Asia were also faced with the domestic and external challenge of development. While colonialism served as a brusque introduction into the twentieth century 'civilization' of industrial power and consumerism, the postcolonial states had to pioneer their own paths for sustaining their populations' livelihood as part and parcel of their holistic rhetoric of liberation. Development was officially interpreted to refer to any programme of infrastructural construction and economic planning that contributed ultimately to the enhancement of the overall population's living standards. This would logically mean building a modern economy upon the legacies of colonialism. For states that had waged intense armed struggles to attain independence on the scale of Indonesia and Vietnam, development took on a revolutionary character that was at once internal and external. Their ideologies guided them through a worldview that transcended the divide between the domestic and external: international structural imbalances in trade and investment were as much a stultifying force as domestic ignorance and backwardness in skills. Likewise, for states such as Burma, Cambodia, Laos, Malaysia and Singapore, which were buffeted by their neighbours' popular revolutionary zeal, development could not have been pursued in peaceful isolation even if their leaders intended to. The more integrated capitalist economies of Brunei, Malaysia, Philippines, Thailand and Singapore could perhaps be said to have been disciplined by the worldview of the free market to lean towards pro-western orientations to varying degrees. The Cold War only hardened these official leanings. Ironically, despite these ideological differences in approaching development, virtually every single state adopted state intervention to direct economics towards political ends. It is often argued that Southeast Asian capitalisms were 'ersatz' rather than orthodox copies of World Bank prescriptions; they shared some commonality in practice with the Marxist and socialist states. Furthermore, both developmental camps in the region agreed that economic dependence upon external powers would be a given, despite their ideological dogmas.

In tandem with this realization, came the recognition that peace among one's Southeast Asian neighbours was ultimately desirable as a necessary foundation for consolidating whatever gains that could be made from state economic planning and dependencies towards the wider world economy. The original five founding members of ASEAN – Indonesia, Malaysia, Philippines, Singapore and Thailand – crystallised this understanding by forming a vague, open-ended regional organization to dampen the possibility of military fratricide leading to economic retardation. In the 1970s, ASEAN tried to consolidate its identity by adopting the Indonesian rhetoric of 'national resilience leading to regional resilience'. Jusuf Wanandi, a prominent ASEAN advocate among influential Indonesian political circles at the time, has famously explained it this way: 'if each member nation can accomplish an overall national development and overcome internal threats, regional resilience will automatically result much in the same way as a chain derives its overall strength from the strength of its constituent parts' (Quoted in Acharya 2001: 58). The isolationist tendencies of Burma/Myanmar continues to somewhat defy this logic. Nonetheless, even the post-1975 communist 'club' of unified Vietnam, Cambodia and Laos came to acknowledge that the Soviet-inspired model of pan-socialist economic brotherhood failed dismally to produce a viable socialist island of progress that could remain aloof from the capitalist economies. The implosion of the Soviet bloc between 1989 and 1991 was another important lesson for community-building in Southeast Asia. This led to the enlargement of ASEAN between 1995 and 1999 when the communist states, and Burma/Myanmar, were accepted as members of ASEAN.

One can thus hazard that learning to be 'community' via ASEAN membership required a large degree of local agency in mapping out a path of coexistence that could accommodate a consensus of views on national security. This was a security that related to ameliorating postcolonial borders and developmental considerations. As will be seen in the following subsections, viable regional international society in this context had to have its sociality articulated through local initiative; preferably through a mixture of consensus and the ability to accommodate lowest common denominator paths of progress.

Characteristics of ASEAN as Regional International Society

Reciprocating tolerance and obfuscation of threat perception

Firstly, one must consider how ASEAN overcame interstate animosity to actually operationalize community through its diplomatic procedure. The first two characteristics can be labelled as *the infinite reciprocation of tolerance* and the *discursive obfuscation of threat perceptions*. As explained earlier, accidental sovereignty that came with decolonization created antagonisms among contiguous statehoods that were helmed by elites pledging to modernize their peoples and economies through a combination of scientific applications and redress of historical injustices. This situation of energising popular attitudes and seeking an outlet for nationalist energies generated a significant set of moral, diplomatic and military problems for the new states. It was convenient to argue (Osborne 1970, Leifer 1972, Colbert 1977) that this was straightforward political realism in elite thinking. Every one of the new states, so goes this logic, saw no need for substantiating the standard anti-colonial slogans of pan-Asianism and Third World solidarity when the world economic pie appeared to be shrinking and the Cold War forced local authorities to declare rigid allegiances. The difference that the more enlightened non-communist elites made in creating ASEAN was to extend realism into a sensitive formulation of neoliberal cooperative restraint. Learning from the pre-1967 conflicts facilitated such new thinking. Nationalist energies could still be generated by each of the new nation-states but at the very least, war should not result from them. Hence the original 1967 Bangkok Declaration announcing ASEAN's formation, together with the Treaty of Amity and Cooperation (TAC), the Southeast Asia Nuclear Weapons Free Zone (SEANWFZ) declaration and assorted declarations on security cooperation specified adherence to the pacific settlement of disputes among member states. Furthermore, each of the original five member states regarded one another to be fellow victims of common afflictions in achieving national security. The Bangkok Declaration stated that its member states should be 'conscious that in an increasingly interdependent world, the cherished ideals of peace, freedom, social justice and economic well-being are best attained by fostering good understanding, good neighbourliness and meaningful cooperation among the countries of the region already bound together by ties of history and culture' (Bangkok Declaration 1967). This was explicitly interpreted by the 1976 Declaration of ASEAN Concord issued in Bali which stated 'The stability of each member state and of the ASEAN region is an essential contribution to international peace and security. *Each member state resolves to eliminate threats posed by subversion to its stability, thus strengthening national and ASEAN resilience*' (Bali Concord 1976).

The principal problem gleaned from the pre-1967 experiences was that internal peace and development could be greatly enhanced if external security among each of the contracting states could be achieved between themselves. The latter would firstly require a large reservoir of toleration for ideological differences, the impossibility of relying exclusively on great power guarantees and a sense that weakness could be seen as a virtue by some other diplomatic currency (Leifer 1999). Secondly, the toleration of ideological differences also meant that pre-existing nationally-derived alliances with great powers could be retained under a vague clause stating that 'all foreign bases are temporary and remain only with the expressed concurrence of the countries concerned and are not intended to be used directly or indirectly to subvert the national independence and freedom of States in the area or prejudice the orderly processes of their national development' (Bangkok Declaration 1967). Thirdly, toleration meant postponing any deepening of the regionalism process in relation to economic integration, social integration and any 'supranationalization' of political authority. Fourthly, all intractable bilateral territorial disputes ought to have been indefinitely postponed for amicable resolution. Fifthly, the practice of toleration also manifested itself in the tactically hazy reference to the consistency of demonstrable actions with an 'ASEAN spirit'. The latter code meant that third party ASEAN members could signal to their fellow members engaged in a dispute to cool their rhetoric and implement immediate measures to de-escalate a standoff. In view of the practice of such toleration, one might argue that the absence of any formal outbreak of war amidst intermittent skirmishes over disputed boundaries, insurgencies in border zones, diplomatic fisticuffs, and government organized demonstrations outside embassy compounds, is a sure sign of achievement for toleration *as* diplomacy.

Toleration within ASEAN is conjoined with what I label the discursive obfuscation of threat. To keep the parties engaged in a latent or simmering dispute from straining toleration towards the penultimate step before war, ASEAN's diplomatic *modus operandi* often involves crafting language that avoids assigning explicit blame or naming enemies even if these categories are blatantly obvious. Some ascribe this to the genuine practice of 'Asian Values' (Haas 1989, Koh 1992), but others make the case that this is simply the professional ethics of classical diplomacy that predated the twentieth century. Nonetheless, it is a feature of ASEAN that as far as possible, no 'national face' should be lost whenever any infraction is committed *within* the community of ASEAN. Witness for instance, the reaction of ASEAN members to the Thai-Cambodian dispute over the ownership of a Buddhist temple in the border zone in 2008–9, or the way ASEAN provided diplomatic cover for Myanmar's recalcitrance towards external help in the wake of Cyclone Nargis in 2008. In the case of the border temple dispute, ASEAN was deliberately marginalised by both parties, and they left it to the Singaporean chair of ASEAN, at the time, to declare that 'both sides reiterated that they would handle the situation in accordance with their ASEAN and international obligations' (Purba and Hotland 2008). Furthermore, there were tentative signals that Cambodia welcomed four particular ASEAN members to mediate – Indonesia, Laos, Singapore and Vietnam – whereas Thailand did not indicate full agreement with such a 'contact group' proposal. Ultimately, both Thailand and Cambodia reiterated their non-negotiable positions, thereby 'freezing' the dispute, while de-escalating their tense standoff through bilateral negotiation following internal changes in the Thai government, and a renewed electoral mandate in Cambodia. All this occurred without any direct intervention from ASEAN. This demonstrated the relative autonomy among ASEAN states in deciding the standards of conflict mitigation without the mediatory role of great powers.

In another example, Cyclone Nargis struck Myanmar in May 2008 and much in line with the response from the international community, ASEAN offered help immediately for disaster relief. The government in Myanmar first denied the scale of the humanitarian emergency, and subsequently, put out the rhetoric that foreign aid NGOs and governments could be exaggerating their claims of devastation and human displacement in order to threaten Myanmar's national security. The military junta was especially wary of accepting aid offers from French and American naval vessels deployed outside its maritime limits. ASEAN members could only obliquely criticise the military regime's attitude individually. On the other hand, in speaking through the ASEAN Secretary-General, they offered constructive engagement towards Yangon by discussing the needs and logistics of helping the people in the Irrawaddy Delta that were most affected by the Cyclone. ASEAN was officially pleased to comply with whatever strictures and procedures that the

Myanmar government required of outsiders. By mid-June 2008, it was assessed that a combination of individual resourcefulness on the ground and private aid efforts retrieved the situation for the Cyclone survivors. A team of 250 ASEAN officials was subsequently allowed in to assess the damage and produce a conclusive report on the disaster even as the government continued to insist that outsiders, including UN staff, adhere to sovereign procedures for continuing humanitarian work (IHT 2008). ASEAN's chair, Singaporean Foreign Minister George Yeo, claimed credit on the organization's behalf for persuading the Myanmar government to allow the entry of foreign aid (Koh 2008). In this way, every national government's face was saved, the ASEAN process resumed normality and a recalcitrant member, in the name of regional sociality, was tolerated. In this regard, an aura of mystique has arisen over the nature of the 'ASEAN Way'.

This diplomatic procedure received its most graphic elaboration in the then Singaporean Foreign Minister Jayakumar's speech on the occasion of the thirtieth anniversary of the organization:

> The members of ASEAN come in different shapes and sizes, ranging from a city state to a vast archipelagic state, and with populations ranging from to 300,000 to 200 million. Despite this, no ASEAN member state enjoys veto power. Decisions are made by consultation and consensus (*musyawarah* and *mufakat*). All members have an equal say but when decisions are made, the consensus is respected…The second principle is of non-interference in each other's internal affairs, a principle which is also enshrined in the UN Charter and in international law. Most of us have diverse populations, with significant differences in race, religion and language, all of which are highly emotive issues. The surest and quickest way to ruin is for ASEAN countries to begin commenting on how each of us deals with these sensitive issues. Each of us deals with them in our own way, in our common effort to achieve harmony and stability in our societies (1997).

Some academics have even added that the consensus-making reveals a formula of '10-x' whereby the majority reaching consensus would respect the dissenter's decision to gracefully abstain by maintaining silence on the final communiqué (Anwar 1997, Haacke 2003: 49–51).

The ASEAN Way was likewise employed to find an interim formula for working out a conflict avoidance mechanism concerning the ongoing South China Sea island disputes centred on the Spratlys and Paracels. China, Taiwan and Vietnam have competing claims on the Paracels, while the more complex Spratlys dispute involves China, Taiwan and four ASEAN states – Brunei, Malaysia, the Philippines and Vietnam. The Spratlys straddle not just the main shipping lanes of that part of the Asian seas, but the surrounding seabed contains significantly large oil and gas deposits. China had raised tensions since the late 1980s by proclaiming official maps and a national law claiming jurisdiction over the islands and much of the adjacent waters; it fought a few naval skirmishes with its weaker rival claimants, intensified air and sea patrols in the area, arrested fishermen from claimant states in the vicinity of the islands, and even built concrete military installations on some islands previously controlled by the ASEAN claimants. Utilising ASEAN's, by then institutionalized, formal dialogue channels, China was persuaded to sign up to an ASEAN initiated South China Sea Code of Conduct in 2002 that de-emphasized military solutions to assert ownership of the islands while encouraging the joint exploitation of oil and gas deposits beneath the seabed. The timing was also propitious since Beijing was concerned with countering the suspicions of its southern neighbours as well as of Japan and the US that China's emergence as a great power would be following a less than peaceful path. Furthermore, China wanted to avoid stoking tensions with ASEAN in line with its interest in expediting economic collaboration with them as well as demonstrating a viable alternative to Japanese and American leadership in East Asian security. More recently within the context of rising Sino-US tensions under the Obama Administration over nuclear proliferation, differences over handling North Korea and economic disputes over trade and currency manipulation, the US appeared to side with ASEAN by indicating that Washington was prepared to adopt a constructive role in the South China Sea dispute. While Beijing chose to view this American statement as a red flag to its ambitions, ASEAN states stood to gain from reminding Beijing of the Code of Conduct, while Washington scored political points within ASEAN and against Beijing by merely appearing to tilt in favour of Beijing's rivals without attacking Chinese brashness directly. At the close of the second US–ASEAN summit in 2010, the joint communiqué merely warned of threats to the regional peace and maritime security of the area without openly naming Beijing or the South China Sea. Room for a diplomatic climb-down was thus created in the process (Chua 2010).

The puzzle of 'face saving' as a diplomatic device is perhaps best explained through culturalist arguments unique to Asia. Southeast Asia, in particular, is widely known to have imbibed cultural and religious strains from the important cultural centres of Sinic and Indic civilizations. Ancient Chinese philosophy of the likes of the Taoist and Confucian schools have, for instance, contributed the idea that noble humanity ought never to exceed their comprehension of the universality of facts at any given point in time. Therefore, one should never assume that the other party in any social interaction is either completely in the wrong, nor completely in the right. Instead, each social encounter ought to be treated as an invitation for all parties to reflect upon their moral personalities and intellectual deficiencies. In this way, improved, albeit existential, outcomes can be produced through social interaction among innately given identities.

Fusing Hindu, Buddhist and local animist beliefs, some Indonesians believe that Javanese and Balinese provincial cultures ought to guide what is proper official conduct, regardless of the state of modernization. This is what Clifford Geertz has termed the 'theatre state' (1980). Analysts of the domestic politics of Indonesia attribute this to the hegemony exercised by charismatic personalities in the various leading political parties in the country who happen to have hailed from the historically and administratively more prominent islands in the Indonesian archipelago. Thai, Myanmar and even Vietnamese politics take on similar face-construction qualities when one ponders how indigenous cultural fusions meld with imported religions and ideologies to place a diplomatic premium on preserving one's prestige in all forms of negotiations. In this regard, Lucian Pye's book *Asian Power and Politics: The Cultural Dimensions of Authority* (1985) is the most prominent example of such culturalist analyses of Southeast Asian diplomacy. Amitav Acharya has taken these culturalist arguments furthest through his constructivist approaches to the study of Southeast Asian regional identities and ASEAN's agency (2001, 2009). Acharya has consistently argued that the avoidance of sensitive discussions within official diplomatic forums and the employment of indirect moderated language for admonition, or expressing difference, by foreign ministries is all about creating a uniquely non-western form of 'conducive socio-psychological setting for intramural problem solving' (2001: 70).

I am content to extend Pye's and Acharya's explanations to cover Southeast Asian politics and diplomacy on the basis of personal encounters with Asian diplomats and their frequent indulgence in the practice of producing double narratives of explaining visible outcomes in generic language while expressing private substantive preferences and approvals. In one anecdote, related to the author by a well connected semi-retired diplomat who wished to remain anonymous, it was intimated that while certain medium powers within the region had wished to take a stronger anti-communist line against the Cold War-era policies of Vietnam and the USSR, it was left to the weaker and smaller states to articulate an eloquently strident tone so that it would carry greater diplomatic and moral weight. Thereafter, following the Cambodian settlement and the USSR's implosion, the Vietnamese responded with a conciliatory discourse of catching up with development in the rest of ASEAN. With the proverbial diplomatic feathers massaged into harmony, Vietnam was embraced as an enthusiastic ASEAN entrant with few reservations from the pre-existing members. Through these ways of making accommodation through face-saving gestures amongst themselves, the non-great powers of the region incrementally dissipate the opportunities for great powers to intervene in the region in the transition from the Cold War to post-Cold War eras.

'Soft' features of diplomatic balancing

As is evident from the nature of decolonization, the postcolonial states have had to deal with the future of their relationships with 'emerging powers' among themselves as well as with their former colonisers who also happened to be the western powers and Japan. Australia and New Zealand, often regarded within ASEAN as medium powers, were players in the security order by virtue of both being located in close proximity to ASEAN, and for having fought alongside the British forces during the Indonesian *Konfrontasi* to defend Singapore and Malaysia. Furthermore, Australia had also aided the US war effort in Vietnam between 1964 and 1975. The Cold War also introduced the presence of the USSR and China into the equation. The post-Cold War era introduced India, and both North and South Koreas into the complex power environment. ASEAN's official posture since the Cold War has been to practise inclusive dialogue with all interested intrusive great powers with a view towards entrenching their stake in regional peace. This was, of course, not possible during the Cold War where ASEAN's very formation was intended to add local diplomatic ballast to the western opposition to communist expansionism via Vietnam, Cambodia and Laos. Yet, how was regular dialogue with great powers possible at all, given ASEAN's composition as a club of weak states, of which most could also be classed as small states?

One might explain this through ASEAN's pioneering of an associative balance of power beneath the veneer of cooperative security regimes. One can see this in operation, in relations among its members. As Ralf Emmers explains, the balance of power as revealed by the Southeast Asian experience may operate 'as a policy consideration, rather than as a system, that influences the modalities of regimes for cooperative security' (2003: 52). This operation of an associative balancing is predicated upon two assumptions. Firstly, while the constraining of power is one element in a constellation of security considerations, the former gains magnified importance when one considers the range of policy characteristics of associative balancing: 'the presence of norms and principles, the promotion of a code of conduct, the level of institutionalization and the existence of common interests' (52). In this way, realist modes of bandwagoning are joined to neoliberal notions of the fusion of social power and purpose in regime formation, along with liberal and constructivist notions of erecting ideal-based collaboration. Secondly, the constraining of power 'is dependent on political rather than military means' (52). Therefore, it is likely that regimes that perform services for its members in constraining the powerful in their midst are likely to remain purely diplomatic associations. At the time of ASEAN's formation in 1967, Southeast Asia's states varied enormously in hard power capabilities. ASEAN itself grouped two extremely weak states, Singapore and Malaysia, who had been recent victims of aggression by an almost complete medium power, Indonesia, which had practised low-intensity military aggrandizement (*Konfrontasi*) against the former two. Singapore and Malaysia, in turn, could not count on the support of their equally weak neighbours and instead had recourse to the military guarantee extended by the departing colonial power, Britain, along with its associated Commonwealth medium powers in Australia and New Zealand. Likewise, Thailand was by no means a medium power and clearly relied on the American deterrence extended across from the erstwhile South Vietnam. The Philippines was an aspiring medium power vacillating between joining Indonesia in picking up the diplomatic spoils from *Konfrontasi* and supporting non-communist states in the neighbourhood, while enjoying the US deterrence umbrella anchored both by a 1947 basing agreement and the SEATO alliance. Vietnam and the rest of the Indochinese states were either on the verge of turning communist (Cambodia and Laos) or adhering to self-imposed isolation like Burma/Myanmar.

Although earlier sections of this chapter argued that accidental sovereignty and learning to avoid regional interstate fratricide broadly explained ASEAN's formation, there were also power constraining calculations at work. Evidently, Singapore, Malaysia, and to a lesser extent, the Philippines, wished to constrain the projection of Indonesian power. It was a major feat for Indonesia, under then President Suharto, to consciously pursue a policy of self-abnegation within ASEAN as a turnaround from his predecessor's policy of overt power projection manifested in *Konfrontasi*. The *quid pro quo* lay in the unstated understanding by its neighbours that Indonesia's 'geopolitical primacy' within ASEAN would be respected through a process of consulting Jakarta first on all major matters to be handled by the organization. Jakarta also extracted Singaporean, Malaysian, Thai and Filipino acquiescence to the earlier mentioned clause in the Bangkok Declaration concerning the temporary nature of foreign military bases on their territories. Although this clause has never been faithfully adhered to, it allowed Indonesia to score a propaganda triumph in securing the acknowledgement that Southeast Asian problems should ideally be solved by Southeast Asians. Moreover, Thailand, Indonesia and the Philippines had by 1967 sought to create an anti-communist front to 'balance' the emerging communist axis emerging in Indochina, supported by Beijing and Moscow (Emmers 2003: 55–9). Furthermore, placing Chinese-majority Singapore within ASEAN allowed its neighbours to constrain Singaporean policy should it ever have emerged as Beijing's communist fifth column during the Cold War. Additionally, as mentioned earlier, ASEAN constituted a Southeast Asian front with which to orchestrate an authentic indigenous forum of support for the western powers in their efforts to contain communism throughout Asia.

In these ways, ASEAN was a balance against the military might of the communist powers in Asia even if it hardly possessed a collective military arsenal of any reckonable size. In an ironic way, by serving as a far more credible local source of anti-communist propaganda than the American-supported Saigon regime ever could, ASEAN put Vietnam, China and the USSR on notice that should they attempt to dominate the rest of Southeast Asia they would face legitimately non-communist governments armed with the will to resist them. It helped that despite American reverses on the battlefield in Vietnam, the mere fact that ASEAN vocally supported the American cause and that they would entertain help from the US, was a sure sign of an associative balance of power at work. Furthermore, ASEAN's deliberate creation of linked sets of norms, such as the Treaty of Amity and Cooperation (TAC), and the various statements pledging the non-use of military force, have served to accentuate the contrast between the path of military aggrandizement and a climate of toleration. This was patently the case when ASEAN decided to conduct a sustained diplomatic campaign of delegitimizing Vietnam's occupation of Cambodia between 1978 and 1990. Furthermore, ASEAN's norms were phrased in such theoretical terms that states could sign up to them without compromising national ideologies and regime types. Consequently, the continuous participation of the initial five states served as a demonstration of the efficacy of the ASEAN Way of regionalism amidst the absence of a stronger interstate consensus towards a European Union style arrangement. The accession of Brunei in 1984 further underscored the extent to which ASEAN had developed into a comfort zone for weak states (Emmers 2003: 78–9).

Subsequently, following the Cambodian settlement in 1991, Vietnam joined as ASEAN's sixth member in 1995 followed by Laos, Myanmar and Cambodia between 1997 and 1999. By this time, ASEAN not only appeared as a local victor of the Cold War, it was also the best forum of sociality for states left bereft of an international ideological anchor with the collapse of orthodox Marxism in the USSR and China. Additionally, given the mystique of the ASEAN Way and its toleration of diverse regime types, it was a safe harbour for all of Southeast Asia's developing states. At this point in time, ASEAN appears to be awaiting the accession of Timor Leste following its creation as a breakaway republic from Indonesia in 1999–2002. Given Timor Leste's size and geopolitical circumstances, the path to membership marked by Brunei and Singapore could serve Timor Leste just as well as a constrainer of the bigger powers.

For the intrusive great powers of the likes of the US, China, India, Japan and Russia, the post-Cold War extension of ASEAN into the ASEAN Regional Forum (ARF) offered particular advantages for balancing without placing military assets as the centrepiece of such strategies. At its inception in 1993, the Forum represented ASEAN's answer to suggestions for a new security architecture following the end of the Cold War. For the US, the post-Vietnam War syndrome meant that she would be content to avoid formal military alliances to constrain her rivals in the East Asian area. Instead, following the Nixon doctrine enunciated at Guam by the US president of the same name in 1968, the US preferred to have Asian states bear the primary responsibility for their defence while the US supported their efforts as an ally. Indeed, for the United States, it was convenient if pro-US states within ASEAN could constrain China and the erstwhile USSR while Washington focussed its energies and finance on maintaining its bilaterally-guaranteed military presence in South Korea and Japan instead. This appears to be a fairly consistent posture for American policy from Presidents Richard Nixon to Barack Obama. Washington would in any case favour increased multilateralism and a shift towards the transparency characteristics of the Organization for Security and Cooperation in Europe (OSCE) although it has not been aggressively pushing for its implementation in the ARF.

China, for its part, views participation in the ARF as a means of constraining American power by marshalling an 'Asian lobby' to frustrate Washington's moves to campaign for democratization and transparency in Asia. China's leaders recognise the dilemmas faced by fellow Asian authoritarians in liberalising their polities, economies and foreign relations dealings. Beginning in 2001, Beijing has actively taken advantage of Washington being distracted by the War on Terror to exercise soft power through the ARF and associated channels with ASEAN, such as the ASEAN Plus Three and East Asia Summits, to join a standstill agreement on the Spratly Islands dispute and commencing work on a comprehensive ASEAN-China Free Trade Agreement. In these ways, China is playing by ASEAN's 'rules' and benefitting from doing so.

Of the others, Japan also perceives the benefit in bandwagoning with ASEAN in holding China's behaviour to account, and occasionally summoning an 'Asian community' in pressuring Washington towards maintaining consistency on free trade. On the other hand, Japanese positions in the ARF are no more than a supplementation of the US-Japan security alliance. Both powers watch over each other's interests in the ARF vis-à-vis China. India by contrast is a latecomer to the ARF, having joined in 1996. However, India's presence is significant because of its growing economic clout throughout Asia and its maritime capabilities bordering the vital shipping waterway of the Straits of Malacca. Singapore is unsurprisingly its strongest advocate within the ARF for the simple reason that it counterbalances the diplomatic weight of all the other intrusive great powers as well as Singapore's immediate neighbours, Malaysia and Indonesia. Russia is also attempting to 're-enter' Asia-Pacific affairs through participation in the ARF although its role appears ill-defined for the moment given the Putin-Medvedev team's obsession with Central Asian and European affairs.

Nonetheless, ASEAN's intramural insecurities, particularly among its weakest members, probably enhance the importance of great powers performing the role of cancelling one another's power gravities; this would thereby enhance the diplomatic manoeuvrability of the weak and minor powers (Goh 2007/8). It was therefore appropriate for former ASEAN Secretary-General Rodolfo Severino to write in a recent background brief on ASEAN's workings, that 'the external powers find ASEAN convenient as the convener and hub of regional forums for interaction, ASEAN being benign, harmless, neutral and made up of no less than ten countries. The forums provide additional venues for the external powers not only to engage ASEAN but also to interact with each other bilaterally or in small groups, as the three Northeast Asian powers do on the occasion of the ASEAN Plus Three meetings' (2008: 101).

Open-ended confidence building

Discussion of confidence building in the Southeast Asian region is virtually inseparable from the preceding elaboration of soft balancing. Confidence building in the ASEAN region cannot be compared to the OSCE's precedents, since the ASEAN states are operating with a view towards merely *deepening* the multidimensional coordination of a society committed to the renunciation of the resort to arms as an achievement of community itself. Intramural disputes within ASEAN, and between ASEAN members and intrusive great powers, remain endemic. Even during ASEAN's 'finest hour' in confronting Vietnam with an annual ritual of denunciation at the United Nations (UN) between 1978 and 1990, Jakarta and Kuala Lumpur tended to favour making overtures towards an accommodation of Vietnam and its Cambodian satellite, whereas Thailand, Singapore and the Philippines preferred a harder line against Hanoi and the Vietnamese-installed Heng Samrin/Hun Sen regime in Phnom Penh. Jakarta and Kuala Lumpur had feared Beijing more than Hanoi's influence. While ASEAN's national military chiefs often gather for informal golf games and conferences, there has been no institutionalization of a coordinated military consultation mechanism. Moreover, as elaborated in the preceding sections, ASEAN members entertain varying degrees of consensus over the benign nature of each intrusive great power. The fears of the infringement of national sovereignty escalate further when ASEAN states contemplate the prospect of humanitarian intervention in their backyard. The Indonesian withdrawal from East Timor under UN pressure in 1999 set an uncomfortable precedent, whereby ASEAN contributions to the UN peacekeeping mission in that territory had to be disaggregated from the ASEAN umbrella and each Southeast Asian contingent vetted by Jakarta for political correctness.

Two years earlier, the Asian Financial Crisis had tested ASEAN's use of coordinated central bank interventions to prop up national currencies under speculative attack. Once again, it was a sub-regional response that took place whereby central banks of member states that enjoyed the status of being the original ASEAN founders intervened to prop up their neighbours' currencies. This was, in any case, a series of selective interventions that proved ultimately futile in restoring confidence to the markets. Subsequently, ASEAN in tandem with China, Japan and South Korea produced the 'Chiang Mai Initiative' whereby the 13 states promised a certain amount of consolidated funding for stabilising currencies in the event of a future financial crisis. This has yet to be tested and wealthy Singapore was notably reluctant in 2009 to commit to a tangible upgrade in promising the amount available for rescuing fellow economies. The Severe Acute Respiratory Syndrome (SARS) and Bird Flu epidemics that affected half of the ASEAN states in 2003–5 also revealed a distinct lack of coordination on an ASEAN level. Instead, affected countries had to unilaterally initiate a call for collaboration before an emergency meeting could be set up. The problem of tackling piracy in the Straits of Malacca and the elimination of Al Qaeda-associated terror networks further stretched ASEAN's credibility, when sub-ASEAN caucuses of member states committed far more political and military capital to the efforts than the more distantly affected states.

Confidence-building in ASEAN should therefore be measured in terms of the willingness to coordinate national policies across the board on any particular issue, or in terms of the degree of 'comfort levels' in allowing a region-wide policy position to be uniformly implemented without reference to encroachments upon national sovereignty. The ratification of the first-ever ASEAN Charter on 15 December 2008 by all ten states is a signal of some maturity in open-ended confidence building but it depends on whether any concrete follow-up is possible. This Charter 'binds' its signatories to strengthen democracy, good governance, rule of law and the protection of fundamental human and economic rights of the region's peoples, and aims to ultimately create a single market and production base. Yet, others argue that the fact that ASEAN is 'brewing' incremental layer upon layer of norms for good conduct among its members is a sure signal of progress towards mimicking the liberal peace model of the European Union (Katsumata 2006). The much-bandied talk of driving ASEAN towards a regional code for peacekeeping and other humanitarian intervention is at a standstill given the continuing problems in dealing with Myanmar as 'a member of the family'. Meanwhile, some halting steps towards implementing an early warning system and a disaster relief standby force for population protection in anticipation of tsunamis and earthquakes is a measured indication of progress towards a regional community of fate. This was given impetus by the massive Indian Ocean tsunami of 26 December 2004. A region-wide adoption of demilitarization steps is, nonetheless, still a long way off.

Finally, this 'half empty half full' characterization of ASEAN's open-ended confidence building should be concluded with this encouraging list of the original extra-regional signatures to the organization's much vaunted Treaty of Amity and Cooperation (TAC):

> Papua New Guinea 1998
> China, India and Japan 2003
> Russia, Pakistan and South Korea 2004
> New Zealand, Mongolia and Australia 2005
> Timor Leste, France, Bangladesh and Sri Lanka 2007
> North Korea 2008 (ST 2008)

The United States is conspicuously missing from this list compiled in 2008. With the coming to office of Barack Obama, however, the US performed a *volte face.* On 22 July 2009, on the occasion of another round of the ASEAN Regional Forum, the American Secretary of State, Hilary Clinton, announced her government's signing of the TAC with great fanfare but couched it in the unmistakable terms of candid transparency: 'Amity, as we know, does not mean absolute agreement. There have been times in the past when we have disagreed, and there are sure to be more in the future. But this treaty reflects our commitment to an honest and open dialogue to help us navigate our differences and reach consensus whenever possible' (Clinton 2009). In this way, the US had partially appreciated the advantages of the 'ASEANised art' of diplomatic threat obfuscation, soft balancing and reading confidence building as a formless development. This was further reinforced in the row between China, the US, Japan and ASEAN over Beijing's perceived aggressiveness in re-asserting its island claims in East Asian seas in September–October 2010 on the occasion of the ASEAN Defence Ministers Meeting Plus. In the public presence of his counterparts in the region, the US Defence Secretary, Robert Gates, reiterated the right of the US and other regional states to freedom of transit and navigation and unimpeded economic development in consistency with international law, while he insisted ingeniously that 'the United States does not take sides on competing territorial claims, such as those in the South China Sea'. Not to be outdone, China's defence minister, Liang Guanglie, reciprocated the gesture of dissipating tension through vagary by declaring that 'China's defense development is not aimed to challenge or threaten anyone, but to ensure its security and promote international and regional peace and stability ... China pursues a defense policy that is defensive in nature' (Both quoted in Shanker 2010). With these diplomatic strokes, the sudden 'crisis' was defused through the diffusion of threat speculation and leaving China subtly warned against further predatory behaviour.

Conclusion: The Shape of Soft Community in Southeast Asia

As a laboratory for international society, Southeast Asia might invite sceptics to scorn it as an experiment in sociality that serves itself best as a peculiarly local model of great power management and coexistence with weak states and medium powers. However, this criticism misses the point of how it speaks to the possibility of furthering one's comprehension of a peaceful international society of unequal states. In 'English School' terms, Southeast Asians have only just begun to adore the nation-state as a container of power for development, collective self-respect and self-determination among states. Over almost five decades (1950–1999), they have learnt community through various trials and errors of trying to reconcile their accidental sovereignties stemming from decolonization and the experiences of trying to pursue mutually exclusive economic and political modernization. Recent research has affirmed the value of sociological understandings of ASEAN's existence in this vein (Kivimäki 2008, Jetschke and Ruland 2009). However, these studies have also not fully comprehended the sociology of ASEAN as a society coalescing around particular diplomatic methods. Through these methods, the ten states of Southeast Asia have appreciated Bull's conception of society as an elemental need for self-preservation enacted through some nebulous version of joint pursuit of likeminded goals. Peace among the nascent states and great powers of unequal dispositions became a derived priority. But unfortunately, this peace manifested in the thinnest possible interpretation of the absence of war.

This form of regional international society was locally tailored in its procedures to fit specific conditions of dealing with great and medium powers in Southeast Asia. This chapter has elaborated on four characteristics of a soft diplomatic community as manifested by the driving role of ASEAN. The starting premise was the infinite reciprocation of tolerance that was translated into the discursive obfuscation of threat perceptions. Since all ten neighbouring states interacted through the lenses of suspicion towards one another and towards their respective great power patrons, it could not have been helped that they cooperated using the lowest common denominator of respecting ideological diversity and drawing the ethical line against open military conflict. The wording of quasi-binding local treaties and communiqués served as the building blocks of a society that had to *continually reassure itself of each member's minimally pacific intentions*. Over time, these norms grew ingrained through diplomatic habit – read the 'ASEAN Spirit' or 'ASEAN Way' – and bound local states and intrusive great powers into a community of believers in a particular mode of behaviour that respected inequality peacefully. Unavoidable rivalries and proxy conflicts were conveniently transformed into soft balancing and open-ended confidence building practices. Of course, these very intangible features cannot be compared on an equivalent plane with the current state of the European Union, the most advanced demonstration of regionalism.

Nonetheless, the Southeast Asian experience, writ large as ASEAN's experience, makes an unconventional virtue out of rendering relations between weak states, medium powers, and great powers towards a non-military competitive field that mixes realism with neoliberal characteristics. 'Soft community' is the best description of this condition of regionalism. Why was soft community possible in managing the behaviour of great powers? While this chapter could have emphasised even more the domineering agency of cultural filters at play, this has been treated elsewhere in some detail and subject to equal intensity of contestation (Haas 1989, Haacke 2003, Chong 2004, Acharya 2009). Other reasons lie in the conjunction of learning trajectories experienced by the various Asian leadership elites of the severely taxing and dilemmatic demands of national independence, pursuing dependent economic development and waging territorial wars with one's immediate neighbours utilising scarce resources. The ASEAN experience in moderating great power behaviour is perhaps also a diplomatic constructivist's dream come true: words alone carry weight in defining the standards of desirable and undesirable behaviour within a highly specific local contingent context of postcolonial development. Detractors of a constructivist reading might well counter-argue that ASEAN's diplomacy of discursive moderation was made possible by the operation of an approximate balance of power equilibrium amongst the intrusive great powers themselves (Goh 2007/8). The diplomatic constructivist would then counter that it is through skilful persuasion in grand diplomatic conferences under the monikers of the ARF, ASEAN Plus Three, the East Asia Summit and the innumerable ASEAN-driven Dialogues that a balance of power can be set in motion as the invisible backdrop to entangling the Weak, the Medium and the Great in a regional international society that would bias their members towards political moderation. Perhaps, this really is how norms triumph over pure interests in Southeast Asia.

Chapter 9
Glorification and its Modes: Emulation, Recognition and Acclamation

Alexander Astrov

It is time now to return to the general question of the volume: What does the Russian–Georgian war of 2008 tell us about great power management as an institution of international society? Different theoretical approaches employed by the contributors seem to suggest the same conclusion: The outbreak of the war signified not merely an unfortunate mishandling of an otherwise sound institution but also the inadequacy of the institution itself, in its 'classical' formulation by Bull, for the current global order.

Thus, a policy-oriented analysis of Russian and EU attempts to 'conduct the conduct' of the newly independent post-Soviet states reveals the inability of both actors to translate their supremacy in either 'soft' or 'hard' power into effective management of the regional society of states. Sergei Prozorov relates this failure to the specific postcommunist condition of today's Russia, which he interprets as a localized 'end of history' that renders any return to great power politics impossible: behind Moscow's great-power rhetoric there is a peculiar form of opportunism aimed at the management of the exception that has become a rule in Russia's domestic politics. The US, in turn, according to Irina Papkova, rejects not only what its policy-makers perceive as Russia's great-power ambitions but the idea of greatpowerhood as such. This rejection was most explicit at the time of the Georgian war and since then has been followed up by a pragmatic 'reset' of US–Russian relations reminiscent of the 'classical' great power management advocated by Andrey Makarychev in his analysis of the relations between Russia and NATO. Yet, as argued by Pertti Joenniemi, such a return to great power management, and thus to a 'thin' or 'pluralist' configuration of international society may be problematic within broader EU–US–Russia relations where significant normative pressures require more attention to the position of small states and non-state actors. Furthermore, Pami Aalto's analysis of the 'pragmatic foreign policy' of small states suggests that pragmatism may well be compatible with an activist promotion of 'thicker', 'solidarist' forms of international society. Finally, Alan Chong's account of the history and practices of one such regional society, ASEAN, demonstrates how small states can manage their own society while keeping great powers at bay.

All in all, then, the preliminary analysis of great power management undertaken in this volume suggests a conclusion similar to that already reached by those who focussed on other institutions of international society identified by Bull, such as war (De Landa 1991) or diplomacy (Wiseman 1999): neither war, diplomacy, nor great power management can be considered only in terms of relations between states and therefore, other, increasingly significant actors must be taken into account. Or to put it in terms suggested by Buzan (2004) and cited by almost every contributor to this volume, global order may be transforming from international into world society and the task of theory is to understand this transformation. So, what can further investigation of great power management contribute to such an understanding?

I have argued in the introduction that, contrary to Bull's analysis, the transformation in question does not render great power management obsolete, but significantly transforms the character of 'management', 'power' and 'greatness'. What I want to indicate now is how by focussing on the changing modalities of glorification, we can refine the English School's articulation of the three traditions of international thought generally and its understanding of world society in particular.

The three traditions and corresponding configurations of global order in terms of which the English School understands world politics are summarized by Buzan (2001: 474–6) as follows:

> International system (Hobbes/Machiavelli) is about power politics amongst states, and Realism puts the structure and process of international anarchy at the centre of IR theory. ... International society (Grotius) is about the institutionalization of shared interest and identity amongst states, and Rationalism puts the creation and maintenance of shared norms, rules and institutions at the centre of IR theory. ... World society (Kant) takes individuals, non-state organizations and ultimately the global population as a whole as the focus of global societal identities and arrangements, and Revolutionism puts transcendence of the state system at the centre of IR theory.

It is important for Buzan's reading of the three traditions and configurations of order defined by them, that they co-exist and continuously blur into each other. However, this blurring should be accompanied by the transformation of the English School's key-concepts which may change their meaning while crossing the permeable boundaries of the traditions. In fact, such conceptual blurring is detectable already in Buzan's own taxonomy. Following Ole Wæver's (1992) suggestion that today's Revolutionism is driven by 'liberal political reason', rather than eschatological constructions of the past, Buzan presents the emergent world society as a web of relations between state and non-state actors perfectly compatible with Foucault's account of governmentality outlined in the introduction to this volume. This compatibility may be radicalized further, along the lines of Hardt and Negri's (2000) analysis, so that Buzan's Revolutionism, culminating in a non-imperialist, network-like Empire, would indeed seem to blur with the imperial constructions of offensive Realism. However, one of the defining characteristics of neoliberal governmentality, as argued by Prozorov in his chapter, is precisely its immanence and therefore the rejection of that very transcendence which is

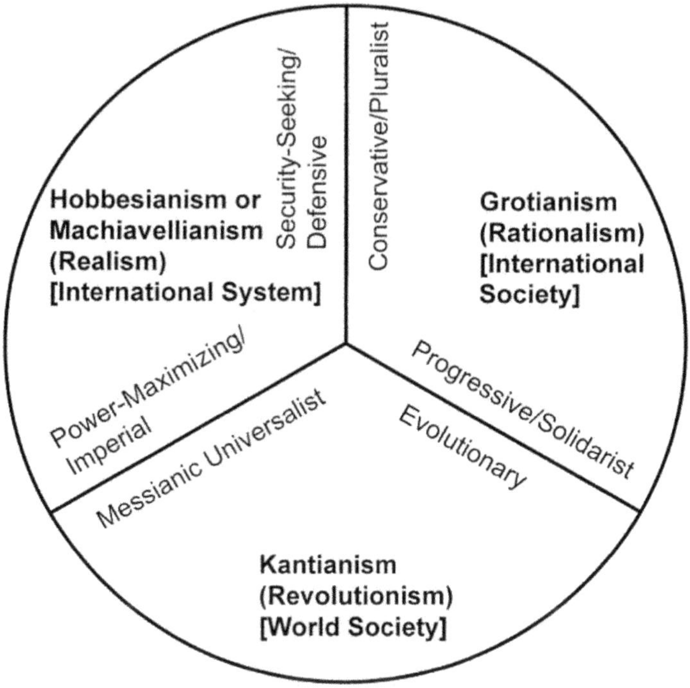

Figure 9.1 The taxonomy of order and traditions in terms of which the English School understands International Relations

supposed to define Revolutionism. Put differently, in this manner we may indeed move from international society to some global, non-Westphalian arrangement. However, in what sense this arrangement is connected to either Kantianism or Revolutionism or, in fact, any strong notion of 'society', remains unclear.

This is where attention to 'greatness' or historical practices of glorification may help to clarify excessive conceptual blurring. One of the beginnings of modern governmentality, according to Foucault, is to be found in the anti-Machiavellian literature that put forward a view of government both multifarious, ranging from the governance of the family to that of the state, and immanent, opposed to the underlying principle of Machiavellian thought: 'For Machiavelli, the Prince exists in a relationship of singularity and externality, of transcendence to his principality' (Foucault 2007: 91). This relationship of externality or transcendence is due not merely to the circumstances of his acquisition of the principality but, as Louis Althusser (1999: 122–3) emphasizes, Machiavelli's focus on the problem of the new prince in a new principality and his repeated insistence that 'one must be alone to found a state'. This singularity of the prince results from a combination of *virtù* and *fortuna*, but it is this very combination that impels him to maximize his *grandezza*: *virtù* is the only weapon he has for taming *fortuna*, yet it is the exercise of *virtù* that exposes him to the vicissitudes of *fortuna* in the first place.

In contemporary IR, this predicament of the new prince in a new principality was explored by Erik Ringmar (1996) through the example of Gustav Adolf's decision to intervene in the Thirty Years' War; a decision which, according to Ringmar, cannot possibly be explained on utilitarian grounds. Ringmar's (150–1) own explanation hinges on a close reading of Machiavellian themes in Gustav Adolf's self-understanding, the most prominent among them being that of both men and states as self-governing subjects without any 'foundations', 'proud self-fashioners who created their selves through the sheer powers of their imagination' and for whom to be 'great' or famous 'was not simply a matter of being socially appreciated or popular, but instead a matter of being reputed *some-one* or famous for *some-thing*; to have a socially recognized identity'. In the end, it was the interplay of unrestrained self-fashioning, what Hume would later call 'the jealous emulation of each other's glory', and desire for recognition that forced Gustav Adolf to demand from Austria by force what it was not prepared to grant Sweden freely.

This interplay explains why Gustav Adolf, a Machiavellian, could also be an admiring reader of Grotius: 'By submitting ourselves to a certain set of rules we not only choose the "correct" action over the "incorrect" one, but we also identify ourselves – and we ask others to recognize us – as the kind of person to whom these rules apply' (151). The underlying Hegelian logic of the struggle for recognition which here synthesizes Machiavellianism and Grotianism was also employed within the English School to account for the evolution of diplomacy into a truly global system (Der Derian 1987). And more recently an attempt has been made to extend this logic further, so as to account for the inevitable emergence of the world state (Wendt 2003). Since all these accounts remain state-centric, however, their heuristic value for my purposes is limited to the identification of two distinct 'languages' or modes of glorification – emulation and recognition – characteristic of Realism and Rationalism respectively.

To see what kind of glorification may be at work in Revolutionism, consider the following, clearly Machiavellian, statement with which Hans Morgenthau (1974b: 61) concludes one of two short essays about Kissinger's diplomacy: 'The statesman, in order to be truly great regardless of success or failure, must behold himself not as the infallible arbiter of the destiny of men, but as the handmaiden of something which he may use but cannot control. Fortuna smiles only on those who concede her the last word'. Interestingly, this is meant as a reproach or, at least, a caution for the Secretary of State whose 'diplomacy of movement' Morgenthau considers to be perfectly Realist. Furthermore, Morgenthau charges Kissinger with a certain lack of character or *virtù* needed for the attainment of true greatness, and yet at the same time attributes the successes of his diplomacy to this very quality: the lack of any fixed identity. Kissinger is an Odysseus-like *polytropos*, a 'many-sided' character, the one 'of many appearances', who, like a good actor, 'does not play the role of Hamlet today, of Caesar tomorrow, but who is Hamlet today and Caesar tomorrow', which makes him a perfect diplomat but a somewhat incomplete statesman (57).

What is puzzling in this is that the very quality of *polytropos* is what Morgenthau understands as a defining characteristic of a possible alternative global order. This is stated most clearly in the last three parts of *Politics Among Nations* united by a common heading, 'the problem of peace'. Peace, according to Morgenthau (1973: 517), 'cannot be preserved through the limitation of national sovereignty, and the reasons for that in the very nature of the relations among states'. The task, then, is to inhabit the world in urgent need of transformation for which it is not ready yet. What makes diplomacy a 'solution' to this situation is not its connection to power politics as such or its noble past. Rather, it is the versatility and flexibility of the diplomat's mind as opposed to that of the technocrat or the ideology-driven crusader. Versatility and flexibility are important not merely as antidotes to technology but mostly because of their congruity with the task at hand: the gradual transformation of international order in the direction of world state.

World state, as any other state in history, has to be antedated by a 'community' over which it will govern; in this case, the 'world' community. Morgenthau considers two approaches. The first one, which he terms 'cultural', aims at enlarging currently existing 'national' identities and blending them into a global one similar in kind. The second, 'functional', creates new identities and loyalties which gradually overlay the currently existing ones. The attractiveness of the second approach consists in its promise of a dense web of fluid and malleable identities, held together not by cultural homogeneity but by a gradually developed loyalty towards the interrelated practical activities and international agencies through which these activities are organized. Actually-existing states, through their participation in the work of various international agencies where state-identity changes from one agency to the other, demonstrate their preserved capacity for versatility and flexibility which was historically characteristic of diplomacy.

Now, whatever else Kissinger's détente might have been, it was certainly an attempt at putting back into motion the rigid world of the Cold War for the sake of that very versatility and flexibility that Morgenthau himself advocated. Yet, Kissinger's versatility and flexibility were pursued, if not for their own sake, then clearly in the name of the existing international order, rather than Morgenthau's imagined world community. This order, however, was, according to Morgenthau (1974a: 57), unsustainable; and not only on account of the risks dramatically heightened by nuclear weapons and ideological crusading, but also because of the general crisis of the nation-state: 'the technological revolutions of our time have rendered the Nation-State's principle of political organization as obsolete as the first modern industrial revolution of the steam-engine did feudalism'. When put into motion, under these conditions, the nation-state, great and super-powers in particular, rather than restoring the legitimacy of power-politics, indulges in the *Realpolitik* of the spheres of influence and other such techniques which lack the substance of Realism.

Most likely, Kissinger did not need lessons either in the predicament of the new prince in a new principality (this is how he understood himself and the US while in office) or in specific German variations on Machiavellianism. His criticism of Metternich, for example, clearly echoes Schmitt's (1986) critique of 'political romanticism': 'Lacking in Metternich is the attribute which has enabled the spirit to transcend an impasse at so many crises in history: the ability to contemplate an abyss, not with the detachment of a scientist, but as a challenge to overcome – or to perish in the process' (Kissinger 1957: 322). When he approvingly cites 'the great restrainer', Bismarck, it is again difficult not to overhear Schmittian account of katechonic greatness: 'That which is imposing here on earth … has always something of the quality of the fallen angel who is beautiful but without peace, great in his conceptions and exertions but without success, proud and lonely' (Kissinger 1968: 922). What he may not understood, according to Morgenthau, is that without an eschatological conception of history, at a point when history 'ends', however temporary or localized this ending may be, in the absence of a transformative political project, *katechon* degenerates into an opportunistic schemer, an *intrigant*, as argued by Prozorov in the case of Russia, while great power management transforms into an ongoing management of the state of exception.

But what about the idea of *polytropos*, as a positive core of the diplomatic tradition? Can it be reformulated, to refer both to the Machiavellian preference for the singularity and transcendence of a new beginning and the Kantian idea of humanity thus formulated by Hannah Arendt (1971, II: 272): 'man's dignity demands that he is seen, every single one ... in his particularity, reflecting as such, but without any comparison and independent of time, mankind in general'? Since this formulation is based on the Kantian *Critique of Aesthetic Judgement*, let me outline the contours of such a reformulation by drawing on two historical examples of artistic engagement with politics. Separated by almost six centuries of European history, both are nevertheless located on the same boundary within Buzan's taxonomy, the one separating Rationalism from Revolutionism.

The first comes from Quentin Skinner's detailed reconstruction of the pre-Machiavellian formulations of the Renaissance republicanism in the frescoes of Ambrogio Lorenzetti painted between 1337 and 1339. The frescoes present the glory of a well-governed, peaceful republic. Meticulously deciphering the frescoes, Skinner (2002: 111) focusses on a group of young boys performing some ritual on a sun-lit square and argues that the performance is a dance whose function is not merely to express 'the *gaudium* we feel at the rule of *iustitia* and the resulting attainment of *pax* and *gloria*'. The dance is also an artistic expression of citizens' active participation in the life of the city; something which was not to be taken for granted in fourteenth century Italy, where most of the republics gave way to tyrannies. Resulting political theories justified this transformation by associating *grandezza* and *virtus* exclusively with the princes and suggesting that the citizens should enjoy *otium*, a form of good life achieved through contemplative withdrawal from politics (131). By contrast, in Lorenzetti's 'republican' frescoes, according to Skinner's reconstruction, citizens are not only celebrating the glory of the republican city, metaphorically portrayed through light, but are bringing it about by banishing through their performance the condition of *tristia*, resulting precisely from a withdrawal from public life (112–16).

Intriguingly, all the main metaphors reconstructed by Skinner reappear in 1917 in another artistic creation. Now, however, the meaning of some of them is radically transformed. In a letter written to his mother from Petrograd shortly after the February revolution in Russia, Alexander Blok (1983, VI: 274, 281) describes the order that suddenly befell the city: '*the city is in the state of such exemplary order as it has never experienced before.* … These moments, of course, are very dangerous; but danger, if it does lie ahead, is *illuminated*, which has not happened for a long time, perhaps never, not in our lifetime'. Here as well, the pairing of light and order is meant to convey the experience of glory, but now the glory of a revolution. And again, as with Lorenzetti, this order and glory are directly opposed not to the tyranny as such but to 'boredom', that appears in Blok in many different contexts, including his World War I diaries: 'It is difficult to say what is more sickening: that bloodshed, or that idleness, that boredom, that banality' (Mochulsky 1983: 394). The choice of words here is clearly not accidental. At around the same time, Blok's fellow-poet, Osip Mandelstam, composed a series of poems which he later published in a volume entitled *Tristia*. Both men were seriously engaged in studying those very Roman texts which, according to Skinner, influenced Lorenzetti's contemporaries. So, Paul Celan (1986: 61) in his notes to the translation of Blok's *The Twelve* had good reason to believe that the heart of the poem, written already after the October revolution, is its eighth section, beginning with 'O grief, O boring boredom, deadly!'

The most controversial part of the poem, of course, is its ending in which the violent dance-like movement of the twelve revolutionary guards transforms into a ceremonial procession headed by Christ. Even more scandalous, perhaps, were some of Blok's private notes written in response to accusations of blasphemy: 'The terrible thought of these days: it is not that the Red Guard are 'not worthy' of Jesus, Who is with them now; it is precisely that it is still He Who is with them, whereas it should be Another' (Pyman 1980 :305). Yet, it is precisely this 'terrible thought' that may hold the key to the understanding of the transformation through which Rationalism blurs into Revolutionism, while the same constellation of metaphors and ideas changes its meaning from the glorification of a peaceful order to that of the violent revolution.

Most of the evidence pieced together by Skinner comes either from theological texts or religious frescoes painted at the time. In other words, the beginnings of republican political thought are not only Roman, as Skinner insists, but also theological. In this way, Skinner's reconstruction supports Schmitt's famous contention that all political concepts are secularized theological concepts, which, in turn, supports the grounding of the theory of the state in the figure of the *katechon*, the 'restrainer' of lawlessness. However, this connection renders problematic Lorenzzeti's affirmation of republican virtues. If the portrayal of the Sienese governing body is indeed, as Skinner suggests, influenced by Giotto's *Last Judgement*, if the young dancers are indeed influenced by Andrea di Bunaiuto's *Allegory of the Church* (Skinner 2002: 204–5), then both influences refer to an explicitly a-political condition of the end of history in which, according to Giorgio

Agamben's (2007) reading of the theological debates of the time, glorification is no longer related to the interplay of self-assertion/emulation and recognition or *tristia* and republican glory, but appears in the form of continuous acclamation which neither brings about any political change nor allows for the contemplative withdrawal.

Put differently, acclamation is an activity appropriate for a world in which, to paraphrase Blok (1983, IV: 289), 'events no longer happen'. By contrast, the 'greatest temptation' of 'our earthly existence' is precisely the idea 'that *there may be events*. ... We may argue, differ in opinions to the point of mutual hatred, but we are united in our knowledge that … the life of mankind is eventful: world wars do happen, revolutions do happen, Christ is being born'. And events, for Blok, are not possible within the framework of *a priori* given or known laws.

So, 'Another' who should have appeared in the poem, according to the 'terrible thought', is indeed 'the lawless', *anomos*, but it is neither the antichrist whose coming *katechon* is restraining, nor merely the *intrigant* into which *katechon* itself is transforming. Rather, in accordance with Agamben's (2005: 111) re-reading of Paul's letter which Schmitt used to support his theory of the state, it is 'possible to conceive of *katechon* and *anomos* not as two separate figures ... but as one single power before and after' the messianic event. Consequently, no political theology can be grounded in Paul's vision. But what is also revealed in the messianic event is the general lawlessness of messianic time. It is a lawlessness which entails a Kantian 'movement from singularity to singularity and, without ever leaving singularity, transforms every singular case into an *exemplar* of a general rule that can never be stated a priori' (Agamben 2009: 22).

If this is indeed an image of mankind reflected in every individual taken as a Kantian end-in-itself (and also Aristotelian 'good-for-nothing') whose personality cannot be exhausted by any project or any presupposed identity, then we should discard Wight's (1966: 33) articulation of International Theory as pointing towards political theology of 'the ultimate experience of life and death, national existence and national extinction' and re-think instead Bull's (1977: 22) contention that order 'among mankind as a whole is something wider than order among states; something more fundamental and primordial than it; and also ... something morally prior to it' as a more fruitful starting point for a theory of world society.

As far as the role of great power management in such theory is concerned, we may, again, follow Agamben's suggestion that, under the conditions of global 'police' governmentality, glorification assumes the form of continuous acclamation whose task is not to affirm the citizens active political existence, but to conceal and to capture the *exemplary* 'lawlessness' of human life. In this manner, acclamation joins emulation and recognition as the third mode of glorification within the tripartite framework of the English School. In so far as the three configurations of order may indeed be present concurrently in world politics, it would be interesting to investigate empirically how different modalities of greatness and therefore different modes of great power management may be expressed in three different conceptual languages.

Bibliography

Aalto, P. 2006a. The Role of the Northern Dimension in EU–Russia Relations, *The Two-Level Game: Russia's Relations with Great Britain, Finland and the European Union*, edited by H. Smith. Helsinki: Aleksanteri Series 2/2006, 103–22.

Aalto, P. 2006b. *European Union and the Making of a Wider Northern Europe*. London: Routledge.

Aalto, P. 2007. Russia's Quest for International Society and Prospects of Regional Level International Societies. *International Relations*, 21(4): 459–78.

Aalto, P. 2008. Commentary: Yes, But It's the Energy Dialogue That Really Matters. *Europe's World*, Summer 2008: 53–5.

Aalto, P., Blakkisrud, H. and Smith, H. 2008. Policy Recommendations for Northern Cooperation, in *The New Northern Dimension of European Neighbourhood*, edited by P. Aalto, H. Blakkisrud and H. Smith. Brussels: Centre for European Policy Studies, 220–34.

Aalto, P. 2009. European Perspectives for Managing Dependence, in *Russian Energy Power and Foreign Relations: Implications to Conflict and Cooperation*, edited by J. Perovic, R.W. Orttung and A. Wenger. London and New York: Routledge, 157–80.

Acharya, A. 2001. *Constructing a Security Community in Southeast Asia: ASEAN and the Problem of Regional Order*. London: Routledge.

Acharya, A. 2009. *Whose Ideas Matter? Agency and Power in Asian Regionalism.* Ithaca: Cornell University Press.

Agamben, G. 1995. *The Idea of Prose.* New York: SUNY Press.

Agamben, G. 1998. *Homo Sacer: Sovereign Power and Bare Life*. Stanford: Stanford University Press.

Agamben, G. 2000. *Means without End: Notes on Politics.* Minneapolis: University of Minnesota Press.

Agamben, G. 2005a. *State of Exception.* Chicago: The University of Chicago Press.

Agamben, G. 2005b. *The Time that Remains: A Commentary on the Letter to the Romans*. Stanford: Stanford University Press.

Agamben, G. 2007. *Il Regno e la Gloria: Per una genealogia teologica dell'economia e del governo*. Vicenza: Neri Pozza.

Agamben, G. 2009a. *What is an Apparatus? and Other Essays*. Stanford: Stanford University Press.

Agamben, G. 2009b. *The Signature of All Things. On Method.* New York: Zone Books.

Aggestam, L. 2006. Role Theory and European Foreign Policy: A Framework of Analysis, in *The European Union's Roles in International Politics: Concepts and Analysis*, edited by O. Elgström and M. Smith. Abingdon: Routledge, 11–29.

Almond, M. 1994. Bear Hug. *National Review*, 46(25): 22–4.

Allison, R. 2008. Russia Resurgent? Moscow's Campaign to 'Coerce Georgia to Peace'. *International Affairs*, 84(6): 1145–71.

Althusser, L. 1999. *Machiavelli and Us*. London: Verso.

Amnesty International. 2008. *Civilians in the Line of Fire: the Georgia–Russia Conflict.* November, Index 04/005/2008.

Antonenko, O. 2008. A War with No Winners. *Survival*, 50(5): 23–36.

Anwar, D.F. 1997. ASEAN and Indonesia: Some Reflections. *Asian Journal of Political Science*, 5(1): 20–34.

Apunen, O. 2008. The Endgame 1943–44: Finnish/Russian Peace Stratagems in the Context of Allied Coalition Policies, in *Russia Forever? Towards Pragmatism in Finnish/Russian Relations*, edited by H. Rytövuori-Apunen. Helsinki: Aleksanteri Series: 167–209.

Arendt, H. 2005. Introduction into Politics, in Kohn, J. (ed.) *The Promise of Politics.* New York: Schocken Books, 93–153.

Arendt, H. 1971. *The Life of the Mind.* London: Harcourt Brace.

Aslund, A. 2008. Putin's Lurch toward Tsarism and Neoimperialism: Why the United States Should Care. *Demokratizatsiya*, 16(1): 17–26.

Asmus, R. and Holbrooke, R. 2008. Black Sea Watershed. *The Washington Post*, 11 August, A15.

Asmus, R. 2010. *The Little War that Shook the World: Georgia, Russia and the Future of the West*. Basingstoke: Palgrave.

Associated Press Editorial (2008): http://www.msnbc.msn.com/id/26403580/.

Averre, D. 2007. 'Sovereign Democracy' and Russia's Relations with the European Union. *Demokratizatsiya*, 15(2): 173–90.

Bali Concord. 1976. *Declaration of ASEAN Concord Indonesia, 24 February 1976*. Available at: http://www.aseansec.org/1216.htm [accessed: 7 March 2009].

Bangkok Declaration. 1967. *The ASEAN Declaration (Bangkok Declaration) 8 August 1967*. Available at: http://www.aseansec.org/1212.htm [accessed: 7 March 2009.]

Barber, T. 2008. Europe Split on How to Restore Ties with Moscow. *Financial Times*, 27 October.

Bauer, H. and Brighi, E. 2009. Introducing Pragmatism to International Relations, in *Pragmatism in International Relations*, edited by H. Bauer and E. Brighi. London: Routledge, 1–8.

Bauman, Z. 2008. In the Court Where Multi-Ethnic Polities are on Trial the Jury is Still Out. *Ab Imperio* [Online], 9(1). Available at: http://abimperio.net/cgi-bin/aishow.pl?state=showa&idart=2070&idlang=18Code= [accessed: 25 October 2010].

Beissinger, M. 2008. Comments on Sergei Prozorov's Empire in the Age of its Disrepute, *Ab Imperio*, vol. 1, 229–33.

Belin, L. et al. 1997. *The Russian Parliamentary Elections of 1995: The Battle for the Duma.* Armonk, NY: M.E. Sharpe.

Benjamin, W. 2003. *The Origin of German Tragic Drama.* London: Verso.

Bergman Rosamond, A. 2010. *Non-Great Powers in International Politics: the English School and Nordic Internationalism.* London: Routledge.

Best, E. 1972. *The First and Second Epistles to the Thessalonians.* New York: Harper & Row.

Bicchi, F. 2007. *European Foreign Policy Making Toward the Mediterranean.* New York: Palgrave.

Bitzinger, R. 1991. Is the Soviet Threat Moving North? *Christian Science Monitor*, 17 January, 19.

Black, J.L. 2002. *Vladimir Putin and the New World Order.* Lanham, MD: Rowman and Littlefield.

Blank, S. 2003. The Future of Russo-American Partnership. *Demokratizatsiya*, 11(2): 183–97.

Blank, S. 2008. What Comes After the Russo-Georgian War? What's at Stake in the CIS. *American Foreign Policy Interests*, 30(6): 379–91.

Blank, S. 2009a. From Neglect to Duress: The West and the Georgian Crisis before the 2008 War, in Cornell, S.E. and Starr, F. (eds), *The Guns of August 2008. Russia's War in Georgia.* New York: M.E. Sharpe.

Blank, S. 2009b. America and the Russo-Georgian War. *Small Wars and Insurgencies*, 20(2): 425–51.

Blok, A. 1983. *Sobranie Sochinenii.* Leningrad: Hudozhestvennaya Literatura.

Booth, K. 1990. The Concept of Strategic Culture Affirmed, in Carl G. Jacobsen (ed.), *Strategic Power: USA/USSR.* London: Macmillan.

Bordachev. T. 2009. 'Multipolarity, Anarchy and Security', in Ivan Krastev, Mark Leonard, and Andrew Wilson, What Does Russia Think? *European Council on Foreign Relations.* London, 61–6.

Bridge, F.R. and Bullen, R. 1980. *The Great Powers and the European States System 1814–1914.* Harlow: Pearson Education Limited.

Brzezinski, Z. 1994. The Premature Partnership. *Foreign Affairs*, 73(2): 67–82.

Brzezinski, Z. 2008. Staring Down the Russians. *Time*, 172(8): 26.

Bull, H. 1966. International Relations Theory: The Case for a Classical Approach, *World Politics* 18: 361–77.

Bull, H. 1977. *The Anarchical Society: A Study in World Politics.* London: Macmillan Press.

Buzan, B. and Little, R. 2001. Why International Relations has Failed as an Intellectual Project and What to do About it. *Millennium: Journal of International Studies*, 30: 19–39.

Buzan, B. and Wæver, O. 2003. *Regions and Powers. The Structure of International Security.* Cambridge: Cambridge University Press.

Buzan, B. 2001. The English School: An Underexploited Resource in IR. *Review of International Studies*, 27: 471–88.

Buzan B. 2004. *From International to World Society? English School Theory and the Social Structure of Globalization*. Cambridge: Cambridge University Press.

Buzan, B. 2008. *The English School: A Bibliography* (Version of August 2010). Available at: http://www.polis.leeds.ac.uk/assets/files/research/english-school/es-bibl-10.pdf [accessed: 14 October 2010] .

Carothers, T. 2009. Democracy Assistance: Political vs. Developmental? *Journal of Democracy*, 20(1): 5–19.

Carr, E.H. 1939. *Twenty Years' Crisis, 1919–1939: An Introduction to the Study of International Relations*. London: Macmillan.

Celan, P. 1986. *Collected Prose*. Manchester: Carcanet.

CFR. 2009. Opening Remarks by Polish Foreign Minister Radoslaw Sikorski at the Council on Foreign Relations 'Nato At 60' Symposium. Available at: http://www.cfr.org/publication/18666/opening_remarks_by_polish_foreign_minister_radoslaw_sikorski_at_the_council_on_foreign_relations_nato_at_60_symposium.html [accessed: 20 November 2010].

Chandler, D. 2004. The Problems of 'Nation-building': Imposing Bureaucratic 'Rule From Above'. *Cambridge Review of International Affairs*, 17(3): 577–91.

Chandler, D. 2005. Introduction: Peace without Politics? *International Peacekeeping* 12(3): 307–21.

Chernoff, F. 2005. *The Power of International Theory: Reforging the Link to Foreign Policy-Making through Scientific Inquiry*. Abingdon: Routledge.

Chesnakov, A. 2008. O Evrope – Bez Ugryzenia Sovesti, *Russkiy Zhurnal*: http://www.russ.ru/lyudi/o_evrope_bez_ugryzeniya_sovesti [2 October].

Chong, A. 2004. Singaporean Foreign Policy and the Asian Values Debate, 1992–2000: Reflections on an Experiment in Soft Power. *The Pacific Review*, 17(1): 95–133.

Chong, A. 2010. Small State Soft Power Strategies: Virtual Enlargement in the Cases of the Vatican City State and Singapore. *Cambridge Review of International Affairs*, 23(3): 383–405.

Chua. C.H. 2010. No Mention of S. China Sea, just Maritime Security. *The Sunday Times* (Singapore) 26 September, p. 6.

Clinton, H. 2009. Remarks From the Signing Ceremony of the Treaty of Amity and Cooperation Accession, Available at: http://www.state.gov/secretary/rm/2009a/july/126334.htm [accessed: 24 August 2009].

CNN Editorial 2008. http://www.cnn.com/2008/WORLD/europe/08/28/russia.georgia.cold.war/index.html

Cohen, A. 2008. The Sochi Bush-Putin Summit: Last Chance to Improve Relations. *WebMemo Heritage Foundation* [Online], 1877. Available at: http://www.policyarchive.org/handle/10207/bitstreams/13615.pdf [accessed: 25 October 2010].

Cohen, S. 1992. The Election's Missing Issue. *The Nation*, 255(17): 622–4.

Cohen, S. 2006. The New American Cold War. *The Nation*, 283(2): 9–17.

Colbert, E. 1977. *Southeast Asia in International Politics 1941–1956*. Ithaca, NY: Cornell University Press.

Collombo, A. 2007. The Realist Institutionalism of Carl Schmitt, in Odysseos, L. and Petito, F. (eds) 2007. *The International Political Thought of Carl Schmitt*. London: Routledge.

Cooley, A. and Mitchell, L.A. 2009. No Way to Treat Our Friends: Recasting Recent U.S.–Georgian Relations. *The Washington Quarterly*, 32(1): 27–41.

Cooper, R. 2003. *The Breaking of Nations: Order and Chaos in the Twenty-First Century*. London: Atlantic Books.

Cornell, S.E., Popjanevski J. and Nilsson N. 2008. Russia's War in Georgia: Causes and Implications for Georgia and the World'. *Policy Paper*. Central Asia–Caucasus Institute. Washington: Johns Hopkins University.

Cornell, S.E. and Starr, F. (eds) 2008. *The Guns of August 2008. Russia's War in Georgia.* New York: M.E. Sharpe.

Cornell, S.E. 2008a. War in Georgia, Jitters All Around, *Current History*, 107(711), 307–14.

Cornell, S.E. 2008b. Russia Blames the Victim. *The New York Times*, 12 August, A21.

Covault, C. 1992. Russian Instability Draws NATO's Attention. *Aviation Week & Space Technology*, 137(21): 28.

De Borchgrave, A. 2008. Caucasus Caldron. *The Washington Times*, 12 August, A16.

De Landa, M. 1991. *War in the Age of Intelligent Machines*. New York: Swerve Editions.

Der Derian, J. 1987. Mediating Estrangement: A Theory for Diplomacy. *Review Of International Studies*, 13: 91–110.

Deutsch, K.W. 1968. *Political Community and the North Atlantic Area: International Organization in the Light of Historical Experience*. Princeton: Princeton University Press.

Deyermond, R. 2009. Matrioshka Hegemony: Multi-Levelled Hegemonic Competition and Security in Post-Soviet Central Asia. *Review of International Studies*, 35(1): 151–73.

Diez, T. and Whitman, R. 2002. Analysing European Integration: Reflecting on the English School – Scenarios for an Encounter. *Journal of Common Market Studies*, 40: 43–67.

Diez, T. 2004. Europe's Other and the Return of Geopolitics. *Cambridge Review of International Affairs*, 17(2): 319–35.

Diez, T., Stetter, S. and Albert, M. 2006. The European Union and Border Conflicts. *International Organization*, 60(3): 563–93.

Diez, T. and Manners, I. 2007. Reflecting on Normative Power, in Berenskoetter, F. and Williams, M.C. (eds), *Power in World Politics*. London: Routledge, 173–88.

Ditrych, O. 2010. Georgia: A State of Flux. *Journal of International Relations and Development*, 13(3): 3–25.

Donaldson, R. and Nogee J. 2005. *The Foreign Policy of Russia: Changing Systems, Enduring Interests.* Armonk, NY: M.E. Sharpe.

Dunlop, J. 2004. Aleksandr Dugin's 'Foundations of Geopolitics.' *Demokratizatsiya*, 12(1): 41–57.

Edkins, J. 2000. Sovereign Power, Zones of Indistinction and the Camp. *Alternatives*, 25(1): 3–26.

Emmers, R. 2003. *Cooperative Security and the Balance of Power in ASEAN and the ARF.* London: RoutledgeCurzon.

Erlanger, S. 1996. Russia Wants No Return of Cold War, Official Says. *The New York Times*, 11 February, A14.

Erlanger, S. 2008. NATO's Georgia and Ukraine Debate. Relations with Russia Underlie Feud over Fast-track Admission. *International Herald Tribune*, 2 December.

Esposito, R. 2008. *Bios: Biopolitics and Philosophy*. Minneapolis: Minnesota University Press.

Fean, D. 2009. Making Good Use of the EU in Georgia: the 'Eastern Partnership' and Conflict Policy. *Russia.Nei.Visions*, no. 44. IFRI Russia/NIS Centre.

Fedorov, Y.E. 2008. The Sleep of Reason: The War on Georgia & Russia's Foreign Policy. *Research Paper* no. 5. Association for International Affairs.

Fedorov, Y.E. 2009. Russia's View of the 'Reset'. Brief Analysis, *Central Europe Digest*. July.

Foreign Policy Concept of The Russian Federation. 2008. [Online], Available at: http://archive.kremlin.ru/text/docs/2008/07/204108.shtml [accessed: 25 October 2010].

Forsberg, T. and Vaahtoranta, T. 2000. Inside the EU, Outside NATO: Paradoxes of Finland's and Sweden's Post-Neutrality. *European Security*, 10(1): 68–93.

Forsberg, T. and Herd, G. 2006. *Divided West: European Security and the Transatlantic Relationship*. Oxford: Blackwell.

Foucault, M. 1990. *The History of Sexuality, Volume One: An Introduction* Harmondsworth: Penguin.

Foucault, M. 2001. Governmentality, in Faubion, J.D. (ed.) *Power: Essential Works of Foucault, Vol. 3*. London: Penguin, 201–22.

Foucault, M. 2007. *Security, Territory, Population: Lectures at the College de France 1977–1978*. Basingstoke: Palgrave.

Friedman, G. 2008. Georgia and the Balance of Power. *The New York Review of Books*, 55(14), 25 September.

Garst, D. 1989. Thucydides and Neorealism, *International Studies Quarterly*, 1: 3–27.

George, J.A. and Stefes, C.H. 2008. The Fate of Georgian Democracy. *Current History*, October, 344–7.

Geertz, C. 1980. *Negara: The Theatre State in Nineteenth Century Bali*. Princeton: Princeton University Press.

Global security and propaganda dogmas, Available at: http://natomission.ru/en/society/article/society/artbews/5/

Goble, P. 1998. Can Russian Diplomacy Hold Russia Together? *Radio Free Europe/Radio Liberty Newsline* 23 September.

Godzimirski, J. 2005. Russia and NATO: Community of Values or Community of Interests, in *Russia as a Great Power: Dimensions of Security under Putin*, edited by J. Hedenskog, V. Konnander, B. Nygren, I. Oldberg and C. Pursiainen. London: Routledge, 57–80.

Goh, E. 2007/8. Great Powers and Hierarchical Order in Southeast Asia: Analyzing Regional Security Strategies. *International Security* 32(3): 113–57.

Gomart, Thomas (2009. Obama and Russia: Facing the Heritage of the Bush Years. *Russie.Nei.Visions*, no. 39. Russia/NIS Centre. IFRI. Paris.

Gorenburg, D. and Makarychev, A. 2009. Russia's Discourses on Neighbourhood and Identity. *Russian Politics and Law*, 47(5): 3–9.

Gorka-Winter, B. and Kumoch, J. 2010. What is behind Sarkozy's Proposal for Reshaping EU–Russia Relations? *Bulletin*. Polish Institute for International Affairs, no. 125, October.

Gourevitch, P. 1978. The Second Image Reversed: The International Sources of Domestic Politics. *International Organization*. 32(4): 881–912.

Graham, T. 2000. The State of US–Russian Relations and the New Bush Administration. *BOFIT Online* [Online], 13. Available at: http://www.bof.fi/NR/rdonlyres/97DC37E1-35FB-4D17-BA4B-2EF38DE1E4DD/0/bon1300.pdf [accessed: 25 October 2010].

Haacke, J. 2003. *ASEAN's Diplomatic and Security Culture – Origins, Development and Prospects*. London: RoutledgeCurzon.

Haas, M. 1989. *The Asian Way to Peace: A Story of Regional Cooperation*. New York: Praeger Publishers.

Halbach, U. 2006. Säberrasseln und Friedenspolitik in Europas neuer Nachbarschaft. *SWP-Aktuell* 32. Berlin, July.

Handel, M. 1981. *Weak States in the International System*. London: Frank Cass.

Hardt, M. and Negri, A. 2000. *Empire*. Cambridge, MA: Harvard University Press.

Hardt, M. and Negri, A. 2004. *Multitude. War and Democracy in the Age of Empire*. New York: Penguin Books.

Helsinki Plus: Towards a Human Security Architecture for Europe. The First Report of the EU – Russia Human Security Study Group. London and Barcelona, May 2010.

Highlights from the First Strategic Concept Seminar in Luxembourg. Available at: www.nato.int/cps/en/natolive/news_58816.htm?

Hindess, B. 2005. Politics as Government: Michel Foucault's Analysis of Political Reason. *Alternatives: Global, Local, Political*, 30(4): 389–413.

Hobson, J.M. and Sharman, J.C. 2005. The Enduring Place of Hierarchy in World Politics: Tracing the Social Logics of Hierarchy and Political Change, *European Journal of International Relations*: 11–63.

Hoel, A.H. 2008. Best Practices in Fisheries Management: Experiences from Norwegian-Russian Cooperation, in *The New Northern Dimension of European Neighbourhood*, edited by P. Aalto, H. Blakkisrud and H. Smith. Brussels: Centre for European Policy Studies, 54–70.

Holsti, K.J. 1970. National Role Conceptions in the Study of Foreign Policy. *International Studies Quarterly*, 14(3): 233–309.

Holsti, K.J. 1985. *The Dividing Discipline: Hegemony and Diversity in International Theory*. London: Routledge.

Hont, I. 1990. Free Trade and the Economic Limits to National Politics; Neo-Machiavellian Political Economy Reconsidered, in Dunn, J. (ed.) *The Economic Limits to Modern Politics*. Cambridge: Cambridge University Press: 41–120.

Hopf, T. 2002. *Social Construction of International Politics: Identities and Foreign Policies, Moscow, 1955 and 1999*. Ithaca, NY: Cornell University Press.

Hurrell, A. and Woods, N. (eds) 1999. *Inequality, Globalization, and World Politics*. Oxford: Oxford University Press.

Hurrell, A. 2002. Foreword to the Third Edition: The Anarchical Society 25 Years On, in *Hedley Bull. The Anarchical Society. A Study of Order in World Politics*. Third Edition. New York: Columbia University Press, VII–XXIII.

Huysmans, J. 2006. International Politics of Insecurity: Normativity, Inwardness and the Exception. *Security Dialogue*, 37(1).

IHT. 2008. In Myanmar, Surprising Recovery. Resourceful Villagers and Private Aid Averted Starvation and Rise of Disease. *International Herald Tribune*, 17 June.

Independent International Fact-finding Mission on the Conflict in Georgia. 2009. Vol. 1. September.

International Crisis Group. 2008. Russia vs. Georgia: The Fallout. *Europe Report*, no. 195, 22 August.

International Crisis Group. 2009. Georgia–Russia: Still Insecure and Dangerous. *Briefing*, No. 53, 22 August.

Ikenberry, J.G. 2000. *After Victory: Institutions, Strategic Restraint, and the Rebuilding of Order after Major Wars*. Princeton: Princeton University Press.

Ikenberry, J.G. 2009. Liberal Internationalism 3.0: America and the Dilemmas of Liberal World Order. *Perspectives on Politics*, 7(1): 71–87.

Ilves, T.H. 2010a. President of Estonia at the Official Independence Day concert, Vanemuine Theatre. 24 February. Available at: http://president.ee/en/official-duties/speeches/2699-president-of-estonia-at-the-official-independence-day-concert-vanemuine-theatre/ [accessed: 28 November 2010].

Ilves, T.H. 2010b. President of the Republic of Estonia at the Reception Marking the anniversary of Estonian re-independence. 20 August. Available at: http://president.ee/en/official-duties/speeches/4979-president-of-the-republic-of-estonia-at-the-reception-marking-the-anniversary-of-estonian-re-independence/index.html [accessed: 28 November 2010].

Jayakumar, S. 1997. Opening Statement By His Excellency, Professor S Jayakumar Minister for Foreign Affairs and Minister for Law of the Republic of Singapore at the 30th Asean Ministerial Meeting 24 July 1997, Kuala Lumpur. Available at: http://stars.nhb.gov.sg/stars/public/ [accessed: 9 March 2009].

Jetschke, A. and Ruland, J. 2009. Decoupling Rhetoric and Practice: the Cultural Limits of ASEAN Cooperation. *The Pacific Review*, 22(2): 179–203.

Joenniemi, P. 2008. Introduction by Guest Editor: Russia's Narrative Resources. *Journal of International Relations and Development*, 11(2): 121–7.

Joenniemi. P. 2011. Turning into a Sovereign Power: The EU Probed Through the Lens of Neighbourhood. *Geopolitics*.

Jones, I. 2005. *The Epistles to the Thessalonians*. Peterborough: Epworth Press.

Kagan, R. 2003. *Of Paradise and Power: America and Europe in the New World Order*. New York: Vintage Books.

Kagan, R. 2007. End of Dreams, Return of History. *Hoover Institution Policy Review* [Online], 144. Available at: http://www.weeklystandard.com/Content/Public/Articles/000/000/015/426usidf.asp?page=1 [accessed: 25 October 2010].

Kagan, R. 2008a. *The Return of History and the End of Dreams*. New York: Knopf.

Kagan, R. 2008b. History's Back: Ambitious Autocracies, Hesitant Democracies. *The Weekly Standard* [Online], 13(46). Available at: http://www.weeklystandard.com/Content/Public/Articles/000/000/015/426usidf.asp?page=1 [accessed: 25 October 2010].

Kagan, R. 2008c. Putin Makes His Move. *The Washington Post*, 11 August, A15.

Karnish, M. 2008. In Candidates' Approaches, Clear Contrast. *The Boston Globe*, 12 August, A1.

Karp, R. 2007. The Conditionality of Security Integration: Identity and Alignment Choices in Finland and Sweden, in *The Baltic Sea Region: Security Strategies, Power Disparity and Identity*, edited by O. Knudsen. Aldershot: Ashgate 45–72.

Kassianova, A. 2001. Russia: Still Open to the West? Evolution of the State Identity in the Foreign Policy and Security Discourse. *Europe-Asia Studies*, 53(6): 821–39.

Katsumata, H. 2006. Establishment of the ASEAN Regional Forum: Constructing A 'Talking Shop' or a 'Norm Brewery'? *The Pacific Review*, 19(2): 181–98.

King, C. 2008. The Five Day War: Managing Moscow after the Georgia Crisis. *Foreign Affairs*, 87(6): 2–11.

Kissinger, H. 1957. *A World Restored*. Gloucester: Peter Smith.

Kissinger, H. 1968. The White Revolutionary: Reflections on Bismarck, *Daedalus: Journal of American Academy of Arts and Sciences*, 97(3): 888–924.

Kissinger, H. and Schultz, G. 2008. Finding Common Ground. *International Herald Tribune*, 30th of September.

Kivimäki, T. 2008. Power, Interest or Culture – Is there a Paradigm that Explains ASEAN's Political Role Best? *The Pacific Review*, 21(4): 431–50.

Koh, L. 2008. George Yeo gives ASEAN C Grade for its Handling of Myanmar Issues. *The Straits Times* (Singapore), 18 July.

Kopstein, J. 2006. The Transatlantic Divide over Democracy Promotion. *The Washington Quarterly*, 29(2): 85–98.

Koskenniemi, M. 2001. *The Gentle Civilizer: The Rise and Fall of International Law 1870–1960*. Cambridge: Cambridge University Press.

Koskenniemi, M. 2009. Colonization of the 'Indies' – The Origin of International Law? Talk at the University of Zaragoza, 1–48.

Kotkin, S. 2008. Myth of the New Cold War, *Prospect* [Online], 145, Available at: http://www.prospectmagazine.co.uk/2008/04/mythofthenewcoldwar/ [accessed: 25 October 2010].

Kramer, A.E. 2009. Putin's Great Game: Winning Control of Natural Gas. *International Herald Tribune*, 30 January.

Kramer, D.J. 2009. Resetting the U.S.–Russian Relations: It Takes Two. *The Washington Quarterly*, 33(1): 61–79.

Krasner, S.D. 1999. *Sovereignty: Organized Hypocrisy*. Princeton: Princeton University Press.

Krastev, I. 2008. Russia and the Georgia War: The Great-power Trap. *Open Democracy.* Available at: http://www.opendemocracy.net/article/russia-and-the-georgia-war-the-great-power-trap.

Krastev, I. and Leonard, M. 2009. The Spectre of a Multipolar Europe'. *European Council of Foreign Relations*. October.

Kratochwil, F. 1986. Of Systems, Boundaries, and Territoriality: An Inquiry into the Formation of the State System. *World Politics: A Quarterly Journal of International Relations*: 27–52.

Kratochwil, F. and Ruggie, J. 1986. International Organization: A State of the Art on an Art of the State. *International Organization*, 40(4): 753–75.

Kratochwil, F. 2006. History, Action and Identity: Revisiting the 'Second' Great Debate and Assessing its Importance for Social Theory, *European Journal of International Relations*, 12(1): 5–29.

Kratochwil, F. 2009. Ten Points to Ponder about Pragmatism: Some Critical Reflections on Knowledge Generation in the Social Sciences, in *Pragmatism in International Relations*, edited H. Bauer and E. Brighi. London: Routledge, 11–25.

Krauthammer, C. 1993. Russian Earthquake; The Meaning of Zhirinovsky. *The Washington Post*, 17 December, A23.

Kristol, I. 1967. American Intellectuals and Foreign Policy. *Foreign Affairs*, 45(4): 594–609.

Kuchins, A. 2007. The Specter of the Cold War Continues to Haunt Europe. *CSIS Commentary* [Online], Available at: http://csis.org/files/media/csis/pubs/070413_kuchins_commentary.pdf [accessed: 25 October 2010].

Kupchan, C.A. 2010. Why Russia Should Join the Atlantic Alliance. *Foreign Affairs*, 89(3): 100–12.

Laclau, E. 2007. *Emancipation(s)*. London and New York: Verso.

Lake, D.A. 2009. *Hierarchy in International Relations*. Ithaca, NY: Cornell University Press.

Lane, R., Talbott, S., and Watanabe, K. 2006. Engaging with Russia. The Next Phase. *Report to the Trilateral Commission*. Washington.

Lavrov, S. 2008a. Vneshniaya politika Rossii i novoe kachestvo geopoliticheskoi situatsii. *Diplomaticheskiy ezhegodnik.* 2008. Moscow.

Lavrov, S. 2008b. Litsom k litsu s Amerikoi: mezhdu nekonfrontatsiei i konvergentsiey. *Profil*, 38(593), October 13.

Lavrov, S. 2008c. The Role of Cooperation between the EU and Russia and Business Communities of the Parties concerned in the Situation of Financial and Economic Crisis. 10 December. Available at: http://www.mid.ru/brp_4.nsf/054FF6DCD2C14E6DC325751B00501E13).

Lavrov, S. 2008d. America Must Choose Between Georgia and Russia. *The Wall Street Journal*. 21 August.

Lavrov, S. 2009a. Cooperation with CSTO would benefit NATO, February 20. Available at: http://natomission.ru/en/society/article/society/artbews/35/

Lavrov, S. 2009b. NATO has taken Mr. Saakashvili under its protection. Available at: http://natomission.ru/en/cooperation/current/show/45/

Lavrov, S. 2010. Interview with the 'Mir' TV- and Radio-station, July 7. Available at: www.mid.ru

Lazarus, J. 2010. Neo-liberal State Building and Western 'Democracy Promotion': the Case of Georgia. Paper presented at the SGIR Pan-European Conference, Stockholm, September, 2010.

Lebow, R.N. 2001. Thucydides the Constructivist, *The American Political Science Review*, 3, 547–60.

Lebow, R.N. and Kelly, R. 2001. Thucydides and Hegemony: Athens and the United States. *Review of International Studies*, 27(4): 593–609.

Le Duan. 1998. Vision of Victory: Vietnam in 1975. Extract from Le Duan, "Forward to the Future" in *Southeast Asia in the Twentieth Century: A Reader*, edited by C.J. Christie. London: I.B.Tauris, 291–94.

Leifer, M. 1972. *Dilemmas of Statehood in Southeast Asia*. Vancouver: University of British Columbia Press.

Leifer, M. 1999. The ASEAN peace process: A category mistake. *The Pacific Review* 12(1): 25–38.

Leland, S.R. and Hoel, A.H. 2008. Learning by Doing: The Barents Cooperation and Development of Regional Collaboration in the North, in *The New Northern Dimension of European Neighbourhood*, edited by P. Aalto, H. Blakkisrud and H. Smith. Brussels: Centre for European Policy Studies, 36–53.

Lemke, T. 2000. Foucault, Governmentality, and Critique, Paper presented at the Rethinking Marxism Conference, University of Amherst (MA), September 21–4.

Legvold, R. 2002. All the Way: Crafting a US–Russia Alliance. *The National Interest*, 70: 21–32.

Little, R. 2009. Series Editor's Preface, in *Pragmatism in International Relations*, edited by H. Bauer and E. Brighi. London: Routledge, xii–xiii.

Lucas, E. 2008. *The New Cold War: The Future of Putin's Russia and the Threat to the West.* New York, NY: Palgrave Macmillan.

Lynch, D. 2006. Why Georgia Matters. *Chaillot Papers*, no. 86. February.

Lyons, M. 1985. From 'Death Camps' to Cordon Sanitaire: The Development of Sleeping Sickness Policy in the Uele District of the Belgian Congo, 1903–1914. *The Journal of African History*, 26(1): 69–91.

Makarychev, A. 2009. Russia and its 'New Security Architecture' in Europe: A Critical Examination of the Concept. *CEPS Working Document* No. 310.

Maliavin, V. 2004. Rozhdenie politiki iz dukha vizantiystva. *Russkii zhurnal*, October 7. Available at: www.russ.ru/columns/poison/20041007-pr.html

Manning, C.A.W. 1975. *The Nature of International Society*. London: Macmillan Press and London School of Economics and Political Science.

Mayall, J. 1990. *Nationalism and International Society*. Cambridge: Cambridge University Press.

Mearsheimer, J. 2001. *The Tragedy of Great Power Politics*. New York: W.W. Norton.

Medvedev, D. 2008a. Interview with the BBC Television. Sochi, 26 August (http://kremlin.ru/eng/speeches/2008/08/26/2131_type8291type82916_205790.shtml).

Medvedev, D. 2008b. Speech at the World Policy Conference, Evian, October 8. Available at: http://www.kremlin.ru/text/apears/2008/10/207422.shtml

Medvedev, S. 1999. Russia as the Subconsciousness of Finland. *Security Dialogue*, 30(1): 95–107.

Medvedev, S. 1999. Power, Space and Russian Foreign Policy, in Hopf, T. (ed.), *Understanding Russian Foreign Policy.* Philadelphia: Pennsylvania University Press, 15–57.

Meier, H. 1988. *The Lesson of Carl Schmitt: Four Chapters on the Distinction between Political Theology and Political Philosophy*. Chicago: University of Chicago Press.

Mitchell, L. 2009. Georgia's Story: Competing Narratives since the War. *Survival*, 51(4): 87–100.

Mochulsky, K. 1983. *Aleksandr Blok*. Detroit: Wayne State University Press.

Morgenthau, H. 1929. *Die internationale Rechtspflege, ihr Wesen und ihre Grenzen*. Leipzig: Noske.

Morgenthau, H. 1973. Politics Among Nations, New York: McGraw Hill.

Morgenthau, H. 1974a. The New Diplomacy of Movement, *Encounter*, 1974, August, 52–7.

Morgenthau, H. 1974b. Henry Kissinger, Secretary of State, *Encounter*, 1974, November, 57–61.

Morozov, V. 2008. Sovereignty and Democracy in Contemporary Russia: A Modern Subject Faces the Post-Modern World. *Journal of International Relations and Development*, 11: 152–80.

Morozov, V. 2009a. *Rossija & Drugie: Identichnost i Granicy Politicheskogo Soobschestva*. Moscow: NLO.

Morozov, V. 2009b. Western Hegemony: Global Democracy and the Russian Challenge, in Browning, C. and Lehti, M. (eds), *The Struggle for the West.* London, New York: Routledge.

Mouffe, C. 2009. Democracy in a Multipolar World. *Millennium: Journal of International Studies*, 37(3): 549–61.

Mouritzen, H. 1988. *Finlandization: Towards a General Theory of Adaptive Politics*. Aldershot: Avebury.

Mouritzen, H. 2001. Security Communities in the Baltic Sea region: Real and Imagined. *Security Dialogue*, 32: 297–310.

Mouritzen, H. 2011. Wikileaks, South Ossetia and the Russian 'reset', openDemocracy, 4 April. Available at: http://www.opendemocracy.net/print/58836.

Mäkinen, S. 2008. *Russian Geopolitical Visions and Argumentation: Parties of Power, Democratic and Communist Opposition on Chechnia and NATO, 1993–2003*. Tampere: Tampere University Press.

National Security Strategy 2006. [Online] Available at: http://georgewbush-whitehouse.archives.gov/nsc/nss/2006/ [accessed: 25 October 2010].

Neumann, I. 2008. Russia as a Great Power: 1815–2007. *Journal of International Relations and Development*, 11(2): 128–51.

NDEP (Northern Dimension Environmental Partnership News. 2010. NDEP Assembly of Contributors – London 30 November 2010. Available at: http://www.ndep.org/files/uploaded/NDEP%20News%20issue%2021.pdf [accessed: 14 October 2010].

Nicol, J. 2009. Russia–Georgia Conflict in August 2008: Context and Implications for the U.S. Interests. *CRS Report for Congress*. Congressional Research Service.

Nodia, G. 2005. Georgia: Dimensions of Insecurity, in Coppieters, B. and Longvold, R. (eds), *Statehood and Security*. Cambridge: MIT Press, 39–82.

Northern Dimension Policy Framework Document, Helsinki, 24 November 2006. Available at: http://eeas.europa.eu/north_dim/docs/frame_pol_1106_en.pdf [accessed: 14 October 2010].

Oakeshott, M. 1993. *Morality and Politics in Modern Europe: The Harvard Lectures*. London: Yale University Press.

Odysseos, L. and Petito, F. (eds) 2007. *The International Political Thought of Carl Schmitt*. London: Routledge.

Ojakangas, M. 2004. *A Philosophy of Concrete Life: Carl Schmitt and the Political Thought of Late Modernity*. Jyvaskyla: Sophi.

Ojakangas, M. 2005. Impossible Dialogue on Biopower: Agamben and Foucault, *Foucault Studies*, 2: 5–28.

Oldberg, I. 2005. Foreign Policy Priorities under Putin: a Tour d'horizon, in *Russia as a Great Power: Dimensions of Security under Putin*, edited by J. Hedenskog, V. Konnander, B. Nygren, I. Oldberg, and C. Pursiainen. London: Routledge, 29–58.

Osborne, M. 1970. *Region of Revolt. Focus on Southeast Asia*. Rushcutters Bay, Australia: Pergamon Press.

Pain, E. 2009. The Russian–Georgian Armed Conflict. *Russian Politics and Law*, 47(5): 10–25.

Palaver, W. 1996. Carl Schmitt on Nomos and Space, *Telos* 106: 105–28.

Pavlovsky, G. 2000. Proshai, Belovezhje!, *Nezavisimaya Gazeta* 235(2297).

Pipes, R. 1997. Is Russia Still an Enemy? *Foreign Affairs*, 76(5): 65–78.

Pocock, J.G.A. 1990. The Political Limits to Premodern Economics, in Dunn, J. (ed.) *The Economic Limits to Modern Politics*. Cambridge: Cambridge University Press: 121–42.

Political Declaration on the Northern Dimension Policy, Helsinki, 24 November 2006. Available at: http://eeas.europa.eu/north_dim/docs/pol_dec_1106_en.pdf [accessed: 14 October 2010].

Pravda, A. 2003. Putin's Foreign Policy after 11 September: Radical or Revolutionary?, in *Russia between East and West: Russian Foreign Policy on the Threshold of the Twenty-First Century*, edited by E. Gorodetsky. London: Frank Cass, 39–60.

Prozorov, S. 2005. X/Xs: Toward a General Theory of the Exception, *Alternatives*, 30(1): 81–112.

Prozorov, S. 2006. Liberal Enmity: The Figure of the Foe in the Political Ontology of Liberalism, *Millennium: Journal of International Studies*, 35(1): 81–112.

Prozorov, S. 2007. The Unrequited Love of Power: Biopolitical Investment and the Refusal of Care. *Foucault Studies*, 4, 53–77.

Prozorov, S. 2008. Empire in the Age of its Disrepute, *Ab Imperio*, vol. 1, 215–28.

Prozorov, S. 2009. *The Ethics of Postcommunism: History and Social Praxis in Russia*. Basingstoke: Palgrave.

Prozorov, S. 2010. Beyond the Paradigm of Integration in EU–Russian Relations: Sovereignty and the Politics of Resentment, in Nygren, B. and Engelbrech, K. (eds), *Russia and Europe: Building Partnerships, Digging Trenches*. London: Routledge, 81–99.

Purba, K. and Hotland, T. 2008. Singapore turns ASEAN into all work, no play. *The Jakarta Post* 23 July.

Putin, V. 2008. Interview with CNN, Sochi, 28 August. Available at: http://www.government.ru. *Vremia novostei*. 2009. no. 97, June 5.

Pye, L.W. 1985. *Asian Power and Politics: The Cultural Dimensions of Authority*. Assistance by Mary W. Pye. Cambridge, MA: Harvard University Press.

Pyman, A. 1980. *The Life of Aleksandr Blok*. Oxford; Oxford University Press.

Rahm, J. 2001. Russia, China, India: a New Strategic Triangle for a New Cold War? *Parameters*, 31(4): 87–97.

Rachman, G. 2008. Power and Russia's backyard. *Financial Times*. 14 April.

Remizov, M. 2000. Voina, yazyk, nevrasteniya. *Logos*, 2(23).

Rancière, J. 2006. *Hatred of Democracy*. London: Verso.

RFE/RL. 2009. Roundtable: Causes and Effects of the Russia-Georgia War, 9 August.

Rice, C. 2008. *Speech at the German Marshall Fund.* [Online] Available at: http://www.america.gov/st/texttrans-english/2008/September/20080918155132eaifas0.4152033.html [accessed: 25 October 2010].

Richter, J. 1996. Russian Foreign Policy and the Politics of National Identity, in *The Sources of Russian Foreign Policy after the Cold War* edited by C. Wallander. Boulder, CO: Westview Press, 69–93.

Ringmar, E. 1996. *Identity, Interest and Action: A Cultural Explanation of Sweden's Intervention in the Thirty Years' War*. Cambridge: Cambridge University Press.

Rogozin, D. 2008. Washington's Hypocrisy, August 19. Available at: http://natomission.ru/en/society/article/society/artbews/35/

Rogozin, D. 2009. Nato tochka Ru. Moscow: Exmo and Algoritm.

Rose, N. 1999. *Powers of Freedom: Reframing Political Thought*. Cambridge: Cambridge University Press.

Russian Newsweek. 2008. 25 February–2 March.

Rutherford, G.W. 1926. Spheres of Influence: An Aspect of Semi-Suzerainty. *The American Journal of International Law*, 20(2): 300–25.

Rynning, S. 2003. The European Union: Towards a Strategic Culture? *Security Dialogue*, 34(4), December.

Rytövuori-Apunen, H. 2008a. Revisiting the Problem of Trust in Finnish–Russian Relations, in *Russia Forever? Towards Pragmatism in Finnish/Russian Relations*, edited by H. Rytövuori-Apunen. Helsinki: Aleksanteri Series, 121–66.

Rytövuori-Apunen, H. 2008b. The Promises of Pragmatism and Finnish Research. in *Russia Forever? Towards Pragmatism in Finnish/Russian Relations*, edited by H. Rytövuori-Apunen. Helsinki: Aleksanteri Series, 315–31.

Safire, W. 1991. Cold War II Has Begun. *The New York Times*, 14 February, A27.

Sakwa, R. 1996. *Russian Politics and Society*. London: Routledge.

Sakwa, R. 2004. *Putin: Russia's Choice*. London: Routledge.

Schmitt, C. 1985. *Political Theology: Four Chapters on the Concept of Sovereignty.* Cambridge, MA: The MIT Press.

Schmitt, C. 1997. *Land and Sea*. Washington, D.C.: Plutarch Press.

Schmitt, C. 2003. *The Nomos of the Earth in the International Law of Jus Publicum Europaeum.* New York: Telos Press, 2003.

Schmitt, C. 2008. *Political Theology II: The Myth of the Closure of any Political Theology*. Cambridge: Polity Press.

Schorr, Daniel Foreign Policy Vexations: The Cool War, *The New Leader* 77 (14 February–28 1994): 3–4.

Schroeder, P. 1994. Historical Reality vs. Neo-realist Theory. *International Security*, 19(1): 108–48.

Sestanovich, S. 2008. What has Moscow Done? *Foreign Affairs*, 87(6): 12–28.

Severino, R.C. 2008. *ASEAN*. Southeast Asia Background Series No. 10. Singapore: Institute of Southeast Asian Studies.

Shanker, T. 2010. Sea Disputes Dialed Down at Defense Chiefs' Forum. *International Herald Tribune*, 13 October, 1–3.

Shapiro, J. and Witney, J. 2009. Towards a Post-American Europe: A Power Audit of the EU–US Relations. *European Council of Foreign Relations*. October.

Shevtsova, L. 2008. Russian Roulette. *The World Today* [Online], 64(10). Available at: www.chathamhouse.org.uk/publications/twt/archive/view/-/id/1810/ [accessed: 25 October 2010].

Shields, S. 2010. NATO Committed to Georgia Inclusion, *The Wall Street Journal*, 1 October.

Shmelova, M. 2008. Ukraine's Multi-Vector Foreign Policy: Attempt at a Summary. *The Polish Quarterly of International Affairs*, 2/2008: 22–42.

Simpson, G. 2004. *Great Powers and Outlaw States: Unequal Sovereigns and the International Legal Order*. Cambridge: Cambridge University Press.

Singleton, F. 1978. Finland between East and West. *World Today*, 34(8): 321–32.

Solzhenitsyn, A. 1990. Kak Nam Obustroit' Rossiju, *Komsomolskaya Pravda*, Special Issue, September 18.

Skinner, Q. 2002. *Visions of Politics: Renaissance Virtues*. Cambridge: Cambridge University Press.

ST (Straits Times) 2008. About the Treaty [Sourced from the ASEAN Secretariat]. *Straits Times (Singapore)* 25 July.

Stubb, A. 2008. The First Post-080808 Diagnosis: Speech by the Minister of Foreign Affairs at the Annual Meeting of Heads of Missions, Helsinki, 25 August 2008, http://formin.finland.fi.

Sukarno. 1998. Sukarno and the Pancasila Principles. Extract from President Sukarno "The Birth of Pancasila."' in *Southeast Asia in the Twentieth Century: A Reader*, edited by C.J. Christie, London: I.B.Tauris, 131–8.

Talbott, S. 1991. No, It's Not a New Cold War. *Time*, 137(9): 28.

Thomas, T. 2009. The Bear Went Through the Mountain. *The Journal of Slavic Military Studies*, 22(1): 31–67.

Tocci, N. 2008. The EU and Conflict Resolution in Turkey and Georgia: Hindering EU Potential Through the Political Management of Contractual Relations. *Journal of Common Market Studies*, 46(4): 875–97.

Traub, J. 2008. Taunting the Bear. *The New York Times*, 10 August, WK1.

Trenin, D. 2009a. The Lonely Power: Russian Security Policy and the West. *The Security Times* [Online], Available at: http://www.carnegieendowment.org/publications/index.cfm?fa=view&id=22683 [accessed: 25 October 2010].

Trenin, D. 2009b. *Solo Voyage*. Moscow: Carnegie Moscow Center and R. Elinina Publishers.

Tynkkynen, N. 2008. Experiences of Environmental Cooperation between the Nordic Countries and Russia: Lessons Learned and the Way Forward, in *The New Northern Dimension of European Neighbourhood*, edited by P. Aalto, H. Blakkisrud and H. Smith. Brussels: Centre for European Policy Studies, 71–90.

Van Ham, P. 2008. The Power of War. Why Europe Needs It. *Clingendael Diplomacy Papers*, no. 19. Hague.

Vaughan-Williams, N. 2009. The Generalised Bio-political Border? Re-conceptualising the Limits of Sovereign Power. *Review of International Studies*. 35(4): 729–49.

Voskopoulis, G. 2003. U.S. Terrorism, International Security, and Leadership: Towards a US–EU–Russia Security Triangle. *Demokratizatsiya*, 11(2): 165–82.

Wæver, O. 2001. International Society – Theoretical Promises Unfulfilled? *Cooperation and Conflict*, 27.

Wagstyl, S. et al. 2008. Sphere of Intolerance. *Financial Times*, 3 September.

Wallerstein, I. 1980. *The Modern World-System*. Boston: Academic Press.

Waltz, K. 1967. International Structure, National Force and the Balance of World Power. *Journal of International Affairs*, 21(2): 215–31.

Watson, A. 1992. *The Evolution of International Society: A Comparative Historical Analysis*. London: Routledge.

Weber, S. 1992. Taking Exception to Decision: Walter Benjamin and Carl Schmitt, *Diacritics* 22(3–4): 5–18.

Wendt, A. 2003. Why a World State is Inevitable: Teleology and the Logic of Anarchy. *European Journal of International Relations* 9(4): 491–542.

Weston, C.C. 1956. Beginnings of the Classical Theory of the English Constitution. *Proceedings of the American Philosophical Society*, 100(2): 133–44.

Wight, M. 1966. Why is there no International Theory? in Butterfield, H. and Wight, M. (eds) *Diplomatic Investigations*. London: Allen & Unwin.

Wight, M. 1977. *Systems of States*. Leicester: Leicester University Press, 46–73.

Wight, M. 1979. *Power Politics*, edited by Hedley Bull and Carsten Holbraad. Harmondsworth: Pelican Books.

Will, G. 2008. Russia's Power Play. *The Washington Post*, 12 August, A13.

Williams, M.C. 1996. Hobbes and International Relations: A Reconsideration, *International Organization*, 2, 213–36.

Wiseman, G. 1999. *'Polylateralism' and New Modes of Global Dialogue*. Discussion Papers 59. Leicester: Leicester University Press.

Žižek, S. 2004. The Lessons of Rancière, in Jacques Rancière. *The Politics of Aesthetics*. London and New York: Continuum, 69–79.

Žižek, S. 2005. Against Human Rights. *New Left Review*, July–August 2005, 115–31.

Zygar, M. 2009. Suverennaya Diplomatia, *Russky Newsweek*, September 14, 2009.

Index

Bold page numbers indicate figures, *italic* numbers indicate tables.

For Product Safety Concerns and Information please contact our EU representative GPSR@taylorandfrancis.com
Taylor & Francis Verlag GmbH, Kaufingerstraße 24, 80331 München, Germany

www.ingramcontent.com/pod-product-compliance
Ingram Content Group UK Ltd.
Pitfield, Milton Keynes, MK11 3LW, UK
UKHW011012180926
475701UK00004B/700
9781138261297